A Fierce Local

Memoirs of My Love Affair with Ireland

— *Memoirs of My Love Affair with Ireland* —

harvey gould

iUniverse, Inc.
Bloomington

A Fierce Local
Memoirs of My Love Affair with Ireland

iUniverse books may be ordered through booksellers or by contacting:

iUniverse
1663 Liberty Drive
Bloomington, IN 47403
www.iuniverse.com
1-800-Authors (1-800-288-4677)

ISBN: 978-1-4620-3367-6 (sc)
ISBN: 978-1-4620-3368-3 (hc)
ISBN: 978-1-4620-3369-0 (e)

Library of Congress Control Number: 2011916163

Printed in the United States of America

iUniverse rev. date: 11/21/2011

Table of Contents

Introduction 1

Chapter 1   The Unlikely Couple 8

Chapter 2   Dipping a Toe into Ireland 12

Chapter 3   Saying Kaddish in Dublin? 20

Chapter 4   Heading Out of Dublin 30

Chapter 5   Riding at Castle Leslie 34

Chapter 6   Riding at Sligo 42

Chapter 7   A Honeymoon in Ireland 50

Chapter 8   Mary, Adare, O. J., and Clonshire 57

Chapter 9   Harvey's Claddagh Ring and Declan's Turf 68

Chapter 10   Foxhunting with the Clare Foxhounds 73

Chapter 11   The Adare Cottages 91

Chapter 12   Dan Flaxman, Sarah, Dingle, and Mrs. Murphy 102

Chapter 13   How Long Can We Stay? 112

Chapter 14   Thoor Ballylee and a Few Miracles at Knock 122

Chapter 15   The O'Conor Don and a Muddy Carracastle Grave 127

Chapter 16   The Stolen Painting Caper 133

Chapter 17   Muckross House and Ballymaloe 139

Chapter 18   Donagh and Picasso 143

Chapter 19   9/11 147

Chapter 20   Purtill Cottage 153

Chapter 21   "Where Are The Pretty Pubs?" 160

Chapter 22   Donal and Patsy 165

Chapter 23   Margaret 175

Chapter 24   Oirish Time. 178

Chapter 25   Tony, Martin, and the Good Stuff. 187

Chapter 26   The Treacy Kids. 192

Chapter 27   The Limerick Foxhounds Come Visiting 201

Chapter 28   President Bush Visits Ireland, Sort of. 209

Chapter 29   Roger the Hammer 217

Chapter 30   The Purple People Eater. 221

Chapter 31   Hunting with the County Limerick Foxhounds. 227

Chapter 32   "You're a Fierce Local, Harv" 247

Chapter 33   "We're Going to a Restaurant in Rathkeale?" 252

Chapter 34   "Say Nothing to Simon" 256

Chapter 35   The Pleasures of Travel. 261

Chapter 36   What Do Ewes Want? 271

Chapter 37   Harvey Becomes a Full-Blooded Irishman 281

Chapter 38   Reverend Harv 304

DEDICATION

This book is dedicated to my wife, Karen. As my
mother would have said, "So, who else?"

ACKNOWLEDGMENTS

First, thank you to Ireland for being, well, Ireland. And God bless my wife Karen, my soul mate and best friend, for meaning she'd stay with me in sickness and in health, for introducing me to the Emerald Isle, and for sharing with me all of our experiences over the many years we've been "fierce locals" there. Thank you also for proofreading and critiquing the numerous iterations of the manuscript. My favorite of your notes was "You're killing me" placed next to a section where I wrote about why and how much I love you.

Thanks to Michael Castleman, a talented San Franciscan author. Though he didn't know me, Michael answered my call for help and offered meaningful advice and encouragement to a first-time author. One of his invaluable recommendations was, "Have an eagle-eyed editor scrub up the manuscript before even thinking about publishing." Who better than his brother David (deke), an author himself and a senior editor at a publishing house? I owe deke a great debt of gratitude for his insightful assistance in tightening, smoothing out, and buffing my manuscript while cheering me on.

Thank you to my sister and brother-in-law, Carol and Steve Weiss, for their helpful editorial comments; to Rebecca Treacy for translating some Irish phrases for me; and to Tony Treacy for cleaning up some of my Yank errors in an early version. (I know, Tony, a "hound" is always a "hound," never a dog.) And a special thanks to Victoria and Tony Treacy and to their children for their love, friendship, and céad míle fáilte whenever we stay at their Purtill Cottage in Adare, our home away from home.

Introduction

I'm not superstitious, so I placed no significance that when my wife Karen and I left for Ireland in 2006, it was our thirteenth trip to the Old Sod. In fact, it *did* turn out to be an unlucky number. During that trip, I spent a lot of time in the Cancer Day Ward at the Mid-Western Regional Hospital in Limerick.

That year, Karen and I were in the early stages of one of our many extended vacations in Adare when, feeling poorly, I visited a doctor in Croagh (pronounced croak). After telling the doctor about my chronic blood disorder, she drew some vials of my blood and sent Karen and me with them to the hospital lab. Three hours later, the doctor called Karen and said, "Get your husband to casualty (the emergency room) now. He needs a blood transfusion. Fast."

Karen and I first arrived in Ireland in 1988. She was already in love with the country. By 2006, I was too—its people, culture, language, size, food, drink, and *craic* (pronounced crack and meaning a love of news or gossip, and a sense of fun most commonly expressed through a mastery of witty talk). I loved the myths, the blend of ancient and modern sites, the forty shades of green in the countryside, the smell of burning peat, the ever-changing weather, and the horseback riding—almost as much as I was in love with Karen.

Its people are sometimes a bit wary at first, especially in the countryside, but quickly receive even strangers with *céad míle fáilte* (pronounced kaid mealah faultcheh, meaning one hundred thousand welcomes). We experienced this open arm acceptance time and again from one side of the country to the other.

Its culture is rich, imbued with a mix of many different elements. Among many others—these include Celtic tradition—the Brehon Law (originating as far back as 2300 BCE, it contains elements a wee bit ahead of its time, such as the right of women to hold property separately from men), St. Patrick and his conversion of Ireland to Christianity in the fifth century, and of course, one of the most important, the superstar rock band U2.

It has two languages, Irish and English. One-third of the residents speak Irish. Virtually everyone speaks English. All road signs are in both languages, so, for example, the sign as you enter Adare Village is:

> Fáilte go (meaning Welcome)
> Áth Dara
> Adare

But if you think you're guaranteed to understand all you hear spoken in English, think again. Your ear needs to adapt not only to the brogue, which is thicker as you get more into the countryside, but you'll also hear words that just make no sense to you. For example, you might be a tad confused if you heard:

> "Ye need to get to the back of beyonds, but if I was ye, I wouldn't even t'ink of buying a horse from that fella you mentioned. He's a blow in, a Gosson, and his place is just banjaxed, and if I'm wrong about that, well then I'm a gobshite fer sure. Now go get yer fine bit of stuff with whom you've been doin' a line and be off with ye."

The good news is that if you just say, "Huh?" the speaker will tell you that what he just said was:

> "You need to get out of Dublin, but if I were you I wouldn't even think of buying a horse from that fellow you mentioned. He's an immigrant, a young one, and his place is broken down beyond repair,

and if I'm wrong about that, well then I'm worse than an idiot. Now go get your pretty girlfriend you've been courting and get going."

It's only the gobshites who pretend they know more than they do and who end up missing the meaning of the chin-wag (discussion).

Its size by US standards is tiny. The Republic has about 4.1 million people and its land mass is about fifty-two thousand square miles, roughly the same population and acreage as Alabama. Yet, within it, there are stark contrasts: cosmopolitan cities with all the usual amenities and villages so small you'd miss them if you blinked, Croagh being one of the latter. You have a people crazy for every technological gizmo imaginable, and yet country pubs with dirt floors like Ellen's Pub outside of Sligo in the west of Ireland still exist, where one day we tied up our horses and went inside for lunch.

When we first went to Ireland in the late eighties, the Celtic Tiger economy had yet to kick in; that started in the early nineties. With the booming economy came an explosion of pent-up desires, such as better housing, cars, food, restaurants, and retail products and services. In the late eighties, most meals consisted of some overcooked beef, two kinds of potatoes, mushy vegetables, and as a side, another kind of potato. By 2006, we were eating some of the best meals we've had anywhere, including at Ballymaloe (pronounced Bally Maloo) in Shanangarry, County Cork; the Mustard Seed in Ballingarry, County Limerick, and best of all, at the house of those living in Adare who became our dear friends, Victoria and Tony Treacy (pronounced Tracy).

The drink in Ireland is incomparable for two reasons. First, by default, a drink means a pint of Guinness and a Guinness in Ireland is special, and second, a pub is one of the many places where you'll find good craic, fueled a tad by the drink. As for Guinness, if you've had one you're thinking, "It's okay, but it's not worth writing about." Wrong. Guinness doesn't travel well, so if you've had one in the States, you haven't *really* had one. Having a Guinness in Ireland is a bit like a religious experience. There's a ritual to it. The barkeep pours three-quarters of a pint and leaves it near the tap. My first time he walked away to serve another customer. After thirty seconds, I thought he'd forgotten about me and I reached for it. His radar sensed I was about to commit the crime of taking my Guinness before it was ready. "Let her settle, lad. Let her settle. I'll push it to ye when it's ready."

"Sorry." Not yet fully comprehending the seriousness of my offense, I lowered my head a bit, as a few locals looked at me as though to say, *Dumb Yank.*

The barkeep returned to my partially filled glass maybe three minutes later, and filled it to the top, but still wouldn't give it to me. He wasn't punishing me. No Irish bartender will serve a Guinness until it's ready. Later, I learned that means it has to fully bubble to the top, leaving about a one-inch head of a creamy topping. He poured some out and refilled it, allowing it another minute to settle. (In all, I've probably seen 3,276 gallons of Guinness poured down the drain by Irish barkeeps in their never-ending quest to serve the perfect pint.) When he was satisfied that it was properly settled and had a presentable head, good to his word, he pushed it toward me. Even for those, like me, who aren't regular beer drinkers, drinking a Guinness is like drinking a bit of nirvana—the head is like a frothy shake, and the drink is a heavy but velvety stout, rich, and well worth the wait.

The craic alone is worth a visit to Ireland. In the end, it's only because of it that I'm able to write this memoir. At the heart of our times in Ireland are those I've met and their good craic, some strangers and some who we came to know well over the years.

There's Margaret who lives in Adare and cleaned Purtill Cottage for us. Each time she came to the cottage many a cuppa (tea) I poured, imploring her to regale me with yet more local stories.

There's Captain Vinnie Bligh with whom we rode horses on the beaches of Sligo and who taught us the Irish way of talking yourself into getting what you want.

There's the group at Collins Pub in Adare we'd never seen before, but with whom we spent a night laughing, sharing stories, singing, telling jokes, and finally closing the place down.

A couple from Northern Ireland, when we stayed at the Park Hotel Kenmare in County Kerry, gave us a lesson about politics in the North and dealing with the IRA, stories you couldn't get from reading books or newspapers.

The never-ending repartee between Tony Treacy and me is an ongoing duel to see who can come up with the wittier comment. I say it's me. Tony says it's he.

The ancient sites are virtually never-ending. Remember Tara, the plantation in *Gone with the Wind*? It owes its name to the Hill of Tara. In County Meath, there's another hill, the ancient seat of the high kings of Ireland, which includes a passage mound that probably dates back to 3000 BCE. Court and passage tombs, Newgrange being Ireland's most famous, were built around 3100 BCE. There are stone forts, dolmens, and standing stones, some in circles.

At the fort of Brian Boru, you're at the seat of ancient power where, as the high king of Ireland, Boru marched into battle against the Danes with thirty thousand men in 1014 when he was eighty-eight years old, and was ambushed and killed that day after he'd won the fight. We once saw a pub and a related inn being built in County Limerick. When it opened, the pub displayed one of my favorite signs: The Pub of Brian Boru—Since 1765. The sign is no longer there.

Did I say the craic alone is worth a trip to Ireland? 'Tis, but so are the horses. Ah, the Irish horses and the Irish love affair with them. For years before we traveled to Ireland, Karen and I shared this love, but it was only after experiencing it firsthand that we came to know how special it is to ride in a country that lives this passion. We've jumped Irish Thoroughbreds on cross-country courses all over the country. We've taken riding lessons, gone on trail rides, and ridden on back roads, where people in cars pull over, switch off their engines, and hand-muzzle their dogs to be sure nothing spooks one of the horses.

At Purtill Cottage in Adare, where we've stayed for a number of years, we just tack up and ride the Treacy's horses on their thirty acres or go for a hack on the surrounding roads whenever the mood strikes us. I've ridden in two foxhunts, both in Ireland, the most grueling rides I've ever had and among the highlights of my life.

In years past, we've seen the sights. We've been pretty much everywhere. We saw the Rock of Cashel in County Tipperary; we've been in Galway, where we bought my Claddagh (pronounced Clahduh) ring, and stayed in the Connemara region. We've been to Bunratty Castle and the bracing Cliffs of Moher in County Clare, and stayed at Ballymaloe House in Cork, spending nights in its drawing room where one of the owners and other musicians sang and played for hours on end, and guests and locals sometimes stepped up to sing their favorite song.

We've stayed at the O'Conor Don's Clonalis House in Castlerea, County Roscommon. We've been to the shrine at Knock in County Mayo, found Karen's relatives in a muddy cemetery in a church graveyard in Carracastle, and toured Thoor Ballylee outside Gort in County Galway, where W. B. Yeats lived and wrote many poems.

We've ridden at Castle Leslie in County Monaghan and on the beaches near Drumcliffe in County Sligo. We've slept at Dromoland Castle in County Clare, and at the Dunraven and the Adare Cottages in County Limerick. We've visited Glin Castle and explored a replica of a Celtic village where Karen took my photo in a stone chair, a throne similar to one reserved for an ard ri Éireann (a high king of Ireland). We've attended point-to-point races in Nenagh, County North Tipperary, stayed in Dingle, walked on Inch Beach in the southwest of Ireland in County Kerry, and toured Muckross House in Killarney. We've been to Dublin, shopped in Limerick, and stayed overnight on the Aran Islands, where you're thrown back into the times of Gaelic Ireland, the Celts, and early Christians, and where we attended a Mass in Irish.

Now, that we've done all that and a good deal more, what we adore most is just living in the village of Adare. There, we're no longer Yank tourists. Instead, we've become immersed and a part of the life of the village, and come to know so well so many of the local trades people and inhabitants, that we've earned the moniker of "fierce locals."

However, what I'd never experienced in Ireland, or anywhere else, was a blood transfusion. We ended up at the Cancer Day Ward in Limerick where I played Count Dracula as the doctors fed my need for more and more blood. Patients and their loved ones sat on reclining chairs at round tables and struck up conversations. No one ever asked about one another's disease. We all knew that everyone there was receiving chemo, blood, or some other lifesaving treatment. We all knew no one was there for the fun of it. This was a place where death sat patiently and quietly at some of those tables, but in the Irish way, that was no reason to be morose. In fact, it was even more reason to engage in some good craic. Christ, this might be the last time to have a good chat or to tell a joke or to listen to some good stories. I had some of my best-ever belly laughs with other patients around those tables. For me this could have been Ireland at its darkest. Instead, it was Ireland at its best.

During the course of three weeks, on seven separate days, I received twelve units of blood. This was a fair slug, since the typical human body holds ten. As I saw it, by the end of the process, all my American blood, and then some, had been replaced by Irish blood. It's rare enough for a Yank to be considered a fierce local. I'd taken matters to a new extreme. I had now gone where few Americans had ever gone before. I'd become a full-blooded Irishman.

Not bad for a Jewish kid from Chicago.

Aran Islands' Taxi

7

Chapter 1

⌒

The Unlikely Couple

Highland Park is a northern suburb of Chicago that stretches along five miles of Lake Michigan. When my family moved there in the fifties during my Wonder Bread years, it was already an affluent town. Unlike many other suburbs on the North Shore, it had a sizable Jewish population. I grew up in a kosher home. Our family observed the Sabbath (Shabbat) from sundown Friday to sundown on Saturday, which meant my mother recited the blessings over the candles, my dad chanted prayers over the wine and the challah in his beautiful voice, and my sister Carol and I didn't get to go to Friday night high school basketball games.

My mother was steeped in Judaism; she believed in it down to her bones. And when she was raising my sister and me, she passed on to us her love of the religion and its traditions.

My sister and I went to Hebrew school every day after public school, and we went to Sunday school for immersion in Jewish history and tradition. Our family attended *shul* (synagogue) for some Shabbat services, various holidays, and certainly never missed attending Rosh Hashanah and Yom Kippur services (the High Holy Days), fasting on Yom Kippur being something of a rite of passage into Jewish adulthood.

Our friends and those we hung around with were all Jews. What I knew about Catholicism wouldn't fill a thimble. I'd never been to a church. I was taught that though Christians believed Jesus was the Christ or Messiah, Jews believed the Messiah hadn't arrived yet. I heard that over time, Christians had done some terrible things to Jews, and some of them thought we'd killed this Christ guy. I always thought if anyone asked, I could explain that our family had nothing to do with it.

At the same time I was growing up, surrounded by Judaism and its customs and traditions, Karen was growing up a nice Irish-Catholic girl in Washington Heights in Manhattan. All four of her grandparents had emigrated from Ireland. Some of Karen's earliest memories are of Irish rebel songs and the St. Patrick's Day parade.

Karen had all the sacraments possible for a young Catholic: baptism, confession, communion, confirmation, and later, marriage. Her dad was a cop on the NYPD. She attended parish schools, went to Mass regularly, and through her teenage years, went to confession weekly. Though the Duffy family lived in an all-Irish neighborhood, it was bordered by an all-Jewish neighborhood. It's easier in a suburban environment to live a more insular life, as I did. When you grow up in a city, as Karen did, in a neighborhood filled with apartments in which people of different ethnicities live virtually next to one another, it's more likely that you'll have more interaction. So while the only "host" I knew growing up was someone who threw a party, Karen grew up eating bagels, lox, and cream cheese, knew the Hirsch's—Holocaust survivors, who owned the local grocery store where she bought candy—and that on Saturdays, not Sundays, the Jews celebrated their Sabbath.

Even in Karen's more ethnic-mixing neighborhood, however, the dividing line was puberty. When it came time to start dating, the Irish-Catholic and Jewish kids who'd played in the same playgrounds, retreated to their respective corners, dating only among their own. Karen was supposed to marry a nice Catholic boy and she did. She had no children. I was supposed to marry a nice Jewish girl and I did. We had three daughters. Karen's marriage lasted four years; mine lasted eight.

As a young married woman, Karen moved to San Francisco. She took a job, essentially as a Girl Friday, with a small company that was gearing up to sell products to copper mines in the Philippines. As it turned out, the company became successful, and she ended up a partner in a business that consumed much of her time for the next three decades.

While Karen was developing her business career, I was a student at Berkeley and then at Northwestern Law School in Chicago. While still at Northwestern, I married my first wife whom I'd met while both of us had been students at Berkeley. Born and raised in San Francisco, she wanted to live in the Bay Area, so within a year of graduating from law school, we moved to a town just north of the Golden Gate Bridge.

I started my career as a lawyer after joining a San Francisco law firm. Karen knew one of the attorneys there and called, looking for someone to be in touch with her partner who had a legal matter to discuss. As destiny played out its hand, I was the one given the assignment, but even after I'd met her partner it took some time before Karen and I first met. Life's chances are thin. There are so many ifs to our most critical connections.

Karen and her partner were at a basketball game one night. She spotted a man in the crowd whom she'd never seen before. Years later she still holds in her mind the image of his face, what he was wearing, how his hair was combed, and the sudden sensation that she was looking at the man with whom she'd want to spend the rest of her life, a sensation that she brushed off as quixotic and childish, but she looked at him again. As the game ended her partner also spotted the man and waved hello. Amazed that her partner knew the man about whom she'd just had a fanciful delusion, Karen asked who it was. "That's Harvey Gould, the attorney who I just met through your contact." Eerie.

After my wife and I separated in 1976 and divorced a year later, I was busy adapting to living alone for the first time, working hard as a young trial lawyer, being a single father, and doubling up on work during the week to keep my weekends free for my children.

Separately, Karen was likewise busy, which meant working full and hard weeks, often including weekends and taking up to four business trips to the Far East annually for three weeks or so per trip. When she was home, her niece and nephew occasionally stayed with her for a weekend, and sometimes the three of them joined my children and me at a park, and then at a restaurant.

I started seeing Karen in a different light. My kids adored being with her, and stripped of her executive surroundings, I was falling madly in love with her. She was successful, bright, driven, beautiful, and had impeccable taste. She's the best judge of character I've ever known. And, of course, she was the forbidden fruit, a blonde *shiksa*, every nice Jewish boy's secret dream.

Years after my divorce, I started to use all my wiles to get Karen to marry me, but she flatly refused. Having made her choices, she wasn't about to slip into a role with someone else's children that she'd avoided for herself. She didn't want to compete with my former wife. She wanted to be "Karen" to my children, not a stepmom. She was ready, willing, and able to guide them, but not to raise them. Try as I might, and I tried mightily, Karen remained resolute. She was a catch well worth the wait, so it wasn't until sixteen years after we met and twelve years after my divorce, that Karen and I married.

Though I knew I'd found my soul mate, living together should have been rough. Each of us had lived alone for many years, and we were set in our ways. Still, adjusting to married life with Karen was a piece of cake. Without ever discussing them, we simply made numerous compromises. What other couples found to be stresses of living together, or "working at marriage," we handled seamlessly. Marrying Karen is the single happiest and smartest thing I've ever done. Falling in love with the land of my new wife's ancestors and making Ireland our home away from home was a close second.

Chapter 2

Dipping a Toe into Ireland

Karen was a Duffy whose father was always going on about being descended from Brian Boru. In the sixties when she was nineteen, she first visited Ireland, tracing the trip in reverse that her grandparents had taken to the United States. She knew her grandmother had come from Derrinacartha, a tiny village in Mayo, and her grandfather had come from Cloontia, a small village in Roscommon, a mile or so from Derrinacartha. Mayo and Roscommon were two of the hardscrabble counties where, as in many parts of Ireland, it was tough to scratch out a living.

When Karen got to Cloontia, she asked if anyone knew Bernard Duffy, her father's first cousin. (Her dad's name was John B. Duffy, the *B* for Bernard.) A villager said, "Jest go down this road till it tarns to dirt. Then ask the first person ye see."

The first person she saw was a young girl. Karen asked her if she knew the Bernard Duffy family. The child said, "Yes, Bernard Duffy is me da."

The young girl took Karen into the family cottage and introduced her to her mother Margaret, who was probably in her midthirties, certainly no more than forty. The main room of the cottage had a dirt floor. A pot of food was cooking over the fireplace. There was no indoor plumbing. Margaret was proud that they'd just "changed roofs," which Karen took to mean that they'd gone from thatch to shingles. Bernard and Margaret had three children—Ned, John, and Margaret. They also had one cow and a donkey. Mother Margaret sent daughter Margaret into town by bicycle to get some bread. When she returned, the bread was served with jam and tea.

Margaret told Karen that Bernard worked in Liverpool for six months at a time. Obviously, the farm alone didn't earn enough to support the family.

On the mantel of the fireplace was a picture of Karen's grandfather. This was her heritage. The hard-luck life in Cloontia in the 1960s, let alone what it must have been like when her grandparents left Ireland sixty years earlier, is why, when her grandmother finally made it to the States and was asked if she wanted to return to visit Ireland, she scowled and said, "No. Why do ye think I left?"

Karen was transfixed by the serendipitous nature of it all, how each of us is a product of luck, pluck, and circumstance. It could just as easily have been her cooking dinner over that fireplace, except that her father's father chose to leave Ireland two generations earlier, knowing that he'd never again return and never again see the land and people he was leaving, whereas Bernard's father had stayed. It was a connecting moment, but it also was chilling.

Margaret knew the family of Karen's grandmother and directed her to her grandmother's house. There Karen found the remnant of an old cottage, left to go to seed, and a new cottage built next to it. The woman who answered the door was married to a descendant of Karen's grandmother, but she wasn't welcoming. She didn't invite Karen in, saying, "You don't look like any of them." She announced that she was from Tipperary as if to say, *I'm better than those born here.*

Even with the unpleasant end of her search for her roots in Ireland, Karen's attachment to the land of her ancestors remained deep and warm. She'd landed in Dublin on that trip and traveled across the country to get to the family homesteads. It was a beautiful trip, and her first exposure to the forty shades of green that dot the countryside and surrounding hills. Her entire childhood had been wrapped up in stories and myths about Ireland, and she was not just a Catholic, she was an Irish-Catholic. She felt deeply the centuries-old plight the Irish had suffered at the hands of the British. The potato famine, about which I knew nothing until Karen came into my life, tied her even closer to the Irish, because she grew up feeling the pain of it. She knew that during the famine, of three and a half million Irish, nearly a million died of starvation and disease caused by the blight that destroyed the potato crops, and another million emigrated in a desperate effort to escape its ravages, during a time when Ireland was exporting food to England. Even then, though, she knew instinctively what many years later a BBC survey would confirm: Ireland was the most content country in Europe. She knew that even with its suffering, it was a land of laughter, beauty, myth, art, culture, dance, and an unbendable spirit—and that a love of all this was in her blood.

As Karen grew closer to agreeing to marry me, she wanted more and more to introduce me to the land of her heritage. Since Ireland and horses go together like love and marriage, going to Ireland on a horseback riding trip seemed the perfect introduction.

* * * * * * * * * * * * * * * * * *

In the early eighties, Karen and I took up horseback riding as our primary form of relaxation. In 1988, we took a horseback riding trip to the Old Sod with our riding instructor, Jann, her future husband, Michael, and Bernadette, a friend and another riding student of Jann's. The trip was spectacular, and though it was strictly limited to the horse world, my first experience of dipping a toe into Ireland was so grand I wanted to return.

The five of us flew to Dublin, the largest city in Ireland, near the midpoint of the country's east coast. What's hard for many Americans to wrap their heads around is the age of so much of Europe, and of course, other parts of the world. To us, old means a town that ten years earlier didn't have a Walmart, some other big box store, or a multiplex movie theater. But the year we arrived, in 1988, the city was celebrating its birthday. Not its one hundredth birthday. Not its five hundredth, but its one thousandth.

The city is deemed to have been founded in 988 by the Vikings. Being no dummies, they built their settlement by Dubh (Black) Linn (Pool) (later the River Liffey), the name Black Pool deriving from its dark waters.

It was also deep enough for harboring ships. After the Norman invasion, the high king, acting as the head of Norman land acquisitions, did what in more contemporary times would be known as heavy-handed rezoning. He annexed a nearby settlement. By the combination, Dublin became the capital of Ireland and a key center of military and judicial authority.

Anglo-Norman rule dates from the twelfth century and from the fourteenth to the late sixteenth centuries, Dublin and its surrounding area was known as the Pale, the only area then genuinely under the authority of English law and from which the phrase "beyond the pale" emanates.

From the Irish perspective, the Pale was a boundary from which they were excluded from living. From the British viewpoint, the Pale was not so much to keep the Irish out as to protect themselves from attacks from the Gaels. Why would the Irish possibly want to attack the English invaders? After all, in 1366 all the English did was pass the Statutes of Kilkenny that forbade English settlers from marrying Irish natives, fostering or adopting Irish children, using the Irish language, and Irish modes of dress, and other Irish customs, mandating that English colonists be governed by English common law, not Brehon law, and denying the Irish admission to any English church. Obviously, the Irish just couldn't take a joke, but they'd have centuries to learn English humor. Anyway, by the seventeenth century, Dublin had expanded greatly, for a time becoming the second city of the British Empire, surpassed only by London.

By 1916, in an ill-fated attempt known as The Easter Rising, for the seventh time in three hundred years, the Irish tried to throw off British rule. Based in Dublin, the uprising failed, and the Anglo-Irish War raged for six years. During that war, Michael Collins helped form the modern Irish Republican Army (IRA). He created an assassination squad (the Twelve Apostles) who killed British agents on Irish soil and assassinated high-ranking British operatives in London. The IRA's guerilla tactics, occurring at the end of World War I, took their toll. The British military, politicians, and public were war-weary and started looking for a way out. Eventually, they agreed to treaty negotiations.

Michael Collins led the Irish negotiating team that resulted in a treaty that kept the six northern counties in Ireland under British control, while creating a Free State for the rest of the country. Hence, to this day you have Northern Ireland and the Republic of Ireland.

Many considered the treaty that Collins brokered as a sellout; others thought it the best solution under the circumstances. This internal dispute led to the Irish Civil War in 1922–1923 during which Michael Collins was assassinated.

I'm not sure whether these terrible periods were given any quasi tongue-in-cheek names, but doing so would have been typical of the Irish. For example, during the British occupation of Ireland in the twentieth century before the Republic was created, the most hated troops were the elite, and often brutal, Black and Tans, getting their name from their black boots and tan slacks.

Today, throughout Ireland, in any pub, you can order a black and tan, and you'll get a mixed pint of two beers, one black, and one tan. Couldn't beat the British militarily? Then, make a beer out of them. Then, too, what the rest of the world called World War II, the Irish dubbed the Emergency.

Also, starting in the late 1960s and lasting for about thirty years was a period of bloody violence between elements of the Catholics and Protestants in Northern Ireland. In came the British military again, though ostensibly neutral, viewed by most Irish republicans as an occupying army, using excessive force against the Catholics. It became common for areas to be encircled with barbed wire. Bombings, assassinations, and retribution killings were common. The violence was relentless. Some Irishmen, imprisoned by the British, starved themselves to death on protest hunger strikes. What name did the Irish give this period? Hell in Eire? No. Times of Blood? No. It's was dubbed the Troubles. Even at and after times of disaster, the Irish manage to turn a phrase that almost mocks the true horror that surrounds them.

This Irish trait reminded me of a TV show I'd seen years ago about the early days of the American rocket program. Many rockets were blown up, either right on the launch pad because of identified problems or within seconds after liftoff, as the rocket was wobbling violently, about to go off course and wipe out some nearby town. The US government, however, never referred to these as failures; they were dubbed "unscheduled disassemblies."

The difference was that in the States, such bureaucratic doublespeak was intended to avoid calling failures what they were. Irish phrasings for their horrible times are the ultimate in craic, a way of dulling the pain, not hiding from the truth.

It wasn't until the 1960s that Dublin began to modernize. Eventually, the city's infrastructure grew dramatically with massive private and state development. Still, with all the sophistication of a burgeoning and increasingly expensive city, some well-known Dublin street corners are still named for a pub or a beloved business that used to grace the site before it was torn down to make way for progress. These people may have become sophisticated, but they still know where the real values lie.

According to historians, when Dublin was founded as a Viking settlement it had no Walmarts, but its people still managed to survive. Today, not only is it the capital of Ireland, but it also has one of the youngest and fastest growing populations of any European city. Continued development in Dublin has been emblematic of the economic growth of the country. In a European-wide survey by the BBC in 2003, Dublin was deemed the best capital in Europe in which to live, although it's now ranked as the world's sixteenth most expensive. It has the fourth highest wages of any city worldwide, ahead of New York and London. As part of the Celtic Tiger growth (challenged since the onset of the global recession starting in late 2008), although Guinness has been brewed there since 1759, Microsoft, Google, Amazon, PayPal, Yahoo! and Pfizer, among others, had European headquarters and/or operational bases in Dublin and its environs and Intel and Hewlett-Packard had large manufacturing plants in a nearby suburb.

Although Dublin is a large city by most standards, the entire country is still tiny by European, let alone American, standards. In 2007, Ireland's total population was about 4.1 million (only recently showing an upward trend for the first time since the potato famine of 1845). The Dublin region has about 1.2 million people, just slightly less than 30 percent of the Republic's entire population.

Yet, you wouldn't know the country is small judged by its artistic talents measured on a worldwide basis. For example, Dublin has produced three Nobel Prize winners for literature, more than any other city in the world: William Butler Yeats, George Bernard Shaw, and Samuel Beckett. It has also produced a few other writers who hardly can be called slackers: Oscar Wilde, Jonathan Swift, Bram Stoker, James Joyce, J. M. Synge, and Sean O'Casey, among them.

In 1904, Yeats and others founded the Abbey, with the express objective of promoting indigenous literary talent, which helped launch the careers of Yeats himself, Synge, and Shaw.

In modern times, if you think of excellent singers or groups, again the Irish have a disproportionate piece of the pie. These include U2, the Fureys, Chris De Burgh (remember "Lady in Red"?), Enya, Clannad, Sinead O'Connor, the Corrs, the Frames (the movie *Once* featured the Frames' lead singer Glen Hansard and one of his songs, in collaboration with his costar in the movie, won an Oscar in 2008 for Best Song from a Film). There's also Thin Lizzy, Altan, the Clancy Brothers, the Chieftains, the Boomtown Rats and its lead singer Bob Geldof, the Cranberries, the Dubliners, Jim McCann, Christy Moore, the Pogues, Dolores Keane (one of my favorites, and right up there with her) Mary Black, Phil Coulter (if you've never heard "The Town I Loved So Well," listen to it and get a lesson in the Troubles), and so many more performers that the list could go on forever.

The central theme of *How the Irish Saved Civilization* by Thomas Cahill is that much of the basis of Western Civilization would have been relegated to the dustbins of history had the Irish monks of medieval times not copied Roman and Greek manuscripts, the Bible, and other vital works.

To this day, the *Book of Kells*, a world-famous manuscript produced by Celtic monks, is on display at Trinity College. The book, produced in 800 CE, contains a stunning example of insular art. Dublin has a number of large art galleries throughout the city, including the Irish Museum of Modern Art, the National Gallery, the Hugh Lane Municipal Gallery, the City Arts Centre, the Douglas Hyde Gallery, the Project Arts Centre, and the Royal Hibernian Academy.

Dublin is also a center for sports, headquartering Ireland's organizations for Gaelic football, soccer, rugby, and hurling. It has a national aquatic center, several racecourses, and basketball, handball, and hockey stadiums. It has shopping galore, most famously, and traditionally on Grafton and Henry streets, plus one of the largest shopping centers in Europe, in Dundrum.

Dublin is also the primary educational center in Ireland with three universities and a total of twenty third-level institutes. The University of Dublin, the oldest university in Ireland, dates back to the sixteenth century. Trinity College was established by Royal Charter under Elizabeth I. It was closed to Catholics until Catholic Emancipation, a process spanning the late eighteenth and early nineteenth centuries, by which many of the restrictions on Catholics, imposed by a series of English laws dating back to the mid-sixteenth century, were reduced or removed. After Catholic Emancipation, however, the Catholic hierarchy itself banned Catholics from attending Trinity College until 1970. (I guess this was initially based on a moral view that Catholic students should not attend a college steeped for hundreds of years in Protestant doctrine and orientation. That view prevailed until the church acknowledged that the religiosity of the instruction from Trinity had abated and what remained was an extraordinarily solid level of secular education.)

But wait. The Irish may have contributed more than their fair share to the fine arts, but Dubliners still know the value of a pint or two, so you'll also still find a pub on almost every street across the city center.

With all that Dublin and Ireland did have to offer, the one thing I knew that Ireland didn't have much of was Jews. When we arrived in Dublin in 1988, I was mourning the death of my father, and I hadn't even thought of trying to find a synagogue where I could say Kaddish, the Jewish prayer for the deceased, while we were there.

Chapter 3

Saying Kaddish in Dublin?

My father died in October 1987. Upon the death of a loved one, numerous observances are mandated by Jewish law, but it's up to the individual to decide which, if any, he or she will follow. One is that all in mourning say a prayer, the Kaddish. Another is that you sit *shiva*, meaning, among other things, that for the first seven days after the death, you remain inside a house and members of the community come to pay their respects.

To say Kaddish you must have a *minyan,* a congregation consisting of at least ten adult Jews. You can have a service with less than a minyan, but you can't say Kaddish without one. Kaddish is said as a part of regular morning and evening services seven days a week. (Orthodox Jews say prayers three times daily.) Typically, services are at 7:00 a.m. and 6:00 p.m. Not all synagogues hold these daily services, so if you're saying Kaddish you seek one out that does and that arranges for a minyan at all services. You say Kaddish for eleven months. Because of the large commitment involved, and because I'm not particularly religious, I tried to rationalize my way out of saying Kaddish.

I made my pitch to my sister's rabbi while we were sitting shiva at her house. Last time I'll pick a rabbi as a foil. He told me that of the many healing and other positive elements that came from saying Kaddish, one was that you'd find groups ready to help in the strangest of places. Before he became a rabbi, and at a time when he hadn't even considered himself particularly religious, he was saying Kaddish for his father when one day he found himself in a small town in Iowa. "I was in a local drugstore and asked the owner if there was a synagogue anywhere within driving distance."

"'No,' said the owner. 'Why do you want to know?'"

"I said, 'I'm saying a prayer for my father that can only be said in a congregation of Jews.'"

"'Oh, so you're saying Kaddish?'"

"Surprised that this old fella in the middle of a small Iowa town knew about Kaddish, I said, 'Yes.'"

"He said, 'Be here tonight at six. I'll make sure there's a minyan for you in the back room.' He was good to his word. In the middle of the cornfields of Iowa, I was able to say Kaddish for my father, because nine strangers took time out of their lives to be in the back room of a drugstore to make sure that a man, whom they'd never met before and would never meet again, would be able to honor his father's memory."

It was an inspiring story, but I was still looking for a way out with a minimum amount of guilt. As I was contemplating my next move, the rabbi asked, "Did your father say Kaddish for his parents?"

"Yes, he did." But, I quickly added, "He said it was a great burden, and often he was the one left holding the bag to get the ninth or tenth person to come to the minyan."

Then, I tossed in what I thought was the clincher. "My father told me on many occasions not to say Kaddish for him when the time came."

By this time, the rabbi had his left arm across his stomach. He used it is as a perch for his right arm, and his right hand was on his chin.

Uh oh, I thought to myself. *He's not convinced, and he has that meditative look of Rodin's The Thinker.*

Now stroking his chin, the rabbi said, "Tell me. Did he say don't? Or did he say *don't!*"

Meekly I conceded, "He said, don't."

The rabbi said, "Then do! Your father wasn't forbidding it; he was saying he wanted to spare you the burden. Don't take him up on that. Honor his memory."

Damned if this rabbi was going to let me off the hook. He'd deftly blocked my excuse by turning my father's "don't" into a "do" (I swear rabbis are alchemists). Cornered, and out of respect for my father and for my mother, who was then still alive, I committed to say Kaddish for my dad. (A few years later I said Kaddish for my mom.)

In saying Kaddish, I discovered real priorities. I'm not a morning person, but I never missed being at synagogue by 7:00 a.m. I scheduled meetings for afternoons, but always told people in advance that I'd have to leave no later than 5:15. Many people take that to mean "around 5:15," perhaps 5:30, or 5:45, or if necessary, 6:15. When I stated my outside departure time, however, I always emphasized that I meant not one minute later and, at times, I left meetings before they concluded. I remember getting some furrowed brows from people obviously thinking that this was a funny way for a "downtown" lawyer to act, but the deeper into saying Kaddish I became, the stronger I felt about my commitment.

More times than not, I'd see many of the same people at the morning and evening services, and we developed a natural bond. Certain prayers vary as the year progresses, so I felt the seasons passing like never before. I felt close to my father in a way that helped me with the suffering of his loss. The rhythm of attending services daily imparted a sense of tranquility.

Initially, I'd thought that saying Kaddish was an outdated and silly custom, but in the end, the experience humbled me. I came to understand that sometimes wisdom is borne of the experience of tens of millions of people who, over thousands of years had felt the same grief I was then undergoing. They'd said Kaddish and by doing so, though they still knew the pain of the loss, they'd emerged feeling some peace. In a sense, they passed down to me the benefit of their experiences and by doing so helped bring me some serenity.

Fast forward to May 1988 and our first trip to Ireland. Karen and I landed in Dublin on a Friday night. I said, "I feel funny. This is the first time I'm not saying Kaddish since October."

"Why don't you make a few calls and see if you can find a synagogue?"

I literally broke out laughing. "Kaddish in Dublin? You've got to be kidding. Are there even two thousand Jews in the whole country?"

"Just make a few calls."

This was one of those times when "Yes, dear" was the quickest way to put an end to a silly suggestion. *I'll look at the phone book, find no synagogues, and that'll be that.* To my surprise, I found the name of a synagogue. I called. I was told its regular Sabbath services were the following morning, and I was welcome to attend. I had my back to Karen as I was talking. Slowly I hung up the phone. Even more slowly I turned around. There she stood, her head slightly tilted to one side, her arms crossed in front of her, the fingers of one hand doing a slow drumbeat against an arm. "Well?"

"Services are at nine, but we're a bit late for dinner right now, so I think we need to get going."

She smiled that smile of complete satisfaction, said nothing more, and turned to get ready for dinner.

The next morning I was a nervous wreck. Never before had I even conceived of going to a synagogue in Ireland, but there I was, not only about to go, but to say Kaddish for my father. What if the services were in Irish? What if I sat in someone's regular seat? What if, when I walked in, everyone pointed a finger at me, like in the movie *Body Snatchers* and started screaming in some horrible tone, "American! American! Get him!" So I did what I always do when I'm nervous. I arrived forty-five minutes early, hoping to "blend" with the crowd and find some corner in which to hide. I must have been a military scout in a former life. Of course, the shul was shut tight when I arrived, so rather than being able to hide, I was standing on the street, sticking out in public like a sore thumb.

The doors finally opened. I decided to wait five minutes. If no one came within that time, I could leave and tell Karen there wouldn't have been a minyan, anyway. I was framing my argument.

It's not my fault that not enough people were there. What did you expect? This is Ireland, not Manhattan."

Just then, congregants began to pour into the synagogue.

Well, that argument won't work, I thought to myself. *I can't lie to Karen, especially about a religious ceremony.*

I entered and then had my next surprise. The seating for the women was separate and upstairs. I shook my head and laughed quietly. You've got to be kidding. *The first time I'm attending services in an Orthodox shul is in Ireland? This proves that God has a sense of humor.*

In the States, the area where the service is performed is always in front, exactly like in any church. Those leading the service are on a raised platform, called a bema. Here, there were two raised platform areas, one in the front and one smack in the center, sort of like a theater in the round, an arrangement new to me, but apparently fairly common in European synagogues.

In my continuing effort to blend, assuming the service would be led from the front bema, I edged about three-quarters of the way back from it and sat down. Damn. The seats all had plaques with names on them. So, on top of everything else, I *was* going to be tossed out of my seat when Shlomo Cohen showed up. This was not turning out well.

I busied myself looking at a prayer book. All in Hebrew. Double damn. Now I couldn't get away with saying, "I had to leave. It was all in Irish." Then, too, there'd be no cheating during the service through recitation of a lot of English, as you'd find in a nice reform synagogue in the States. I'd really have to fake it. I knew the Kaddish cold, so that was okay, but giving myself the benefit of the doubt, my ability to read Hebrew was maybe a C+. I saw in my mind's eye more outstretched arms with fingers pointing and screaming, "American! American! Get him!"

I was trying to come up with some excuse for leaving and how to do so without causing too much of a fuss when I thought I heard a voice from behind me.

"What's yer name, lad?" I turned around and saw a leprechaun in a silk top hat and tails.

"I beg your pardon?"

"What's yer name, lad?"

I *almost* blurted out, "Why, it's Dorothy and I'm from Kansas and I want to go home."

"Lad, yer name?"

"My, my name is Harvey. Harvey Gould."

"No, lad. In Hebrew. What's yer name in Hebrew?"

I couldn't remember anyone ever asking me my Hebrew name. I managed to croak, "Chanan Laib."

24

"And what are ye doing in Ireland?"

I was slowly beginning to realize that I must have slipped through the looking glass into Alice's Wonderland. I hadn't fully registered that this leprechaun, wearing a top hat and tails, and with an Irish brogue thick enough to slice, was actually an Orthodox Jew, talking to me in a synagogue in Ireland. None of this made sense. All Irish were either Catholics or Protestants. I think I mumbled something brilliant like, "Oh, not much. Just here to enjoy your country."

He tipped his hat and quietly walked away. I wondered if he was heading off to report this encounter to the Mad Hatter.

I was still in shock and consequently had lost the thread of my plan of escape when the service started. *Oh, boy. I'm in for the long haul.* At least I hadn't been tossed from my seat, but I then realized that the service was emanating from the bema behind me, so I had my back to those conducting the service, making me feel that much more like an idiot (in Ireland, an eejit).

After awhile, I got into the swing of things and calmed down. It looked like I might survive this ordeal. At one point, I turned around and there was the leprechaun along with three other men in top hats and tails, each sitting on a corner of the bema. I'd never seen anything like this, but these men were the *shomrei Shabbos*, or the Guardians of the Sabbath. They were to make sure that all was conducted properly—perhaps including a new rule never again to allow a Yank to sneak into their midst.

We reached the part of the service where the Torah is taken out of the ark. The Torah is read three times a week: on Mondays, Thursdays, and Saturdays. In every synagogue all over the world, the exact same *parsha*, or portion, of the Torah is read on the same day. One person chants the parsha aloud, but others are called up for the honor of chanting prayers before and after the parsha readings. When called to do these prayers you're given an *aliyah* (literally meaning to go up), which is considered a high honor. In the States you know beforehand if you'll be getting an aliyah. Among other things, this means you can brush up on the prayers, if necessary, to make sure you don't stumble when the time comes for you to chant them for real. When one is called to the Torah for an aliyah, the

Torah reader calls up the designated person by chanting his name, in an Orthodox shul, by his Hebrew name.

I was still trying hard to appear small when I thought I heard "Chanan Laib" in the midst of a long string of unintelligible Hebrew chanting. Then came a pause that seemed to last an eternity. I turned around. The leprechaun was standing on the bema, beckoning me with his index finger and a wink.

I pointed to my chest, raising my eyebrows, without words asking, *Me?* He nodded.

Oh, my God! They're giving me an aliyah! If I screw this up, they'll revive the Old Testament punishment of stoning!

I walked up to the bema looking far steadier than I was feeling. As in all synagogues, there were placards with the prayers. In the States, and in almost all reform and conservative synagogues, the placard is a cheat sheet, an English transliteration of the Hebrew blessings. No such luck. The prayers on this placard were, thank you very much, in Hebrew only. Now, I've chanted these blessings many times. I'd gone to Hebrew school, and had my bar mitzvah. But all that went out the window. Here, now, I was just a weak-kneed, know-nothing Jew still wondering if I could make all this go away by closing my eyes, clicking my heels quickly three times, and saying, *There's no place like home. There's no place like home.* When that didn't work, I did what trial lawyers always do when faced with a challenge. I gave myself a quick talking-to, thinking, *Quit being a pansy. You can do this.* Then I belted it out, gaining strength from hearing my own voice. (In case you haven't noticed, lawyers love to hear their own voices.)

It worked. I finished the first round of blessings just fine, but I still had a second set to chant after the parsha. My confidence was up and I was standing there, trying to get the first word of the second set of prayers firmly in my brain, when one of the men standing on the bema next to me did what Jews all over the world do during services and what Catholics simply cannot understand. He started talking to me.

"So, why are ye here?"

"Oh, just traveling."

"No, I mean why are ye in synagogue?"

"Oh. I'm saying Kaddish for my father."

I thought I'd given the man a heart attack. He took on a sickly pallor. He immediately walked away from me to hold a meeting with two other men on the bema, including the leprechaun. Slowly, he walked back and said, "According to Halacha (Jewish law), you must deny yourself certain pleasures during mourning. Being called to the Torah is the ultimate pleasure, so when you're saying Kaddish, you can't have an aliyah."

It wasn't raining, but I knew I was about be struck by a lightning bolt. He continued, "But since we called you and obviously you didn't know, go ahead and finish the prayers." In other words, on a very close vote, the remainder of my aliyah wasn't vetoed, which undoubtedly would have been a first in Jewish history.

By some miracle, I remembered the first word of the second set of prayers and that's all I needed to navigate the balance safely. When I finished, all on the bema shook my hand, honoring me by saying "Yashe Koach," traditionally said to one who has just actively participated in the Torah reading, although I thought it more likely that most of them wanted to wring my neck.

I returned to my seat where I remained for the rest of the service without looking back again. I recalled my discussion with the rabbi who had found a minyan in the back of a drugstore in a small town in Iowa. "Let's see," I pictured telling the rabbi, "wasn't I the guy who told you I'd never end up needing a minyan in an unlikely place? Oy vey."

As the service neared its end, I leaned forward, went into a mild trance, and saw my dad's smiling eyes. He loved a good story and what had just happened was a doozy.

"Son, you've outdone yourself this time."

It was for you, Dad. I screwed things up a bit by accepting the aliyah, but I did the prayers, and I just said Kaddish for you—in Ireland. By the way, how was my chanting?

"You did a fine job. You were right on tune. Not quite as good as your old man, but pretty good. And son, the rabbi you talked to about saying Kaddish for me was right. I did mean 'do.' And God bless you for doing it."

Don't get me all choked up now, Dad. I have to get back to Karen after this service ends.

"Tell her I heard her advice last night to try to find a synagogue where you could say Kaddish. Remember when I gave her a kiss the first time you brought her to us and I said, 'Welcome to the family'?"

I remember.

"Well, this time you give her a kiss *for* me and tell her I knew what I was doing."

That'll be easy. Bye, Dad. We'll talk again.

"Good-bye, son."

After the service, the leprechaun asked me to join the congregation for the Kiddush—after a Sabbath service all members retire to another part of the synagogue and say prayers over wine and bread. Then, the congregation does another thing that Jews always do as a community: eat together. Sometimes there's also schnapps so you can have a drink, all very friendly.

Meanwhile, even after my chat with my dad, I was still embarrassed about my aliyah faux pas, and I didn't want to extend my embarrassment by mixing with the congregation in a social setting just to hear them say, "So you're the lad who …"

I was visualizing a story in the local Jewish press: "A dumb cluck Yank took an aliyah at an Orthodox shul in Dublin while he was still mourning the death of his father."

I wanted out, so I made my apologies to the leprechaun, skulked out of the synagogue, scurried back to the hotel, and gave Karen a blow-by-blow of what had just happened.

The first thing she asked me was, "Why didn't you stay for the Kiddush?"

She knew what it would take me a number of return trips to learn: the Irish don't run from such situations. They embrace them. And now I know that if I had it to do over again, I'd have laughed it off, gone to the Kiddush, and had a few schnapps. Then I'd have shared some stories with the leprechaun and others in the congregation. I'd have laughed with them about my mistake and convinced them to agree to give me an aliyah every time I returned to the Old Sod.

In return, as I'd ask for my third schnapps, I'd have offered a toast, "*L'chaim!* (To life!) And thank you for the honor of the aliyah that you granted me today. I'm sorry I didn't know that I should have refused it. I meant no disrespect, but I still loved chanting the prayers, all the while thinking of my father, may his memory be for a blessing. May you have *shalom bayit* (peace in your homes), and may we share in the future the same spirit of joy that we shared today."

I would have made friends for life with every Orthodox Jew in Ireland. The congregation would have hoisted me on their shoulders and danced around the room (another mourning violation) as I would have yelled, "Another schnapps!"

But this was my first trip to Ireland, and I was still an eejit.

Chapter 4

Heading Out of Dublin

After remaining in Dublin for a few days, it was time to leave for our horseback riding trip. We were heading first to Castle Leslie in Monaghan, on the border with Northern Ireland, and then to Sligo.

The first order of business was to pick up our two car rentals at the Dublin Airport.

Michael and I handed over our reservations. The man behind the desk looked up our information, took a moment to study it, and then asked, "How many of you will be in each car?"

I answered, "Two in one car, three in the other."

"And how much luggage will you be carrying?"

Michael said, "Eight suitcases, plus totes."

"No way all of you will fit in the cars you've reserved."

Being savvy travelers, we knew that the role of car rental agents all over the world is to get you to upgrade to a larger and more expensive car. Michael and I exchanged a knowing glance that we weren't about to be shagged lightly.

I asked, "Can we see the cars to judge for ourselves?"

"No problem a' tall," the man said politely. "Just walk down to the far end of the car park where you'll see the cars in numbered areas. Drive the cars around the airport circle, ending back up in front of the airport. There's a lane for rented cars."

Off we went to pick up the two cars we'd reserved, a bit full of ourselves for avoiding the scam.

It took perhaps twenty minutes to get the cars back to the front of the airport. The lane for the rented cars was just a narrow strip with iron posts on each side to guide you to the correct place to load up your luggage.

This was my first experience driving a car in Ireland, done in the English style. The first time is always a shock and a challenge. The driver's seat is on the right, and we'd reserved stick shift cars: automatics were probably up to three times as expensive. With the gearshift on the floor, you shift with your left hand so the whole thing is backward to us Yanks. Then, once you get out into the flow of traffic, everything is really backward. But we'll get to that.

Meanwhile, Michael and I managed to retrieve the two cars and drive them, somewhat awkwardly, to the front of the airport where Karen, Jann, and Bernadette waited with the luggage. We tried three or four different versions of loading the bags and finally thought we'd succeeded, until my ever-practical wife pointed out that with many of the bags now in the backseats, the five of us should see if we could fit. It turned out we could—if Bernadette and Jann rode on the roof. We gave up the ghost. The guy behind the desk was right. These cars were too small. Somewhat sheepishly, Michael and I headed back to the car rental desk. Karen, Jann, and Bernadette settled onto a patch of grass next to the cars, somewhat amused at our predicament.

I mumbled, "We think we need the next size car."

"Won't work."

Michael said, "Well, we almost had everything in the first cars we tried, so the next size up should be just fine."

"Here are the keys. I'll see you again when you want the bigger cars."

Michael and I, a tad less full of ourselves than the first time, left to return the wrong cars and get the right ones. We pulled up to the loading curb. After another twenty minutes trying to pack everything and everyone in, we were reduced to the ignominy of returning to the guy behind the counter, tails tightly tucked between our legs. This time, he just held out two new sets of keys and said nothing. We half smiled, exchanged keys, and headed off a third time for the cars. By now, the thrill was gone. We just wanted to get on the damn road to Castle Leslie.

I pulled my car up to the front of the airport. Michael, a bit cranky by this time, turned his head for a moment too long as he was driving to the loading area, and smashed right into one of the posts. The window on the driver's side was down. As he repeatedly smacked his steering wheel, I'm sure I'm not the only traveler who heard him shout, "Fuck! Fuck! Fuck! Fuck! Fuck!" Just as he was finishing his venting, a *garda* (police officer) walked over to us, and we wondered if we were about to see what the inside of a garda station looked like.

The officer said, "Now, lads, you've got to be moving along. Get your gear into your cars and be off with you."

I didn't bother saying that we'd pretty much been trying to be off for about an hour, as we'd struggled to find the right cars for our gear. Instead, I said, "Yes, officer. We'll be gone in just a moment."

We threw our luggage inside. It and the five of us all fit easily, just as the smug rental car agent had told us all along. We dashed back into the airport to sign the papers, and finally we were on the road for Castle Leslie.

By then, we were used to sitting in the wrong driver's seat and shifting backward, but now we were also on the wrong side of the road. On the highway, the left lane is the slow lane; to pass a car, you pull into the right lane. When you come to a roundabout (the European version of an intersection with traffic from different entry points feeding into it), the right-of-way is to drivers coming from your right. It takes awhile to get the feel of first looking in that direction for oncoming traffic and it takes practice to know which lane to get into as you enter a roundabout, which depends on the exit you want to take out of the roundabout.

As we headed out of the city, Michael handed me a set of maps and said that as soon as we got to a safe spot, we'd pull over and he'd review the route he'd laid out for us to get to Castle Leslie.

There are two kinds of people in this world: map lovers and those who either are neutral to maps or hate them. Michael is a map lover. I'm not. Michael loves the way maps fold and unfold. He loves to spread a map on a big, smooth table and study the national highways, from county roads to local roads, which usually mean a flat tire within five minutes from nails stuck in the mud. He adores using magic markers to highlight his proposed route. He revels in researching the likely kinks in the route and how best to navigate around them. Me, I just want a general idea of where I'm heading and worry later about how to finesse getting there. Michael would have loved traveling with Lewis and Clark. I probably would have mutinied.

After we were a mile or so out of Dublin, Michael found a safe place to pull over, and dutifully, I pulled in behind him. He ran back to our car and began to unfold the map as he approached us. I was holding my ground. I didn't take out my map. Just as he arrived at our car, he was already explaining the route we'd take, where the problem spots were, and how we'd get around them. I let him go on for a full minute as he leaned through the window and pointed to his map spread across my lap. Finally, I said, "I've got an idea. Why don't you lead and I'll follow you?"

"Okay," he said, hurt that I didn't want more detail about the mapped route, but I knew I'd won the day, because he was already folding the map.

"Just don't lose me!" I yelled as he walked back to his car.

He raised a hand in recognition of his obligation not to lose us. He led. I followed. We arrived at Castle Leslie without a hitch.

Chapter 5

Riding at Castle Leslie

Bigger than its American cousin and with more endurance, the Irish Thoroughbred has what riders refer to as heart, not just a willingness to carry its rider, but its own love of riding and courage to take on challenging jumps.

Irish children start riding at an early age and quickly learn the rules. It's unacceptable to return a horse in a sweat; if you've been out for a hard ride, you walk your horse the last mile or so before you dismount to let him cool down. When a rider dismounts, and before tending to her own comfort, first she runs up the irons (the stirrups), loosens the horse's girth, lifts the rear of the saddle to let air get to his back, and then removes the horse's saddle and bridle. She puts on his halter, gives him a good pat on the neck, and a treat—a lump of sugar or a carrot or two. Then she can take off her helmet and take some water herself. If it's warm out and her horse is still overheated, she gives him a good hosing to cool him down.

It's not that American kids don't love horses. They do. It's just that for the Irish, it's in their blood. They've seen their parents handle horses, and they learn the lessons by example, and in doing so, discover the grander lessons—respect for animals, compassion, and responsibility, the extent to which others rely on us, and critically, that we are not at the center of the universe.

Even those Irish who don't ride respect the horse and its place in their history. Castle Leslie (where years later Paul McCartney and Heather Mills were married) was a perfect introduction to the country for those who shared in this love.

Jann knew Sammy (Samantha) Leslie, a riding instructor and one of the owner/operators of Castle Leslie. That was our reason for going there. Castle Leslie is in Monaghan, right on the border of Northern Ireland. At the time we were there, the castle wasn't available to guests. Instead, twenty or so of us riders slept in bedrooms in the hunting lodge. (The castle was later refurbished and apparently now is used for guests.) Everything revolved around horseback riding. On the first day, already in riding clothes, all guests had breakfast together. Then, we went outside where the horses were brought to us, all tacked and ready to go, which Karen and I came to call "the Irish way." Back home, before you're ready to ride, you catch your horse in the pasture, bring him in, groom him, pick his feet, and put on his tack (saddle, bridle, and sometimes other special equipment). The Irish way was sheer heaven. After asking a few preliminary questions about our riding experience, the instructors matched horse to rider.

On that first day, after we'd all mounted, we were taken into an outdoor riding ring where the instructors put us through some fairly mild paces to be sure we knew at least the basics of riding: hold the reins properly, post correctly at the trot, sit the trot, canter, and do so on the correct lead. We also popped over a few small jumps. In short, the proprietors wanted to assure themselves that the group was devoid of any buffoons who didn't know how to ride well enough to go on the planned excursions.

At this stage, the instructors changed around a few horse-and-rider combinations having gained a few clues, for example, about which riders might be more capable of handling a particularly headstrong horse.

There was no pressure. If you wanted to remain in the riding ring the whole time and take lessons, you could do so. If you wanted to go out on the one thousand acre, cross-country course and jump until you dropped, it was fine with them. If you wanted to go out on the cross-country course, but ride from hilltop to hilltop without doing any jumping (hill topping), right this way.

Jann, Michael, and I all may as well have had an *L* branded into our foreheads for *Lunatic*, because we were part of the group of jumpers. Although Karen also took some jumps on the cross-country course, her preference, and Bernadette's, was to be part of the group that took dressage lessons and some trail rides, including hill topping.

I figured I was in for a more than a decent ride when I saw my mount, a black stallion. The first clue was that he was the size of a mountain. The second clue was that his name was Turbo. The third clue was that his mane was roached. Think of a big kid with a Mohawk haircut. When I mounted him, I felt like my head was on a level with treetops. In fact, while other horses grazed on the grass (although you shouldn't allow your horse to graze when he's fully tacked up), the fourth and final clue was that Turbo pulled out and munched on—bushes.

Unlike foxhunting, as I'd learn in later years, the kind of pleasure riding we did at Castle Leslie isn't as constant. When you ride and when you stop is at the discretion of the instructor, but there's a mix of walking, trotting, cantering, hand galloping, and for the lunatics, jumping over the man-made, cross-country obstacles, intentionally built at different degrees of difficulty. Still, even with the occasional stops, the riding was both exhilarating and difficult.

On our first day, I was bringing up the rear of a single file line of horses going downhill amid a fairly dense copse of trees when I thought I heard a faint call from the front of the line, "Okay, are we ready for a wee trot?" (If you ride in Ireland, don't be fooled when your leader asks if you're ready for a "wee" trot or a "wee" canter. To the Irish "a wee trot" means one that lasts so long that your legs are burning, "a wee canter" means one that continues until you're sweating, oxygen deprived, and you can't even feel your legs anymore.)

Meanwhile, since trotting downhill through trees is not my idea of fun, I opened my mouth to say, "Can you wait till we're all on the flat?" But I never got out more than "Can" before the line ahead of me took off. I said to Turbo, "Okay, buddy. Your job is to avoid detesticularizing me." (Who cares if that's not a word? I sure as hell knew what I meant and it was a close call.)

After a number of wee trots and then walks, and after we took in the beauty of the surroundings, we had some "wee" canters. Many who don't ride think that the horse does all the work, and there's really no exercise for the rider. So a bystander watching us spend three hours or so riding might say, "When do these people get a workout?" I thought the same until I began riding, but believe me, when you're in the saddle for hours at a time, even with resting periods in between your wee trots and canters, you return with a warm and weary body.

At Castle Leslie, after three hours of riding in the morning, we had lunch and a brief rest period, and then went out again for another three hours of riding. Six hours in the saddle is a lot of riding in a day. In the States when Karen and I take lessons, both our horses and we get a good workout, though we either take or share a one-hour lesson.

After day one at Castle Leslie, everyone is feeling fit, a "good" tired, and for those who made it without a mishap, a bit cocky from making it without coming off the horse.

Day two you still feel good, but a tad more tired and a little stiff.

The end of day three is when the fun starts. At the end of the riding, no one can walk up the stairs without pain. The guys try to tough it out and climb without holding onto the handrails, but eventually you hear, "Oh, my God. I didn't even know I had muscles there." People grunt and groan, taking those stairs at the oddest angles I've ever seen, bending this way and that, some leaning heavily to one side or the other, depending on where their muscles are the sorest. Here's the trick. If you can make it through that third day (mounting and just sitting in the saddle, on the fourth day is no easy trick), you'll be fine. We were at Castle Leslie for six days and the riding, the scenery, the meals, and the camaraderie all made for a spectacularly memorable experience.

It's hard to describe jumping, but for me, it's a momentary and complete sense of freedom. Lifted off the ground on the back of an animal (actually, you should be standing in your stirrups to take weight off the horse's back), who weighs perhaps twelve hundred pounds, you have this brief sensation of weightlessness. At the same time, you can't get so lost in the moment that you forget to ride your horse. Jumping can be deadly business, especially cross-country jumping, where you're jumping immovable objects and sometimes, even when you do everything right, you can get into serious trouble.

Harvey in a Jump Competition in California

Years earlier in the States, Karen and I were spectators at a cross-country class taught by J. Michael Plumb, a former Olympic equestrian silver and gold medalist. Most of the spectators, not including us, were parents of children who were taking a lesson that day. One of the students was a teenage girl whose horse refused a complicated jump three times in a row. Plumb ordered her to bring her horse in front of the jump, hold him there, and hit him repeatedly as hard as she could with her riding crop or bat. As she did so, some in the crowd gasped.

Plumb turned to the crowd and said, "Apparently some of you are upset to see me teaching a teenager to strike a horse. Well, if you're going to ride a cross-country course, age is irrelevant. All that matters is that you and your horse do it correctly, because ridden incorrectly, it can be deadly. If a horse refuses a jump because of rider error, I blame the rider and instruct her how to correct her mistakes. If a repeated refusal is the horse's fault, as this time, then immediately he must be punished in front of the jump he refused. I hope that this will prevent a future disaster and avoid him ending up seriously hurting or killing himself and the rider. If you don't like the risks or the necessary training, then you should have your children find another sport."

With that, he turned his back on the spectators, returned to his lesson, and on the fourth attempt, the horse took the jump.

No one said a word. No one left the course. There was no more gasping. Plumb was right, I've carried his lesson with me, and occasionally, when I'm being a bit of a cowboy doing jumps, I say, *Hey, this is deadly stuff. Be serious. Do this right. You and your horse could end up injured or dead if you do it wrong.*

Show jumping consists of a jump course within an enclosed arena. The jumps include verticals, spreads, and double and triple combinations usually with many turns and changes of direction. Though it's dangerous, the jumps aren't stationery so a horse may knock down a rail, but it also can crash through a jump or throw you over his head into one, and you'll be getting up slowly and gingerly, or worse. However, on a cross-country course, there are no rails to knock down; all the jumps are immobile. If you take the jump but don't clear it, the result can be disastrous.

At Castle Leslie when we went out to ride cross-country, the leader took a jump first, and then invited others to do likewise. Next, she took a combination of two jumps, then three, and so on until she built her own mini-jump course for us to follow.

One day, our leader took us from a pasture into a wooded area by first jumping over a fence. From there, she showed us a series of jumps, one of them an "in and out"—that is, a set of square logs completely enclosing an area. You'd damn well better jump in and out properly or you'd spend the rest of your life in that tiny boxed-in space.

After we'd each taken the series of jumps she'd shown us, the leader told us that if we wanted, we could repeat the seven jumps in reverse. I said,

"Sounds great" (as I spent more time in Ireland, that would become, "That's grand"), and the instructor said, "Then off you go." And off I went.

Everything was going swimmingly. I'd taken the first six jumps and loved it, but in my reverie, I overshot the path to the last jump by perhaps twenty yards. Beyond the correct turn, I saw a trail that I mistook for the route to the final jump from the woods into the pasture. As I turned into it, I put my leg on Turbo to signal him to pick up speed. Big mistake.

You should always look ahead for the next jump, so you can gauge at what pace to bring the horse into it, pick the spot where you want to take off, line up the horse for the center of the jump, adjust his speed, and so on. But as I looked ahead, instead of seeing the jump I recalled, I saw a ten-foot cyclone fence. Because I'd urged Turbo to pick up speed and he'd obliged, he raced toward that fence ready to jump it or die in the effort, and of course, kill me as part of the deal. Worse, because the area was wooded, there was no place to turn. Even in my panic, I realized that turning off the path and into trees wasn't a sensible solution, so I used my "boy energy" like I've never used it before or since. Stopping a Sherman tank with your arms and shoulders is no small feat, particularly when you've just goosed the accelerator, but impending impalement on a cyclone fence is a great motivator. With maybe four to five feet to spare, I got Turbo to stop, and to this day, I swear that horse turned his head to me and said, "Sissy. I could've made that jump." I just sat on his back, breathing heavily, my heart racing.

Ever so slowly, we turned around, went back to the correct pathway, and easily took the final jump, my heart still thumping as a deer's after being caught in headlights. The instructor said, "That took a bit longer than I'd figured. Was there any problem?"

"No problem a' tall. We were just enjoying the sights."

I slept exceptionally well that night, happier than I can ever recall being alive and not sliced into a thousand pieces.

The beauty of the scenery and the thrill of jumping were memorable. Especially amazing was just being on the roads with the clippety-clop of our horse brigade when a car would pull over to the side, the driver would turn off the engine, and if a dog happened to be in the car, roll up the windows and hand-muzzle the dog to prevent it from barking. The drivers knew you don't want a horse spooking anytime, less so on a road, and even less so on wet pavement, often the case as we'd ride in the rain. We'd all give a light salute to the driver, who always saluted back.

I've ridden on roads in the States, where it seems that it's almost a game to see who can spook the horse first or perhaps more fairly, where there's simply no real understanding of how dangerous spooking can be to horse and rider, especially on a roadway, and especially if it's slick from rain. The difference in Ireland was being in a country that reveres the horse and to whom horses still play an ongoing part in daily lore. Still, every time I saw a driver pull over I just thought, *I don't believe it. I love it, but I don't believe it.*

Before we left Castle Leslie, we had one day off from riding and took a short tour of the area by car. At one point, we were obliged to cross into Northern Ireland, where we quickly came face-to-face with the Troubles, crossing a British military outpost with soldiers in battle fatigues carrying assault weapons. We were asked for identification. None of us had any with us, thinking we were just out for a simple country ride. Once they heard our accents, they let us pass, but not before telling us that there had been an "incident" the previous night and admonishing us on future outings to carry identification, as it was likely we'd be stopped routinely. Eight hundred years later and this was still an occupied land. Apparently, we were beyond the Pale. The Brits. Gotta love 'em.

Chapter 6

⌒

Riding at Sligo

After leaving Castle Leslie, our group headed to the next spot Jann had selected for our riding holiday: the Rectory, the house of Captain Vinnie Bligh in Drumcliffe, County Sligo. Captain Vinnie Bligh? It's true. You can't make up stuff like that. Vinnie was a retired captain in the Irish Army, making his living by leading horseback riding treks and using his house as a B&B. We had breakfast and dinner at his house; lunches were picnics packed by Vinnie's wife that we ate on the trail. Again, we rode every day, but the riding was different from Castle Leslie.

First, instead of mounting our horse each day from the same point, Vinnie arranged the preceding night to transport the horses to a new starting location, so each morning he'd drive us there, and we'd ride across a different terrain. Second, our group comprised his only riders—a small clique, tight and friendly. Third, this was the first time that season these horses had been ridden. They'd been feeding in open pastures most of the winter where the grass was well salted from the ocean sprays. So, these horses were as high as some of those who'd spent the Summer of Love in San Francisco and then never remembered it. (As Willie Nelson once famously said, "If you remember the sixties, you didn't live 'em.") Finally, unlike Castle Leslie, where we were confined to a huge area controlled by the landowners, much of it with trails and prearranged cross-country courses, in Sligo we were riding across patches of public and farmland and the terrain varied from fairly rugged to beaches, so the type of riding varied to fit the terrain.

When Vinnie paired me with my horse, it seemed that a theme had begun to develop during this trip. At Castle Leslie, I rode Turbo who was solid black, the size of a mountain, and ate bushes for a snack. Vinnie put me on Ben Bulben, a solid gray mare, and because of her size, properly named—after a local mountain. Ben Bulben was fine at the walk, but every time I put my leg on her to ask for a trot, she reared. It may have looked cool when the Lone Ranger's Silver went up on his two hind legs, but it scares the hell out of you and it should. If that horse falls over on you, you're dead. Possibly, she is too, but you definitely are. I'd never had a horse rear on me before and thank God, it's never happened since.

Jann was not just a friend, she was our riding instructor, so I kept telling her that my horse was rearing every time I gave her the leg signal to trot. Jann kept insisting I was being ridiculous. "Everyone overdramatizes and says their horse is rearing, when she's just prancing."

Right then, Vinnie yelled, "Is everyone ready for a wee trot?" and he took off. I put my leg on Ben Bulben and up she went on her two hind legs.

As Jann pulled ahead of me, I heard her yell, "Holy shit! She is rearing!"

I managed to hang on until Ben Bulben got over her scary habit, and then we got down to business. Vinnie's one rule was that we were never allowed to get in front of him, a sensible precaution to prevent riders from getting out of control. Still, Michael and I decided that we wanted to ride like the wind and get a tad out of control. So, we often held our horses back, let Vinnie and the rest of the group get a quarter-mile ahead of us, and then ripped to the back of the line at a mad hand gallop, standing in the stirrups the whole way. Just as Vinnie was turning around, we'd have just reached the back of the line, had our horses back in a walk, donned expressions of angelic innocence, and appeared to be casually looking around at the scenery. Vinnie remained suspicious, but we continued to play our game as the women shook their heads at our high school antics.

New to us was riding on beaches. At one point on one beach, Vinnie told us we could canter and we did. Karen canters, but it's not her favorite gait. She doesn't particularly like speed, and feels a loss of control at a faster gait. Still, she was being a good sport and put her horse into a full canter. She started pulling away from me, her horse obviously feeling his "salt" and deciding to have a good solid stretch of his legs. Well, this wasn't going to happen to my woman. Macho Harv to the rescue. Of course, I'd seen millions of movies where the cowboy pulls alongside of a runaway horse with some damsel in distress desperately trying to hold on while the cowboy casually grabs the reins and brings the horse slowly to a halt. Not to be outdone, I urged my horse on and started pulling up to Karen. The problem was her horse must have thought, *The race is on.* And he wasn't about to lose. He slipped into fifth gear and was literally gone like a shot. I've never seen anything like it.

Years later, when I read the book and saw the movie *Seabiscuit,* the true story of one of the winningest American race horses in history, what jumped out at me was a scene in which Seabiscuit ran a head-to-head match against War Admiral, the favorite to win a race dubbed the Match of the Century.

Seabiscuit's regular jockey was injured, so he counseled the substitute rider to gain the lead, but then intentionally hold Seabiscuit back. "Let War Admiral come up on him. When the Biscuit sees his eye and knows he's being challenged, release his reins, leg him on, and put the whip to him. He'll burst into a gallop no horse can match." And that's exactly what happened in that race at the Pimlico Race Course in Baltimore in 1938.

Meanwhile, back on the Sligo beaches in 1988, unwittingly I was riding War Admiral to Karen's Seabiscuit, who was up to the challenge. I was at a flat-out gallop, when her horse pulled away from me as if I was standing still, shooting past Vinnie like a rocket. Oops. Not exactly what I'd visualized.

Then I looked up and perhaps a quarter-mile straight ahead, I saw an outcropping of rocks. There was no way around them. Either your horse stopped, or you'd be like Wylie Coyote in one of those many cartoons where all that's left is his outline after falling from some mountaintop or shot from a cannon and into a cliff.

I knew Karen was scared to death, but instinctively she did the right thing. She stood in her stirrups and rode him out. No way could she muscle him to a halt and knew if she even tried, she'd fly off the horse and at that speed, even falling on sand is no guarantee that you won't end up with a broken neck. Unbelievably, as the horse got close to the rocks, he started to ride in a wide circle and ever so slowly, finally came to a halt.

I can sum up Vinnie's attitude: he was not pleased. From then on, I never again challenged Karen's horse. If I had, although she's not a violent woman, she'd likely have killed me.

We spent one Saturday evening at a local pub in Drumcliffe, a short walk from the Bligh's residence. To get to the pub, we walked by a cemetery where, as it turned out, the famous Irish poet and playwright, W. B. Yeats, is buried. We read the inscription on his tombstone: "Cast a cold eye on life, on death. Horseman pass by!" What I didn't know until sometime later is that the inscription came from the last lines of one of his final poems titled, "Under Ben Bulben," inspired by the Sligo countryside and its nearby mountain. Yeats's gravesite is one of the few attractions in Drumcliffe, and the next day when we saw people gathered at the cemetery, Michael said, "We're not witnessing an actual funeral. They don't have much to do in Drumcliffe, so as a local attraction, they bury Yeats every Sunday."

We also had a special treat in Sligo. One day at lunchtime, instead of stopping and having our picnic packed by Vinnie's wife, we dismounted, tied up our horses loosely to hitching posts, and entered Ellen's Pub. I don't remember what I ate, but for the rest of my life I'll remember the sensation of getting off our horses, hitching them to a post, and strutting into a pub for a meal and a pint.

During that lunch, we learned that Ellen's Pub was one of the few places in the locality that hosted regular sessions of live Irish music and dancing. We returned the next night to get a real slice of Irish life, stepping into a world that seemed 150 years old. Ellen's Pub was the genuine item. It had dirt floors and honest-to-God local musicians playing the fiddle, the guitar, and of course, the bodhran (pronounced boreon), a shallow handheld drum that you beat to create a hypnotic rhythm.

But what really got us that night was the dancing. The men and women were seated on benches against the walls on opposite sides of the room. When the music finally moved them, the men crossed the divide and extended their hands. Once a couple started there was no halfway to this dancing. From the outset, they were flying, hands tightly tucked at their sides, eyes straight ahead, expressionless faces, and feet hitting the dirt hard at a phenomenal pace, certain to break someone's spinal cord. Somehow, there were no vertebral injuries. The five of us did our best to join in, but it was hopeless. These folks were off in a different world and all that we could do, really, was watch in awe and have a few pints, and then a few more.

Then it was time to go back to Vinnie's house. Karen, Bernadette, and I had come in one car. Jann and Michael had come in theirs. They left before we did, so we were on our own, and saying that Ellen's Pub was out in the country and far from Vinnie's, is like saying the Milky Way is out in space and far from earth. The pub was so far out in the country that none of us really had a clue about how to get back from where we'd come, and all we had was the moonlight as a guide—no Michael and no maps. I'm not saying that we'd had too much to drink, but I will say the talk in the car was animated, and as we approached an intersection, Karen and Bernadette, without hesitation, told me to turn right.

Now, I'm the first to admit that my sense of direction is about as good as the vision of the three blind mice. Still, something was nagging at me to turn left. Maybe it was a vague memory of over which shoulder I'd seen the moon on the way to Ellen's, maybe it was something else. But all my instincts were telling me to go left. On the other hand, I trusted Karen's sense of direction more than mine, so I turned right.

There we were, the three of us, feeling no pain and heartily enjoying a good laugh when all of a sudden I saw the road peter out at the edge of a bog, essentially a wetland that over time, accumulates peat, which is a deposit of dead plant material. Once peat is formed and cut, it's a wonderful material to burn, giving warmth and a pleasing earthy scent, also used in some single malts for a heavy flavor.

While the bog is still forming, though, going into one is a bit like sinking into a tar pit. Worse yet, bogs occur where the water at the ground is highly acidic. Think the comic book character, *Swamp Thing*. In short, had I not stomped on the brakes I'd not be writing this book. Instead, the American Embassy would still have an unanswered circular about three missing Yanks, last seen at Ellen's Pub somewhere on the outskirts of some village not far, as the crow flies, from Vinnie Bligh's house.

Wouldn't you know it? For the first time in my life I'd been correct. We should have turned left. As I ever so slowly backed up the car to a point when I could turn around, it was suddenly so quiet that you could hear three Yanks breathing.

The next day we were off for another ride. Along the way we came to a man standing at a gate. Vinnie told us to stay mounted, not say a word, and await his further command. He dismounted and walked up to the man. We sat on our horses, more or less quietly. For about twenty minutes Vinnie and the man had a splendid blabbering time. Finally, they shook hands, Vinnie remounted, the man opened the gate, and we entered at a walk, and then picked up a nice trot. Once we were safely out of view from the man at the gate, Vinnie stopped.

When we pulled up to him, he told us about the grouchy German farmer who'd never before allowed him to ride across his land. He said this was the first time he'd ever had a chance to talk to him while he was out for a ride. When we asked what he said to convince the man to change his mind, we learned a key to Irish thinking.

"I never mentioned a thing about wanting to ride on his land. The first thing we talked about was the weather. Then we talked about our children. Then we talked about the local sports teams. Finally, he asked if I'd like to ride across his land. I said that would be grand if he thought it made sense. And so we shook hands, he opened the gate, and now I've got what I've been trying to get for many years."

Thus, we learned the art of Irish circumspection: never ask directly for what you want. If you do, you won't get it. Instead, talk about anything and everything else until the other person, who knows damn well what you're after, offers it to you.

Deep within the German's property, unwittingly, Bernadette put her leg on her horse and it started trotting away from our group, not particularly fast, but bouncy. Vinnie told us to stay put while he went after her. The four of us remained in our saddles and watched Bernadette slowly trot away from us. She bobbled a bit before Vinnie caught up to her. Then, with no visible sign of commotion, Bernadette slid off her horse in what seemed like slow motion. Vinnie reached her and dismounted. We expected to see her get up, remount, and ride back to us.

Instead, Vinnie signaled for us to come to him. We rode up to find Bernadette in obvious pain. We stayed with her while Vinnie took off on his horse to get to a car he could drive into the field, and as it turned out, take her to a hospital to set her broken collar bone. The whole thing was surreal.

I've taken some bad falls and I've seen many, but this was so slow and seemingly innocuous that somehow it just didn't seem fair to result in a significant injury. While she'd been at a walk, her horse apparently mistook what he thought was a cue to trot. Bernadette was caught off guard, unprepared for the changed gait, which was bouncy. She couldn't keep her balance, slid from her horse, and in a fall that should have ended with no injuries, she ended up falling at exactly the wrong angle and seriously hurting herself.

On our last day, the rest of us were back on the beaches near Mullaghmore on the Donegal Bay, Michael and I again acting like naughty high school boys. Suddenly, as though painted by Walt Disney, we saw a castle seemingly floating on the water and appearing to be within reach. The beauty was so stunning that it actually made us all shut up, no small feat for our group. We continued to canter along the water's edge, and as the visage became larger, we pulled up. Vinnie told us that what we were seeing was Classiebawn, the castle where Lord Louis Mountbatten summered for thirty-five years.

In 1979, ten years into the Troubles in Northern Ireland, by then with two thousand dead and twenty thousand injured, seventy-nine-year-old Mountbatten went on his fishing boat with his daughter, son-in-law, their fourteen-year-old twin sons, his mother-in-law, and a young local, the "boat boy" for the summer. Two members of the IRA detonated a remote controlled bomb they'd placed underneath the boat, blowing it to smithereens, killing Mountbatten, one of his grandsons, his mother-in-law, the boat boy, and injuring the others.

Though Mountbatten had taken no part in the politics of Northern Ireland, he was a member of the British Royal Family and was close to Prince Charles. He was also the last Viceroy of India, a highly decorated member of the British navy, England's first sea lord (a post some years earlier held by Winston Churchill), and chief of the British Defense Staff from the midfifties until 1965. He had served as commander in chief of the Allied forces in the Mediterranean for NATO in the early fifties, and had helped produce a twelve-part television series titled, "The Life and Times of Lord Mountbatten." His career, close ties to the Royal Family, and stature as a British icon, made Mountbatten an ideal symbolic target for the IRA to take down. Suddenly, we envisioned blood, body parts, and death in the nearby waters and on the beach, and the fairy castle didn't seem so magical.

We spent a quiet last night in Sligo going out for a few pints and thinking about all we'd experienced on our trip. For me, seeing the forty shades of green as we drove across parts of Ireland, barely avoiding impaling myself on a cyclone fence, marveling at the Irish respect for the horseback rider, jumping the most beautiful cross-country course I'd even seen, encountering a military road block, lunching at Ellen's Pub and returning to see Irish step dancing as it's meant to be done, almost disappearing into a bog, riding in Sligo, Bernadette's surreal mishap, witnessing Yeats's weekly burial, and hearing a grim tale of the Troubles.

As that trip ended for us, I was well satisfied that I'd begun a long friendship with a country, its culture, and its people. I knew that Karen and I would be back. I didn't know then that it would be the following year—for our honeymoon.

Chapter 7

A Honeymoon in Ireland

Only one thing could top the riding trip: finally getting Karen to marry me.

In the fall of 1988, I was incapacitated and had my first of three back operations. Although the pain before the surgery was real enough, and afterward there wasn't much I could do for myself for about six weeks, I might have overdramatized the amount of help I needed by just a "wee" bit. The result was that for the first time, Karen moved in with me even though we'd known each other for fifteen years, and I'd been divorced for eleven. By then, she'd also had a failed marriage and one particularly emotionally abusive relationship, and she placed no stock in men's promises of fidelity and eternal love. For my part, I knew we belonged together for the rest of our lives, and we had a tender loving relationship as comfortable as a cat taking a nap in the afternoon sun.

Of course, I courted her parents as much as I courted her. Who says the way to a woman's heart is through roses? I say it's through her mother. Though her dad was wary of me, fearing my secret plot was to marry Karen and convert her to Judaism, John B respected me, and we had some great talks about history, literature, and politics. I stayed away from sex and religion. I'm not a complete dummy. He liked me and grudgingly came to accept that if his strong-willed daughter wanted to marry me, she would, and he'd hope for the best.

One down, three to go.

By that time, my mom was confined to a wheelchair. Six months a year she stayed with my sister in Highland Park, the other six months with me. Although Karen and I worked full-time, Karen arranged dinner for the three of us nightly; on Friday nights, she joined on the blessings over the candles, the wine, and the challah. Karen and my mother shared a love of books and traded recommendations. Karen got her books on tape. They also talked about history, literature, and politics (Karen, also no dummy, stayed away from sex and religion.) During this period, my mom's wariness about Karen and her secret plot to convert *me* to Catholicism softened. She saw her as a bright and caring woman, in Jewish terms, a woman of valor. She also knew that with Karen, her son was a happy man, and in the end, that is what she wanted most for me.

Scorecard: two down, two to go.

Karen's mom, Mary, took one look at my relationship with my mom, and that was enough for her. She said to Karen, "You can always tell if a man will be a good husband by watching how he treats his mother. He treats his mother with love and respect. This is a good man. He'll make a good husband."

Three down, one to go.

For a few years in the most general terms, Karen had said that at the right time, we'd get married. To me, that meant when both of *us* were in wheelchairs. So, after eleven years of loving this woman, doing my damnedest to accept her reasons for us not getting married, and often feeling frustrated by the wait, I finally gave her an ultimatum. I said, "Either we get married or stop seeing each other." I've never been so scared in my life, deathly afraid she might say, "Then as much as I love you, we must stop seeing each other." I hadn't decided whether I'd then grovel, retract, beg, cry, fake a heart attack, or some combination.

What she said was, "Why can't we just live together? Why do we have to be married?"

I said, "Because I don't want to make it easy for you to leave. I want a public commitment—rings and all."

She paused a few moments, stroked my cheek, and said, "You know how much I love you, don't you?"

"I think so, but prove it and marry me."

"Marrying you won't make me love you any more, you know."

"I know, but I want you to be by wife, and I want to be your husband."

She stared deep into my eyes, smiled, and said, "Since you're being a stiff-necked Jew about this, okay. Let's set a date."

I breathed again.

And so in July of the following year, after we'd known each other for sixteen years, and after I'd pursued Karen for about twelve, we were married and took a two-week honeymoon, the first in Venice and the second in Ireland. The original plan had been to spend two weeks in Ireland. Then, one night early in 1989, we attended a fund-raising auction. One of the items was a week's stay at an apartment in Venice. When the bidding started, Karen raised her hand, and she never lowered it. Eventually, other bidders got it: she wasn't going to be outbid. As the gavel fell, she turned to me, gave me a kiss, and said, "This is my wedding gift to you. We deserve to spend the first week of our honeymoon in one of the most romantic cities in the world. Now do you believe that I love you?"

"I never doubted it," I lied.

Venice *was* romantic. We ate at restaurants along the Grand Canal and toured the glassworks on the nearby island of Murano. We had lunch at an outdoor café on the island of Burano where we bought a hand embroidered, linen-and-lace tablecloth and matching napkins that we still use for special occasions, as well as a remarkable piece of lacework of two horses, handmade by local nuns.

We drank Bellini's at Harry's Bar, a tiny hole in the wall where the drink was invented and where routinely Ernest Hemingway drank way too many. We fed the pigeons in San Marco Square, exactly where I'd seen footage of my mom doing the same thing in 1938. Lazily, holding hands, we strolled along the narrow and twisty streets. We also went to a quadrangle of apartments where in the fourteenth and fifteenth centuries the *campo gheto* iron foundries were located. Starting in 1516, gates were installed outside the quadrangle and Jews were locked in nightly. From this compelled closure and the nearby ironworks, the word "ghetto" derives. On the perimeter of the quadrangle is a succession of synagogues. Mounted on the walls of one were *ketubot* (Jewish marriage contracts) many hundreds of years old. Inspired by them, when we returned home we had our own *ketubah* prepared by local artists. Its images include the Rialto Bridge over the Grand Canal, a gold medallion Karen gave me as one of my wedding gifts that reads: *Je t'aime plus ou'hier moins que demain,* (I love you more today than yesterday and less than tomorrow), and of course, shamrocks and the green hills of Ireland.

* * * * * * * * * * * * * * * * *

We continued our honeymoon in Ireland, staying first at Dromoland Castle in County Clare, and then at the Park Hotel Kenmare in Kenmare, County Kerry.

Dromoland Castle is a luxury hotel with a long and winding driveway that leads you from the main road, through its own golf course, past its own lake, and up to the entrance of the hotel. For a long period from the tenth century forward, what's now the land on which Dromoland Castle resides was home to the O'Brien's, the royal Irish family.

The first building constructed on the site was probably a tower house in the fifteenth century, but the land wasn't always so idyllic. Dromoland roughly translates into Hill of Litigation, named for good reason. For three hundred years after the tower house was erected, the site went through disputes, possessions, attempted repossessions, and a variety of legal claims. Where was I when they needed a good trial attorney? There were leases and subleases; one owner fled during a seventeenth century rebellion, while another, in line to inherit the place, was killed in battle.

This previous site of squabbles was now, for us, a place of tranquility with its beautifully manicured links and lush gardens and scenery. Our suite was downstairs. At first that seemed a bit dodgy, since I thought we were being put in a dungeon, but the room actually opened onto a private area in the garden, away from the madding crowd.

Karen was a bit nervous about returning to Ireland. Our trip the previous year had been pretty much all horseback riding, and you just can't go wrong in Ireland on a riding trip. This time, we'd be absorbing more of the country itself. She knew that she loved it and felt it in her bones, but here was her Jewish husband from Chicago who hardly had any inbred affinity for this land. So, it was with some trepidation that she took me back. But Karen had certainly done us just fine in selecting Dromoland as our second honeymoon location. And it didn't take long for me to fall almost as in love with the land of Karen's heritage as I was with her.

One night we had a drink at a bar where a local singer performed mostly traditional Irish songs. A fairly large group of Americans there spanned three generations. They asked for all the Irish songs on which they'd grown up: "A Mother's Love is a Blessing," "Sweet Rosie O'Grady," and others. Without realizing it, the Americans weren't asking to hear *any* traditional Irish songs. They were asking to hear all the songs written by immigrants after they'd emigrated to "Amerikay." The fact is the performer, and most Irish, knew none of them. What I soon learned is that virtually every *traditional* Irish song has one or more of the following themes: fighting the British, hating to leave Mother, death, being shipped off to Australia as a convict for fighting the British, death, being drunk, love that proves false, being hung in the morning by the British, broken hearts, starvation, dismemberment, death, and death.

Still, we joined in with this group singing a cappella, since the performer couldn't help. Karen, of course, knew all the songs. But the real kick was that the patriarch of this group was a retired NYPD cop, as was Karen's dad, and a current security officer at a bar in New York, the Inwood Lounge. More than one of Karen's young male cousins had routinely been thrown out of the same joint (in one instance, thrown through its plate glass window), the same cousins who'd become successful securities brokers on Wall Street.

After we'd been there awhile and this family learned that we were on our honeymoon, they insisted we pick a song we wanted to hear. At that point, Karen had said I played guitar and sang. That did it. No way was I getting out of that room without playing and singing, not an easy trick when you know "Hatikvah" (the Israeli national anthem), but not "Carrickfergus." I ended up playing "House of the Rising Sun," figuring a rousing song about a house of prostitution in New Orleans would go over well in a pub in a fancy hotel in County Clare. Besides, my mind had gone blank, and I couldn't think of anything else. It made no difference. My performance met with applause as raucous as though Van Morrison had just finished a set.

We went riding one day at a nearby equestrian facility. Though it was nowhere as thrilling as our experience the prior year, still, we were in the saddle again in Ireland and that felt good. No, it felt grand.

One night we had dinner at the Dunraven Arms, a hotel in Adare, a lovely village in County Limerick. We liked the hotel, learned that the Clonshire Equestrian Centre was nearby, and thought it might be nice to stay at the Dunraven on a return trip.

After a few days, we were off to stay at the Park Hotel Kenmare in the town of Kenmare in Country Kerry in the southwest of Ireland. The hotel dates from 1897, is in a beautiful setting overlooking the Kenmare Bay, and at the back are stairs that lead all the way down to the water.

To get to Kenmare, you traverse the Ring of Kerry, a beautiful drive that offers many lures to take you off the main road for a particular vista, park area, or some other attraction, but even if you stay on the main road, you see some gorgeous scenery. As we traveled farther south, we started seeing palm trees. In Ireland? What the hell did they think this was, the Caribbean? But there they were, plain as day.

Entering the town of Kenmare is a pleasant experience. The town, sometimes known as The Jewel in the Ring, is filled with restaurants, arts and crafts shops, and shockingly, pubs, lots of pubs. My intent was to take ten seconds of footage of every pub in Kenmare on a roll of film (this was back in the Super 8 days when a roll of film lasted three minutes), but I ran out of space well shy of my goal. In town one night to have dinner at one of the local restaurants, we got a taste of real Irish folk music played where and how it should be played—in a pub with many locals singing along, the rest more interested in finishing their pints.

We met a Catholic couple at the hotel. They were from Belfast. The man was an attorney by trade, but he and his wife owned and operated a pub and a restaurant. They told us that the IRA shook down many local establishments for cash, theirs included. When they finally said no, they were bombed out—twice. They told us, "More Catholics have to stand up to the IRA. That will eventually weaken them as an obstacle to peace in Northern Ireland. At the same time Protestants have to reign in their paramilitary organizations for the same reason."

Karen asked, "And if that doesn't happen?"

The wife said, "If Catholics and Protestants continue to attack each other with bombings, retribution killings, and other atrocities, the violence will continue to spiral out of control. If each side says enough, and refuses support to the paramilitaries, eventually the Troubles will get resolved."

Karen said, "But isn't the heart of the problem religious differences?"

The husband answered, "We don't think so. We think that the core of the problem is more economic and eventually, if left alone, things will work out."

It was interesting to get a perspective from folks living what was then going on, rather than reading about impersonal newspaper accounts that simply reported the violence.

In 2004, President George W. Bush was in Ireland for a brief visit and a European Union meeting. The rumor was that his advance team had tried to place the presidential party into the Park Hotel Kenmare, but the hotel was booked and the manager actually said no to the President of the United States. As I discuss in detail later, former President Bush was strongly disliked in Ireland. Thus, many hearing of the hotel manager's response to the presidential request hoisted a few pints to his good health. Instead of staying at the Kenmare in 2004, the president stayed at Dromoland Castle. Obviously, Karen and the presidential travel planners shared similar tastes, but we got both hotels we wanted, while the president had to settle for his second choice.

From Kenmare, it was back to Shannon and home. Once again, Ireland had left its mark, and I knew that we'd be back often. I was right. So far, besides our 1988 and 1989 trips, we've returned in 1991, 1994, 1996 (for my first foxhunt), 1998, 2000, 2001, 2003, 2004 (twice—once for pleasure and once for my second foxhunt), 2005, 2006, and 2007, and we have every intention of returning many more times.

Chapter 8

⌒

Mary, Adare, O. J., and Clonshire

We'd planned on going to Ireland in the summer of 1994 with Karen's mom and dad, but unexpectedly, Karen's father died in late 1993. Mary acknowledged it would be good to get away for a bit, so she agreed to join us. Karen and I remembered during our honeymoon having dinner at a restaurant at the Dunraven Arms Hotel in the village of Adare and liking the hotel and village, so we decided we'd stay there with Mary.

So on June 18, 1994, we checked in. Here's how I know exactly the date that we arrived. On that day, (June 17 in Los Angeles) the news broke that O. J. Simpson, the famous retired American football player and former Heisman Trophy winner, was in a surreal car chase. He'd just been charged with the murder of his ex-wife, Nicole, and her friend Ron Goldman. He was scheduled to surrender, but instead got into his car with a friend, and slowly drove along a freeway, the LAPD behind him. This scene, right out of a Fellini film, was caught on camera by helicopters following both Simpson and the police.

Also notable on that date was that an entire banquet room at the Dunraven Arms was set up with huge television screens for locals who were watching Ireland play in its first-ever match in World Cup soccer. (What Americans call soccer the rest of the world calls football.) There are numerous playoffs just to get into World Cup competition, and the championship is awarded only once every four years. If Americans think that American football is top dog in sports viewership, they're mistaken. In 1994 and 2006 about ninety million and ninety-eight million, respectively, watched the Super Bowl. Big numbers? Nah. According to the *Federation Internationale de Football Association* (FIFA), the global governing body for World Cup soccer, the World Cup finals for 1998, 2002, and 2006, respectively, drew global audiences of 1.3 billion, 1.1 billion, and 715 million. Even allowing for hype, the fact remains that it's no contest. World Cup soccer rules. It certainly did at the Dunraven on the night of our arrival.

Anyway, unfortunately for Ireland, it was matched against Italy in the first round. Italy had never lost a first-round match, and by some odds makers, was a 40–1 favorite for the game. Still, all of Ireland was in a sports frenzy, because the Irish team had qualified, even if against an unbeatable opponent. Then, in a stunning upset, Ireland won that game, 1–0.

The crowd at the hotel went nuts, exploding with ecstatic cheering, and drinking one hell of a lot of Guinness to lubricate their enthusiasm. They weren't alone. That night, all across the country, the Irish flag waved from many a honking car late into the night. Although Ireland was knocked out of the World Cup in the second round, it had beaten the Italian team, which had the second most World Cup championships, and nothing could dampen the mania that spread across the country that night and for many days thereafter.

For her part, Mary was unimpressed with all the hoopla. She was perhaps the only soul in the Old Sod that night not consumed with the Irish bid to advance in the World Cup. She was enthralled with the LA police, in replay after misbegotten replay, slowly following O. J. Simpson on a freeway in his now-infamous white Bronco.

During the next few days, it was hard to get Mary out of her room, as CNN repeatedly reported every minor detail about the case as it began to unfold. We learned who O. J.'s attorneys were. We learned the police had forensic evidence, but couldn't disclose it. Breaking news story: Nicole and Ron Goldman had been lovers. Corrected news story: they weren't. News flash: Nicole had eaten at the restaurant where Ron was a waiter; she had left her sunglasses there, which he was returning. Correction: it might not have been sunglasses. Still further correction: the police couldn't say what he was returning. In short, we learned a whole lot of nothing, but when you have a twenty-four hour news cycle to fill, you fill it with everything under the sun, garbage and all.

Mary, when we could pry her away from the television and after she'd vocalized a thousand questions and speculations, handed down her verdict: guilty.

Karen and I, meanwhile, were reacquainting ourselves with our surroundings. The Dunraven is a fine hotel. Sensing we'd return there and knowing it never hurts to be acquainted with the boss, I introduced myself to Louis Murphy who, with his brother Brian, is a comanager and perhaps co-owner of the Dunraven; the ownership issue has always been shrouded in secrecy. I'd also heard that Louis was the go-to guy to set you up with a horse and get you into a foxhunt.

After opening pleasantries, I told him I was interested in riding in a hunt. As though he hadn't heard me, Louis talked about everything except what I'd asked him. He didn't say yes; he didn't say no. Instead, he asked how many times we'd been to Ireland, talked about the weather, the Dunraven, Adare, the weather, how long we'd be staying, and the weather.

As we left to spend the day in the village, I was confused as to whether I'd been unclear, but I shook it off.

There's only one way into the Village of Adare and that takes you right onto Main Street. By many it's deemed the prettiest village in Ireland. The entire commercial part is roughly the equivalent of two or three city blocks long, but it's jam-packed with antique shops, restaurants, jewelry stores, clothing stores, pubs, some houses—and many of the buildings have thatched roofs. Not that I'm judgmental, but if this village doesn't take your breath away, you're a hard-hearted, cold-blooded dullard with no eye for romance or beauty.

Just as you enter the village from the City of Limerick side, on your left is the Adare Manor, the former seat of the Earl of Dunraven, titled by the British Crown as early as 1800 and given the lands that now constitute all of Adare, and more. As is true of so many of the stately manors in England and Ireland, the descendants of the original owners couldn't afford to maintain the properties, which eventually were deeded to the state as a part of a national trust or sold and turned into fine hotels on sprawling estates. That was how the Adare Manor came to be a first-class hotel and golf course. Ditto for Dromoland Castle.

Though we knew then that we'd just entered a special village, we didn't know that Adare would become the place where we'd plant our roots in Ireland.

Our first full day there, we ripped Mary away from CNN to walk the village. We had lunch at a pub, tea at a restaurant, and visited a church where, in years to come, Karen would light enough candles to burn down the country. We had dinner at the Dunraven's formal restaurant, the Maigue, named after the river on Adare's outskirts.

Karen and I planned to ride a bit at Clonshire Equestrian Centre, about a ten-minute car ride from the hotel. Karen wanted to take dressage lessons; I wanted to risk my neck on its cross-country course. This left us with the minor dilemma of what to do with Mary on our riding days. Even she wasn't willing to sit in front of the TV an entire day, waiting for some juicy new morsel about the O. J. case. She was welcome to come with us, but it's boring to watch others ride, especially when you're not into it, and for Mary the most significant fact about horses was that they made really big and disgusting poops.

Mary enjoyed staying in the village on a few occasions when we'd ride at Clonshire. We suggested that she take a one-day bus tour of the Ring of Kerry. She resisted mightily at first, but eventually relented, took the tour, and had a smashing time. So, she learned to occupy and enjoy herself during those times that we rode. Still, as soon as she'd return from an outing and before we'd go to dinner, she tuned in CNN to get her O. J. fix.

For us, riding at Clonshire was a treat. Its grounds are large, though not as massive or beautiful as those at Castle Leslie. Clonshire, however, also had its own cross-country jump course and enclosed and outdoor riding rings. The first time we went, we had a riding lesson scheduled for the two of us, and we found the manager of the facility, Sue Foley, quickly. We liked her straight away. She's about as big as a minute, unpretentious, and friendly. After we'd signed all the necessary waivers about death and dismemberment she asked us about our level of experience. Then she paired us up with horses, delivered "the Irish way." After we mounted, Sue had us ride in the indoor arena to evaluate our level of expertise.

As Sue was gauging our riding ability, I thought back to the time that Jann introduced us to two other students as potential additional participants for our Ireland riding vacation in 1988. I'll call the boyfriend of this duo Bill; I'm changing his name to spare the guilty. All Bill wanted to know was how much we'd be able to jump. I considered him pushy in pursuing a singular agenda, rather than being interested in the overall trip, but I had no doubt from his one-track mind that he was a seasoned jumper. After Bill and his girlfriend left, Jann told us not only had he never jumped before, but also he was a neophyte rider. Either Bill had a death wish, or he wanted to prove he was Clark Kent, hidden cape and all. Whatever his problem, we wanted no part of him; Jann, Michael, Bernadette, Karen, and I were unanimous that Bill wouldn't be joining us. It's eejits like him who get not only themselves killed, but others with them. It was eejits like him I'd be reminded of the morning of my first foxhunt, wondering then if I'd morphed into Bill. It was eejits like him who Sue was looking to ferret out in her indoor arena—braggarts with little, if any, experience to back up the big talk.

After riding in Clonshire's indoor arena, we graduated to the outdoor ring. There, Sue watched as I took some jumps to see if I qualified to go out onto the cross-country course.

Sue was satisfied enough with my jumping skills in the outdoor arena that she sent me off with Katie, her sister-in-law, but she was correct to test me beforehand. To take jumps, you must coordinate a number of different elements. You need contact with the horse's mouth via your reins but without pulling too tight. You need to round him up so he's relaxed and paying full attention to you; his neck properly flexed and bent, rather than with his nose high in the air and him out of control. You must moderate the horse's pace, be on the correct lead heading into the jump. You have to keep your arms tucked close to your sides, thumbs up while keeping your seat, thighs, shoulders, and arms relaxed to avoid the horse feeling your tension.

If you're riding with your seat in the saddle, you need to know when to stand in your stirrups with your knees bent, leaning into the roll pads, keeping your heels down, head up, and moving your hands forward up the horse's neck to give him his freedom as he takes the jump. This avoids "hitting him in the teeth" with the bit, which not only hurts the horse, but also breaks his concentration.

While airborne, you should never look down. A jumper's mantra is, "Look down and that's where you'll end up." Instead, midair you must already be viewing the upcoming jump, mentally setting up to take the next obstacle. If it requires a change of direction, you have to change his lead upon landing. (At a canter, the correct lead means having the right front leg taking the longer of the strides if you're cantering to the right and vice versa.) You have to do half halts (a soft closing of your hands on the reins) to slow your horse to adjust for the number of paces to the next jump, or pick up his speed, as required, so he'll take off from the correct spot. You must keep your "leg on" the horse to give him confidence, but also know when he needs extra encouragement by more leg, a kick, or use of your riding crop. Between each jump, both horse and rider must remain balanced and focused. And more. In short, you have to know what in the hell you're doing. As J. Michael Plumb had said years earlier, jumping is dangerous even when done properly. The risk increases when you're full of ego and false bravado.

When all is said and done, you're sitting on top of an animal that weighs roughly twelve hundred pounds, and you and he are vaulting over some obstruction. The possibilities include your horse hitting the barrier with his front legs going up, or his hind legs coming down; refusing the jump; taking the jump, but stumbling on the opposite side, any of which can cause serious injuries; or sailing over the jump as properly intended with horse and rider feeling those exhilarating moments of weightlessness when it all just comes together. As you feel your horse launch both of you over the obstacle into an instant quietness, time seems suspended as the two of you, in harmony, are airborne, and momentarily free of gravity. The sensation is thrilling.

In light of Sue's approval for me to go onto the cross-country course, each time we returned to Clonshire that season, Katie and I tackled it. A few times Karen came out with us, but her preference was to remain in the outdoor arena taking dressage lessons with Sue, who later confided that she, too, far preferred dressage to jumping, as most sane people do.

Dressage is another form of riding. It derives its name from a French term and commonly means "training" or "working." Its purpose is to get a horse to develop its natural athletic capabilities in as relaxed a manner as possible, thus making riding her as a pleasure horse that much more enjoyable. The horse must learn to respond to aids from the rider to make various moves, and pick up different gaits at precisely the correct location in the dressage ring. Taking a dressage test is not unlike a figure skater doing compulsories, in which each skater is required to perform exactly the same moves in precisely the same proscribed sequence. As with skating compulsories, the many different dressage tests range from the fairly simple to the extraordinarily complex that only Olympic level athletes can perform. In both skating compulsories and dressage events, all competitors in a particular class take the same test; each skater or horse-and-rider team, as the case may be, being judged not against one another, but against a theoretical perfect performance.

No matter which form of riding you love most, though, dressage is the linchpin. If on the flat, with no required jumping, you can't learn correct body position and proper methods of communicating with your horse, and you can't teach your horse to respond to your aids, you won't be able to control and ride your horse correctly while jumping. Both dressage and jumping require focus so both forms of riding are wonderful ways to get your mind off everything else.

It's also a democratic sport, the only Olympic one in which men and women compete dead even with each other—no separate men's events and women's events, and no spotting of points for women as compared to men. Equestrian events are also the only Olympic sport where a human and an animal team up as co-athletes, both needing to be fit and in harmony.

At Clonshire, Sue Foley never pushed. She wasn't looking to create Olympic athletes, but to improve the riding of those who wanted lessons and to provide an enjoyable and safe activity. Still, once Karen and I proved to her that we were able and willing to take things to the next level, she had the horses and the riding course or dressage movements to challenge us. As we returned to Clonshire and Sue got to know us, she always had our horses ready. Mine, routinely, was Jack. The first time I rode him she told me, "He's a great jumper, but he gets antsy if you take too long to mount him."

"Why?"

"He's missing his left eye because of a disease."

Great, I thought to myself. *One-Eyed Jack.*

I took her advice and used a mounting block to get on him quickly. I remember thinking, *Terrific. Am I nuts? I'm going onto a cross-country course with a half-blind horse.*

As it turned out, he was steady as a rock and true at every jump. If I did my job in controlling his gait, adding more leg when necessary, bringing him in at the proper angle and as close to the center as possible, and staying out of his face when he took off, he took care of me perfectly.

Indeed, I'd learned by then that if I thought I was approaching at the wrong angle or wasn't set up or balanced properly, I'd pull out of the jump rather than take it. At the same time, I jumped confidently and without fear. More accurately, I didn't show fear. Any rider who takes a challenging enough jump course likely will have to overcome some degree of apprehension. However, even when you feel it, the trick is to convey that you are utterly confident, a lesson of which I'd be reminded some years later during a hunt. Though big, horses are sensitive animals. Think of one in a field swishing his tail when a fly lands on him. If he can feel a single insect on his butt, he can certainly sense if a rider on his back is tense or hesitant. It's a circle. If your horse feels that you're reticent about a jump, he'll get reticent about the jump. Often, that's when accidents happen.

After I'd complete a sequence of jumps successfully, Katie yelled, "Brilliant!" Who was I to disagree with her?

As I took harder and higher jumps, she allowed me more latitude to push my limits, trusting that although I had some cowboy in me, I wouldn't take undue risks.

She added more jumps in sequence, sometimes with short distances in between, sometimes long. She added some required riding from open fields into dark wooded areas, which can spook a horse unless the rider takes him in with solid control and confidence. She added jumps going uphill and down. She made turns sharper, chose patterns that made me change directions frequently (and thus, change leads), added some in and out of water, and some that had leafy branches on top making it scarier for the horse, thus requiring absolute control.

Eventually, we'd pull up together at an area with jumps galore of all kinds in view and she'd say simply, "Off you go," allowing me to make up my own minicourses, often leaving to me the choice of taking easier or more difficult jumps. I always returned to the stable with an incredible high.

On our last day of riding at Clonshire that year, Katie set up an entire show jump course for me on a large lawn. Of course, it was raining and the grass was slick. I took some of the highest and broadest jumps ever. On landing from one, Jack lost some traction on the wet grass as I changed lead heading for the next one at a canter. Realizing he didn't have enough room to recover to take the next jump, he sat down on his butt and slid—me in the saddle sliding along with him—stopping just as his hind legs were under the jump. Then he stood up and gave himself a good shake, me still on his back. I patted his neck heartily, and we finished off the course without further incident. Karen was there to catch a photo of my favorite refusal of all time.

In the end, our introduction to Adare and Clonshire was perfect. Mary enjoyed herself and conquered a few of her fears including taking a tour on her own. We ate at some lovely restaurants in and around the village. And we found the perfect place to ride. In short, we were sold on returning to Adare on our next trip to Ireland.

As we were leaving the Dunraven, Louis stopped me. "Did you say you were interested in going on a hunt?"

"I did."

"Katie tells me you're a brilliant rider. If ever you're back and interested in riding in a hunt, let me know. I'll set you up."

So *that* was it. He'd heard me when I'd asked at the outset of our stay about riding in a hunt, and then intentionally changed the subject. But he wanted to know whether I could ride well enough to handle it, not just from my own mouth, but from someone whose judgment he trusted. So, he'd had his spy from Clonshire watching me the whole time. He'd said to Katie, "This guy says he'd like to hunt. Let me know if he can handle it." Sneaky, these Irish.

"Oh, I'll take you up on that, Louis. I will most definitely take you up on that."

Harvey Mounted on One-Eyed Jack

Harvey and One-Eyed Jack on a Clonshire Show Jump Course

The Best Refusal Ever

Chapter 9

⁓

Harvey's Claddagh Ring and Declan's Turf

That same trip, Mary, Karen, and I took a four-day excursion to Galway and the Connemara region. Galway's on the west coast with a population of about seventy thousand and has the fastest growing population of any city in Ireland. At the time, we didn't know that Karen's nephew, David, would spend his junior year in college at the University of Galway, where he frequented every pub and even made it to an occasional class.

Of major interest to us was the section known as Claddagh, a fishing village just outside the old walls of the city.

Claddagh is known for a unique design, found on rings in particular, but also on a number of items ranging from necklaces to door knockers. Years later, we even saw an embroidered version on a reverend's stole. The design is of two hands clasping a heart; on top of the heart is a crown. The hands connote friendship, the heart symbolizes love, and the crown represents loyalty. It's the lucky person who can know all three with another. I'm one of the lucky ones.

Over time, "rules" have emerged for the ring. For example, if the ring is worn on the right hand with the hands and heart facing away from the body, it signifies that you're not in a serious relationship. If you wear it with the design facing you that means your heart is taken.

Of a number of different stories about the origins of the design of the Claddagh, the one I like best is of a Galway clansman traveling to the West Indies to earn his fortune, intending to return home to marry his true love. His ship was captured, and he was sold as a slave to a Moorish goldsmith in Algiers. His master trained him in the craft of making jewelry. During his captivity, he made a ring as a symbol of his love for the woman waiting for him in Claddagh. Thus, the Claddagh ring was born. When William III became king, he demanded that the Moors release all English prisoners. The Moorish master was so fond of his slave that he offered him his daughter's hand in marriage and half of his wealth, but the clansman wanted to return home to marry the woman he'd left fourteen years earlier. Upon his return, he gave her the ring, and they were married and, of course, lived happily ever after. I'm probably partial to this version of the story, because I know *exactly* how it feels to have to wait so long for your true love.

During the Irish Potato Famine of 1845–1849, a million people fled Ireland, many with their Claddagh rings, thus creating a greater exposure of its design.

Karen already had hers. Her parents gave it to her as a gift when she was a youngster. I bought one in Galway that trip, and it remains one of my few special pieces of jewelry. I wear it on my right hand, not as my wedding ring, only because my wedding ring is my father's, inscribed with his initials and wedding date, and now, with my initials and my wedding date to Karen. And, yes. I wear it facing me, not because my heart is taken (though it is), but because I love to look at the design.

After spending a day or so in Galway and acquiring my Claddagh ring, we were ready to move into Connemara, a region marked by a rugged landscape bounded on the north, south, and west by the Atlantic, and on the east by the Invermore River and a part of the Maumturk Mountains. With a population of slightly more than eight hundred, Clifden is the largest town in Connemara, but our favorite village in the region was Roundstone with a far more manageable population of about two hundred. It had a wonderfully earthy feel, yet it was artsy, without being cloying. There we bought Mary a painting called *Connemara Girl*, a popular image in the area of a young girl living a hard life. She's barefoot, wears a black shawl over her head, and draped around her body. A goat is on either side of her, one on inclining rocky ground. Upon returning home, Mary proudly hung the painting in her apartment in San Francisco.

While in Roundstone, we also went to the local church so Mary could buy a Mass card. That's when Karen and Mary learned that unlike in the States, in Ireland you don't buy Mass cards at churches. You buy them at chemists (pharmacies), and then bring them to the church after filling out the cards to identify in whose honor or memory you want a specific number of masses said. Mary filled out the card for her brother Jim, who by then had been Brother Peter in a seminary in Perrysville, Missouri, for about forty years. Prior to that, he'd been a paratrooper in World War II. He'd taken on the highly risky assignment for the double pay, so he'd be able to send half of each paycheck to his parents. Meanwhile, Mary's husband—and Karen's father—Johnny landed on Omaha Beach on D-day and lived to come home. I think of these men whenever I feel like I've had a bad day.

* * * * * * * * * * * * * * * * *

Life works in funny ways. Years before we'd come to Ireland together, we'd heard of a pony, born in Connemara, but then for sale in Los Angeles. At the time, we were looking to buy Karen's first horse. We went to LA where Karen rode the pony, Declan. She liked him, but he failed a vet test and we were concerned about taking on an animal with foreseeable health problems. The owner was Willy Leahy, himself something of a legend in the Connemara region. He owned hundreds of horses, routinely led groups on rides on the Connemara Trail (Jann had ridden with him some years earlier), owned a number of properties throughout the area, and had a reputation as a shrewd businessman. Eventually, I called him to talk turkey, or in this case, pony.

Though over the years Karen and I bought eight horses between us, never before or since have I discussed buying one quite like the conversation I had with Willy.

"Lad, the job of vets, especially in Amerikay, is to fail horses that are fer sale. They do it because they're spooked by all the lawsuits that Yanks conjure up. They do it to help buyers get lower prices. They do it because it's in their bones to do it."

"That may be so, but we really don't want to buy a horse just to have nothing but problems."

"Lad, I'll tell you what we'll do. You arrange to have the horse trailered to yer barn. Keep him for six weeks, or three months, or six months. I know the horse is sound, so once you and your wife are satisfied that he is, send me a check. If you're not satisfied, just send him back to the barn in Los Angeles and you owe me nothing." Even I had no comeback except to say, "Okay."

After we'd had him for about six weeks and he was rock solid, we sent Willy his check. Some twenty years later, Karen is still riding Declan (named for one of Willy's sons). We've never had a serious problem with him and he's the darling of the barn.

* * * * * * * * * * * * * * * * *

The day we left Galway, we were heading to Cashel House in Connemara. Although I was following the directions in the guidebook, I began to doubt them. We might as well have been driving on the moon. The landscape was hard, rugged, barren, rocky, and desolate—and those were the good parts. It started to seem like some kind of bad joke and that soon some highwaymen would jump out from behind any of a myriad of nearby boulders, brandish their swords, and yell, "Stand and deliver!"

Cashel House couldn't be anywhere near this desolate and forsaken moonscape. After all, it's one of the inns listed in Ireland's *Blue Book*, which until then, had never taken us to such a forlorn spot. If I hadn't known that we were in Ireland, I'd have thought we were in a wet version of the Mojave Desert. Then, just around a turn, we saw the entrance for Cashel House and what a welcome sight it was.

It sits at the head of Cashel Bay with its own tennis court, private beach, and stud farm, from which they breed and export Connemara ponies. Much of the food comes from its own gardens; the rest of its fifty acres are wooded and have walkways.

Throughout Cashel House are a number of sitting rooms, each burning peat in the fireplaces, so you're surrounded by that magical scent. I fell so in love with the smell that whenever in Ireland I buy a supply of peat incense. Then, during the year, I get a whiff of a reminder of Ireland with the touch of a match.

In 1969, one year after Cashel House converted into an inn and restaurant, the place was put on the map when General and Madame Charles de Gaulle spent two weeks there. You don't have to be a general, or the president of France, to understand why they enjoyed their time.

A tranquility hovers over the place. You can lose yourself on the wooded walkways, in the gardens, or on the beach, leaving the world's problems behind, and as Mary found, even O. J.

Karen took a picture of me while we were staying at Cashel House. I'm leaning on a fence overlooking Cashel Bay, wearing an Irish sweater-vest and staring peacefully into the distance. Years later, when I recorded a number of songs that I'd written, we used that picture on the cover of the CD.

Chapter 10

Foxhunting with the Clare Foxhounds

Late in 1994, and having nothing to do with riding, but with a deteriorating spinal cord, I had my third back surgery, this time a spinal fusion.

Because of the surgery, we weren't able to return to Ireland in 1995, but I received plenty of advice from my doctor, friends, and partners, all with the same message: never ride again. I said, "Of course, my riding days are over. With my back problems, what do you take me for, an eejit?" By mid-1995, I was riding again. I find the pleasure so great that the risk is worth it, which I guess is easy to say as long as I'm not paralyzed as a result of some riding accident.

By 1996, I was ready to tackle Ireland again. However, this time, without then knowing how much longer I'd be able to ride, I wanted to do something I'd never done before: I'd dreamed about riding in a foxhunt and by then I wanted to do it—in Ireland. We booked reservations at the Dunraven. Prior to arriving, I was in touch with Louis Murphy. He remembered his parting offer to me and said that he'd take care of the arrangements.

We arrived in November. Hunt season is always during winter. Neither the horses nor the hounds could possibly keep up the pace during the warmer months. Also, the scent of the fox hangs low on the ground in the winter, while rising out of reach in the summer. On the other hand, winters in Ireland aren't friendly. The rain doesn't just come at you from above; it seems to hit you sideways and at all manner of angles, even up from the ground and all at the same time. The wind blows in at you. The skies vary from rainy to cloudy to Old Testament every thirty minutes or so. In short, if you're debating between Hawaii and Ireland for a winter vacation and you're not into foxhunting, I strongly suggest Hawaii.

We met with Louis, who'd arranged for me to ride with the Clare Foxhounds. The site of the "meet," the point of origin for the hunt, was a town called Ruan. There we'd saddle up. Louis told us that in Ruan we should seek out Martin Geoghan (pronounced Gagan).

I asked, "Where's Ruan, Louis? And where do we meet Martin?"

He took us to an eighteenth century map of Ireland and pointed out Ruan. "Can't miss it. You just need to remember to go down this little offshoot near this bridge." Since this map preceded *roads*, the description wasn't exactly what I'd call clear.

"What about Martin? Where do we find him?"

"You'll find him."

Oh, boy.

That night, Karen knew I was a wreck. I laid out every stitch of clothing I was going to wear the next day, each in its own spot on a second bed in the room, right on down to my stock tie and pin. All the while, round and round in my head I was saying to myself, *Why am I doing this? Do I have a death wish like that eejit Bill who wanted to come to Ireland to jump when he was a neophyte rider? I know I'm not good enough to ride in a hunt. I don't even know what it means to ride in a hunt. Why did I trap myself like this? Did I update my will before we left the States? Maybe I'd better cancel. Yes, I'll let Louis know in the morning that I just came down with typhus.*

I didn't sleep. I saw a headline: Stupid Yank Who Didn't Know Arse from Hole in Ground Found Dead with Arse in Hole in Ground. It wasn't the obituary I wanted.

The next morning it was pouring. I couldn't eat anything. I couldn't even look at food. I slowly put on my riding outfit. Karen took a picture of me in our hotel room. I'm wearing my riding clothes, gripping my riding crop like it was my last thin string to life. I have this stupid smile on my face, the kind where you know the person in the picture is saying, "I really hate this, but I don't know how to get out of it."

The ride to Ruan took about forty-five minutes. The whole way there, we drove through what the Irish would call a lashin' rain, whipped into a frenzy and driven by winds that would have given a seasoned sailor a tough time. I kept thinking, *If the hunt is rained out, it's not my fault. I can return to the Dunraven with a mournful look and say, 'Bastards. They called the hunt off because of a drizzle. What sissies. Oh well, maybe next year.'* Then I'd have a few pints and toast my good luck.

I kept hoping we'd get lost. We didn't. We arrived at Ruan. By comparison, Adare looked like a metropolis. In addition to a few houses, there were two pubs and a church. My money was on Martin being in one of the pubs. We walked into one. I wasn't hard to spot. I was carrying my crop and wearing taupe riding pants, a black riding jacket, polished black leather riding boots, a black riding hat, and black riding gloves. My face was twisted in a rictus—not so much a smile as a fixed expression of stark terror.

A woman approached me. "I'm Annie, Martin's wife. Would ye be Harvey?"

I intended to say, *Who? Never heard of any Harvey.* Instead, like an eejit, I said, "Yep, that's me."

Just as I was about to say this was all a big mistake, Annie turned and called out to Martin, who was laughing heartily with some local lads. He wiped his mouth clean of his latest swig of Guinness on the arm of his jacket, looking like he'd just polished off his fourth pint, and then approached me.

"So, Louis tells me you've never been on a hunt in Ireland, lad."

"Actually, I've never been on a hunt, period."

He looked at me, turning his head sideways as if to say, *Don't try to con an Irishman,* but I guess my continued silence convinced him I wasn't lying. While he was still looking at me, he raised his hand and with a voice that must have been heard in the next county yelled, "Michael! A drink fer the lad!"

I got my pint of Guinness. I'm not accustomed to drinking anything stronger than coffee or tea before noon and normally, the idea of alcohol before dinner is revolting. But not that day. It sounded just fine, thank you very much. In fact, if there'd been time, I'd have had pints two and three. After all, I'd seen the signs all over Ireland—Guinness Means Strength—and I wasn't about to argue the issue. Hell, unless the rain saved me, and the hunt was called off, I was about to participate in a ride that was going to kill me.

As luck would have it, just as I finished drinking my breakfast, Martin said it was time to go outside. We left the pub; the rain was down to a heavy drizzle. The hunt was on. I followed Martin to his horse carrier and waited as he off-loaded Seamus. Karen's picture of me waiting again reveals someone looking for an escape hatch. Seamus was bigger than our house in San Francisco. Even knowing I was facing my mortality, I still admired the Irish way and Seamus was gorgeous, all tacked up, groomed, and ready to go.

Martin gave me a leg up, so I could mount Mt. Seamus. Although this was my virginal hunt, Seamus had been through it hundreds of times, and he'd take good care of me. In fact, I kept thinking, *He'll take good care of me. He'll take good care of me.* I didn't believe it for a minute. Still, I appreciated that this was a special animal. I shortened my reins, spread my arms a wee bit, turned my thumbs up, and closed my hands on the reins, sliding them lightly left to right from my shoulders, massaging his mouth. He rounded up his neck, a good sign that he knew what he was doing. Thank God. That made one of us.

I was happy to stall for as long as possible, but Seamus was the boss. He knew what he was there for, and he wanted to get on with it. He started to snort lightly and whinny, and then paw the ground, so I walked him, telling myself that I needed to calm him down, but damn well knowing that the only one of us who needed to calm down wasn't the horse.

The whole village suddenly came alive. People started milling on the roadway. Then the huntsman let the hounds out from their truck carrier. Suddenly I was in the middle of what seemed like a surreal BBC setting of a movie of a hunt, with maybe sixty hounds, tails high in the air, barking, yapping, running around, and the huntsman calling each of them—by name. It was all just a blur to me, but the huntsman was already getting control of his band of barkers.

Riders were mounting and making last minute adjustments to their girths; you don't want your saddle to slip in the midst of a wild hand gallop across open fields, or worse, while jumping a stone wall. Karen pulled my girth a notch or two tighter. I shortened my stirrups so I could stand in them for the upcoming long canters and hand gallops (a two-point position) and the jumps just ahead. I noticed they were breakaways, meaning they had a sturdy rubber strap, rather than leather on the outside. If you lost your balance on a jump, or you were thrown from the horse, your foot would break the stirrup. That way, you'd fall clean, rather than having your foot caught in a stirrup and being dragged to a bad ending. I hoped I wouldn't need them, but it was good to know they were there.

I also noticed a few riders had a stiff leather strap across the front of their saddles. I asked one of them, "What's that?"

"It's a Jayzuz strap."

"I beg your pardon?"

"A Jayzuz strap. You know."

"I don't."

"When yer takin' a jump and you jest know yer about to come off you pray to Jayzuz, Mary, and Joseph to keep you safe as yer grabbin' the Jayzuz strap, hopin' yer prayer is heard and they'll keep you safe and in the saddle."

"Ah ha! I've got it. Thanks."

"No problem a' tall. Have a good ride, lad."

"And to you."

I had no Jayzuz strap. Damn. But even if I had, wasn't sure that the prayer would work for a Jew. Oh well.

All around the village, I heard the clippety-clop of the hooves of fifty or sixty horses on the pavement. Many were snorting or neighing with excitement, knowing that soon they'd be flying across open fields and jumping their hearts out. Some pawed the ground, but by then Seamus was fine. I was still walking him in a nice wide circle, getting him, and a hell of a lot more importantly me, mentally ready for what we were about to start.

Slowly a queue of riders formed. Then the whole group started to walk down the village street in single file and headed to the fields. I put on my bravest face possible and waved to Karen. Some riders, including me, fiddled with the reins; others were calm, having done this a hundred times before. Then the pace of the horses ahead of me began to slow. I looked ahead and saw the queue coming to a halt. A young lad up ahead seemed to be collecting something from the riders. When I got up to him, he held out his hand. I didn't know what he wanted. Was he a beggar? Did they do high fives in Ireland just before you entered the field of your death?

"Cap," he said.

I looked at him and furrowed my brow. I said, "Beg your pardon?"

"Cap," he repeated.

I was wearing one. He took a deep breath, then said, "The fee fer goin' on the hunt."

Ah, yes. Louis had told me I'd pay two fees: the cap, or the fee to ride in the hunt, and a fee to Martin for the rental of his horse. When I asked Martin if he wanted me to pay him for the horse rental before the hunt, he said I could pay when (I think he really meant if) I got back. Maybe he had a lesser fee if the rider died on the hunt. Stupidly, I assumed that because Martin was willing to collect the horse rental after the event, I could also pay the entrance fee upon my return, or they could file a claim with my estate. By the time I'd reached this young man I'd forgotten entirely about the cap.

As it turned out, any horse rental fee is a private matter and has nothing to do with the cap. Each member of the hunt club pays an annual subscription fee. In some clubs, members also pay a nominal cap per hunt. For nonmembers allowed to ride in the hunt, the cap is a larger sum. All fees charged are to raise money to pay the numerous expenses of operating the hunts. In some clubs, the Master of Foxhounds (MHF), the person ultimately in charge, donates his or her time, but the huntsman, who has primary responsibility for the hounds, and the whippers-in, who assist the huntsman, are usually paid professional staff. Fees also pay for the hounds themselves, plus costs for maintaining them in kennels, their training, rental to ride across some of the farmers' properties, and costs to fix some of the inevitable damage done during every hunt. At the time I knew none of this. All I knew, as this young lad had his hand out, was that I felt like the biggest gobshite in the line, and no doubt, many in the queue agreed.

"I'm supposed to pay the cap now?"

He said nothing, but his look established that he was one of the many who concurred with my own assessment of myself at that moment.

"I have no cash with me, but my wife is in the village. You could get the money from her. She's blonde and wearing a red slicker."

"It's okay," said the young lad. "I'll see ye shortly after the hunt."

I picked up the trot just as the MFH, huntsman, and whipper-in, wearing their beautiful livery, scarlet coats, were entering the first field. Within seconds, the hounds took off and suddenly, we were cantering. Still suffering the embarrassment of not having the cash on me to pay the cap, I looked ahead and saw that I was facing my first stone wall during my first foxhunt.

Approaching the wall, my brain wasn't focused on jumping. My reins were too long, and my seat and my legs weren't steady. But with a horde of riders behind me, I had no time to make the many necessary adjustments. So over I went. I bobbled, slid, and almost came off my saddle. Yet I held on, and I didn't even have a Jayzuz strap. It was my best damn bobble ever.

Okay, wise guy, I said to myself. *Back to basics. Breathe. Get your damn seat down in the saddle; let your legs spring in the stirrups and not be jammed in there like they're cemented; shorten your reins, get your legs back, heels down. You're on a hunt in Ireland, boyo. This is the real thing. Could be the ride of your life. You can do this. Don't screw it up. You just had a wake-up bobble; don't blow it.*

I'd ridden cross-country courses in low-level competitions in the States. I'd taken hundreds of hour-long riding lessons, gone trail riding, competed in some show jumping, and had Castle Leslie, Sligo, and Clonshire under my belt. None of that prepares you for a foxhunt.

In a hunt, the riding is long, hard, and with few resting points. In addition, there's no set course, as in show jumping, which takes place within an enclosed arena, and cross-country jumping, which takes place in an open field. Also, the time of a hunt isn't preset. Instead, for long stretches you ride at a trot, sometimes on local roads and sometimes across open fields. At any given time you're with five, ten, or fifteen riders. If you're on the roads, they're in front of and behind you; if in a field, they're in front, behind, and right beside you. Packs of riders automatically form in bunches of ten or so, depending on the riders' speed and mastery.

When the hounds have the scent, you stand in your stirrups in the two-point position for fifteen to twenty minutes straight, with your horse either in a canter or at a full gallop, flying across open fields, hearing the pounding of hooves on the ground, the professionals so far ahead of you they're barely in sight. You're riding so fast and the air is so cold that your eyes water.

Suddenly, you see a stone wall ahead of you and you try to slow down, sitting down in the saddle and using half halts, but your horse is so wired that he just wants to run. And he's the boss. You don't fight him; it's no contest. So you focus on riding the horse, and you let him take the lead as you approach the jump. You launch over a stone wall like a rocket shot from a cannon, and it feels so good that you just shake your head, not believing any of it is real.

I jumped into a field and approached a stone wall on the opposite end. As I legged on Seamus, from my right I saw a horse cantering to the same spot I'd chosen. Within five yards of the wall, I pulled Seamus hard to the left to avoid the inevitable deadly collision. Though he was ready and willing to take the jump, and my adrenalin was pumping hot and heavy, I realized it wouldn't be a good idea to have twenty-five hundred pounds of horseflesh meet in midair at a combined speed of maybe forty miles an hour. I circled him back into the field and waited for others to clear the wall before trying the jump again.

Seamus didn't like being pulled out hard. By doing so, I'd probably hurt his mouth and confused him by stopping him from what he was ready to do. As the field cleared, I put him back into a canter and headed for the wall, but within a few feet of it, he refused for the first time during the hunt. I repeated a few more times. Same result. At least I stayed in the saddle. The farmer on whose land we were riding was in the field. He waved me to come to him. I trotted over.

"What's yer name, lad?"

"Harvey."

"And yer horse, Harvey, what's his name?"

"Seamus."

"Well, that's fine now. So, ye had to pull Seamus up hard like, to avoid a collision and that was the right t'ing to do. But the last few times ye tried to take the jump ye were a bit wild like."

"Was I? I thought I was just taking him in quietly."

"Well, I'd say not Harvey. You were tryin' a wee bit too hard, yer arms flappin', no stopping to the kickin' or the usin' of yer crop, so Seamus here knows yer nervous and not so confident about him gettin' over."

"Really?"

"Aye, 'tis the truth. So, what yer goin' to do, Harvey, is circle him back again, but this time not so frantic like."

"Okay."

"Take him back nice 'n' easy, maybe thirty meters, and don't be takin' him back at the canter. Take him back at a nice easy walk, pattin' his neck the whole time."

"I can do that."

"And breathe, Harvey. Settle down into yer saddle. Let go of the grippin' muscles. Let Seamus here know yer nice and relaxed, not a' tall nervous, and ye've got all the time in the world."

"Relax. Settle into the saddle."

"That's right, Harvey. Then, after you've slowly turned him toward the wall, still walk him ten paces or so, lettin' him know yer in no rush."

"I've got all the time in the world."

"That's the stuff, lad. Then when he feels nice 'n' relaxed, pick up the trot nice 'n' easy, keepin' yer body loose, and takin' a nice deep breath."

"Trot. Deep breath."

"Don't let him break into the canter. Keep yer reins short, but don't pull back too hard which'll jest hit him in the mouth. Keep old Seamus here at a nice steady trot till yer maybe ten meters from the wall. Then, sit deep in yer saddle, breathe out, put yer leg on him firmly, but not frantic like, and ask old Seamus here then to pick up the canter."

"Pick up the canter."

"That's right. Don't get all excited and don't use yer crop. Keep yer arms at yer side, not flappin' in the wind. That'll just get him upset, but keep yer leg on him nice and firm to let him know yer feelin' jest fine, and you're the boss."

"Firm. Not frantic. I'm the boss."

"That's the stuff, lad. Jest go back to how you always do it and you'll see. He'll be jest grand. He'll pick up the canter nice 'n' easy and when he does, stand in yer stirrups, lean forward a bit and let him know yer happy to take the jump. And Harvey, tell him yer sorry ye had to pull him out hard before, but now everything's fine. Okay then, lad?"

"Lean forward. Sorry. Okay then, and thanks."

"Not a' tall. Off you go then, lad."

I did exactly what he'd instructed and as I approached the wall, I patted the horse's neck solidly and said, "I'm sorry I had to pull you out so hard, Seamus, but I'm ready now." Then, I took a nice deep breath, put my leg on him firmly, stood in my stirrups, and slid my hands up his neck. He picked up the canter, and we sailed over the wall.

As I landed on the opposite side, I turned. The farmer was waving and smiling. I saluted him and yelled, "Thanks!" But I know he couldn't hear me as Seamus and I turned into the misty rain and back to the hunt.

* * * * * * * * * * * * * * * * * *

You approach a massive bank that would scare the hell out of you if you looked at it from the ground or took the time to think that you're about to jump over, or into it. Rain is still falling, and you wish your glasses had wipers and a defroster, but you settle for just being able to see, though barely. As you approach the bank, you have to remember to lean back, way back, in your saddle, exactly the opposite of how you're taught to jump in the States. There, you jump on the flat, and you've had it drummed into your head to move forward in your saddle and slide your hands up the horse's withers to give him his head, free of restraint, as you jump. On a hunt, you have to adjust your technique.

Your brain barely registers that while jumping across a monster ditch, if you're leaning way forward in your saddle, you're certain to be thrown over the horse's head and you will land in the dirt on the other side if he makes it. Or you'll end up in the ditch, some filled with water, if he doesn't. You tell yourself, *Sit back; sit down; legs forward.* Somehow, you do, and you actually land on the opposite side, hurling the distance over the huge space, and pounding up mud as you land.

Then you come upon a small knoll in a field. You gallop up, leaning forward to let your horse have his lead, and as he pitches down, leaning way back to provide a counterweight. If you gauge it wrong, you're on the ground. If you do it right, you're rocking forward and backward at an insane speed, loving the sensation, and galloping on with a shit-eating grin.

You hear the hounds ahead in full cry as they give tongue to one another, their way of communicating when they're working a line, meaning on the scent trail of a fox. As you're chasing the hounds, sometimes you jump into waterways, and then scamper up the bank on the opposite side. At times you're in open fields, literally riding with the wind. Other times, you duck as you enter an area thick with foliage, putting your head down and raising an arm to avoid being smacked in the face from branches whipping back at you. Inevitably, some riders come off their horses.

A foxhunt can last anywhere from a little more than an hour to more than four hours. But unlike pleasure riding, and unlike many hunts, on the one with the Clare Foxhounds that day, the only leisure time was once or twice when, at the discretion of the huntsman, we pulled up, not for the sake of the riders, but to give a breather to the hounds and the horses.

It's amazing that with all the seeming chaos—the huntsman leading the hounds with packs of riders forming behind him; hounds giving tongue and running in the lead; the wind in your face bringing tears to your eyes, which, with the rain, you try to clear away with one of your riding gloves while you're at the gallop; your heart thumping at the breathtaking speed, the sound of the thundering pack of horses; horses and riders vaulting over stone walls and sheer banks—it's actually all beautifully organized. No one is allowed to ride ahead of the professionals, and unlike with Vinnie Bligh, no one does.

A field master rides across the general terrain a day or so before the hunt to spot any particularly dangerous patches. Still, on the day of the hunt, you never know exactly the route you'll be taking, so his job remains to ride ahead and caution riders, even if only moments before they're in the area, to give them at least a few seconds to react and try to stay safe.

In the fields, I had no real sense where I was in relationship to Ruan. At times, we backtracked to some portion of the village, typically to jump a stone wall onto the road, sliding a bit because it was wet from the rain, then within two steps, jumping the wall on the other side of the road into another field. Perhaps four or five times during the hunt, Martin appeared at some juncture when we were crisscrossing the village. He cupped his hands and yelled, "Are you okay, lad?"

Thundering past him, I turned my head and yelled back, "Doing just fine, Martin!"

Later, I told Louis how nice it was of Martin to check on me repeatedly. He laughed. "He was checking to make sure that you weren't so tired or riding so poorly that you were going to kill yourself, and more important, his horse. So he was continuing to offer you a way out." Damn. I liked my romantic version better.

Meanwhile, back at the hunt, the villagers knew where the thundering herd was likely to appear and they stationed themselves for the best view possible. Indeed, some had been hunters in their day and were now groupies of a sort, recalling the times they'd been part of the field and jawing about the weather, the route, the riders, and how and what they'd be doing if they were out there. For her part, Karen spent some of her time with one group of old-timers, but most of it in one of the churches lighting candles and praying that I'd come back in one piece. There she was again, trying to burn down Ireland.

Finally, after roughly four and a half hours of the hardest riding I could ever have imagined, the hunt stopped. It was over. I'd quit counting how many jumps we'd taken, but it seemed somewhere north of a hundred. I'd lost track of the trots, canters, and gallops, during which only adrenalin kept my legs from giving out. My face and helmet were splattered with mud kicked up from horses I'd galloped behind across open fields. My riding coat and pants were wet from the rain. My body was soaked with sweat. I never thought I'd think, *Thank God for no more jumps.* But there I was thinking it.

We rested for about ten minutes and I began to relax. I'd hurt my right foot on a jump a few miles back when it struck a tree branch extended partly over a jump; a tough way to be reminded of the principle of an irresistible force meeting an immovable object. I thought I'd broken my big toe. For a good while after that, I had to stand on my toe hard in the stirrup to control the pain, which was intense, so I was particularly glad now that we'd pulled up and the hunt was over.

I was elated, the pain notwithstanding. I'd completed a hunt in Ireland and was still in the saddle. I was marveling at my accomplishment and reveling in the rest period, figuring that soon the huntsman would slowly move us into the center of the village from the last field. But after about ten minutes of milling on the horses, cooling them and us down, I heard a horn in the distance. I looked up and saw a number of the riders gathering together and jumping over another stone wall into another field. *Oh, my God. The hunt isn't over! Here we go again.*

I had to switch gears. I patted Seamus on the neck and said, "I'm really tired now, buddy, so I'm counting on you to do the heavy lifting." He did. We crisscrossed the village again with the young kids whooping, hollering, and urging the riders on as we jumped over more walls into more fields. After another fifteen minutes and six or seven more stone walls, we took one final jump that landed us on the road leading to the village. From that point, we brought our horses back to a walk. This time it wasn't a false alarm. Finally, it was really over.

I touched my left leg, my right leg, each arm, and my head. I was all there. By then I felt a chronic dull throb in my right toe, the acute pain lost in the exhilaration of being a part of this fraternity. After a minute or so at a leisurely trot, we came back to the walk, and entered the center of the village. I had another of those shit-eating grins plastered across my face. With my right leg, I kept reaching for my stirrup, but couldn't find it; I looked down and it was gone. It struck me that on my very last jump, I'd leaned hard to the left, and my right breakaway stirrup had broken and come off. I was coming into the village with one stirrup. On my last jump. I looked up and said, "Thank you, God."

Not only had I stayed the course of this long hunt, but also I hadn't come off my horse once, no small feat. When I spotted Karen among the villagers, I made sure my position on Seamus was as good as I could look, and I raised one closed fisted hand in a salute to Karen, Seamus, myself, and the most phenomenal ride of my life. Karen was waving to me as though I was a conquering hero, home from the wars. I'd seen some riders come off their horses during the hunt. Karen told me she'd seen many back in the village. They'd stopped riding either because they couldn't keep up, or they'd been thrown from their horses and couldn't recover them, or they'd been hurt so badly they couldn't continue. She allowed me my moment of pride. She didn't care. Her praying had paid off. I was alive and in one piece, sort of. (The toe took a good six months to heal.)

I settled with Martin and the young lad who came running to collect the cap. He reminded me what he'd actually said earlier: "No worry. *If you're still alive after the hunt, I'll get the fee from ye then.*" I'd met my end of the bargain: living through the hunt and happily paying the fee.

* * * * * * * * * * * * * * * * * *

Foxhunting stirs passions. To those who ride in or run them, the criticisms are unnerving and unfair, without basis in fact. For those who oppose foxhunting, it's a bloodlust event based on the unseemly sport of killing a fox (or in some localities, hares) for no reason other than the thrill of it.

In 2005, England passed a law that restricts, and in some cases outlaws, foxhunting. I believe that before passage of the bill, it generated something like seven hundred hours of debate in Parliament, precisely because passions run so high on both sides of the argument.

My purpose in writing about the two hunts in which I rode in Ireland is to try to give some feel from the rider's point of view. Speaking for myself and for a number of regular hunt riders I've come to know, it's the riding that matters. From my limited experience, the killing of a fox is barely the point of most modern day fox "hunting." In fact, hunts often end without it, for example, when a fox has gone to ground, meaning when it has gotten into its den or other place of refuge, the huntsman calls off the hunt. Whatever the reasons for the origin of foxhunts, over time, it's evolved into a sport that tests the endurance of rider and horse and certainly creates some of the most challenging riding imaginable.

Karen loves animals and without her support, no doubt many an animal shelter would fold. She hates the idea of a fox dying at the end of a hunt, so for my first one in Ireland, she insisted that I ride with the Clare Foxhounds on a day when they weren't hunting a fox. Instead, they were doing a drag hunt in which a scent has been laid, or dragged across a terrain before the hunt. In this way the hunt, with hounds and all, is strictly for the ride and has nothing to do with chasing, let alone killing an animal. I was seeking a new, different, and challenging ride. I got what I wanted and then some. Indeed, because it was a drag hunt, the riding was probably harder than a regular one when the field pulls up as the hounds stop and start, searching for the scent.

Though this was a drag hunt, as we were mounting, someone said that if a fox crossed the path of the pack, the hounds would take off after it. That's what hounds are trained to do. At least on that day, no fox proved to be that big of an eejit.

Later, when I told friends I'd been in a drag hunt, they hesitated for a second and I'd have to say, "No, I wasn't with sixty cross-dressing riders."

* * * * * * * * * * * * * * * * * *

No hunt is complete until the group retires to the nearest pub, where everyone, without challenge, gets to tell about jumping a ten-foot wall, then into a twenty-foot ditch, and then scampering up the other side with no problem. The rule is, if you survive the hunt, you get to tell any story you want and all others who'd been on the hunt will nod and back you up: "Aye, 'tis the truth. Maybe a twelve-foot wall."

Another seven or eight riders in the hunt were also staying at the Dunraven, so rather than go to a local pub in Ruan, we headed back to Adare and went to the pub there.

At the Dunraven were two Brits who'd been on this hunt and had been riding in them for twenty-plus years. One of them took a bad fall about midhunt, which ended his riding for the day. The other one made it to the end. He asked me, "How did you like the hunt?"

"Well, I thought it was spectacular, but I have nothing to compare it to, because I've never been on one before."

"You mean you've never been on one in Ireland?"

"No, I've never been on any hunt before."

"Well, I've got good news and bad news for you. The good news is that you've just been on the hardest and best hunt you'll ever ride. The bad news is any hunt you ever ride in the future will pale by comparison."

Then he got off his stool and walked around to look at the back of my riding coat. It was "clean," meaning it had no telltale mud on it, evidence that I hadn't come off my horse. He turned to the room, hoisted his pint, and said, "A toast to the lad. He rode his first hunt, a hard one, and he rode it clean. Cheers."

Those in the pub said "sláinte" and "cheers," toasting me.

As I clinked glasses with those near me and uttered my own sláintes, I felt like I'd just won a gold medal at the Olympics. I still feel that way.

The Unlikely Couple

At the Dunraven the Morning of the Hunt with the Clare Foxhounds

Awaiting Seamus

Time for a Leg Up with Martin Geoghan's Help

Chapter 11

⌒

The Adare Cottages

Even in the afterglow of my hunt with the Clare Foxhounds, plus basking a few more days at the sumptuous Dunraven, we came to terms that the joint wasn't cheap. We could afford it for a short time, but it was too pricey for a long-term stay. We learned that the Dunraven also owned self-catering cottages on the opposite end of the village, roughly a ten-minute walk from the hotel.

The cottages, nestled into a cul-de-sac at the end of a small lane off Main Street, had their own parking and office, and were staffed a few mornings a week.

In all, there were eight cottages, named after local towns, including Bruff, Askeaton, Kildimo, Croom, and our favorite and the cottage we always tried to reserve, Castleroberts, which was at the end of the row of cottages so no cars came that far to park, and outside its front door was a view of a church that lit up every night. Each cottage, for rent on a weekly basis at roughly a third the price of rooms at the Dunraven, had two floors—a downstairs consisting of a kitchen, a living room with a fireplace, and a bedroom en suite. Upstairs were two more bedrooms, one en suite, plus a third bathroom and a small room with a washer and a dryer.

Each cottage had a basket of flowers hanging under the eaves by the front door and every day, come rain or shine, more often than not rain,

Joe O'Dwyer came around at 5:00 p.m. to water them, his trusty dog always by his side. Every time he did, Karen and I were at the front window watching him, but Joe always made sure to stare straight ahead. No way would he acknowledge our presence. It took us into our third year to get him to talk to us, and then, the only way it happened was that when it was time for the daily watering, I went out the front door and said something brilliant like, "Isn't it a lovely day?"

"'Tis."

"Looks like the rain's comin' in from the west."

"Does."

From that breakthrough, we worked our way into one and two-sentence discussions. Eventually, we actually got to talking.

Joe was born and raised in Adare and had inherited his uncle's house on Main Street where he still lived alone, never having married. He maintained the grounds at the public golf course at the Adare Manor, traveled around town on his bicycle, fished daily in the early morning hours in the Maigue, and was a sports nut, as were many Irish. This meant, among other things, that when his team played on a particular day, he flew its flag in front of his house. For those sports nuts who drove, they'd put the flag on their car, and if your team won, you'd drive through the village, repeatedly honking your horn. But Joe left that for the kids.

Through the many years we've stayed in the village, of our many pleasures, one is seeing Joe on the opposite side of the street, waving to him and having him, eventually, heartily waving back.

The first year we stayed at the cottages, we also went to the Adare library and met Margaret, the head librarian. Although Karen brought enough books to sink the *Queen Mary*, she wanted more. She found some at the library. We asked if we could check them out. Margaret asked for our address. We said, "The Adare Cottages." She said that was fine, but asked for a ten-punt deposit (the euro came along some years later), refundable when we returned the last book we'd checked out.

In later years, we came to know Margaret better. Karen and Margaret recommended books to each other. Karen checked out books Margaret suggested. Margaret told us about guest lecturers, and during our second year at the cottages, through Margaret we got library cards, which we still proudly carry and use every time we're in Adare. With the cards, we no longer had to make the deposit. Man oh man, we were practically natives.

We also toured an old factory in nearby Croom. In its heyday, it churned out flour using the power of the Maigue to work its machinery. Its engines, restored sufficiently, produced enough flour that one of the guides gave us a bag as we left. In turn, we gave it to a gardener who also worked at the cottages. He doffed his hat, thanked us profusely, and the next day, gave us scones his missus had baked from our gift.

That year we met Richard, owner of a country sportswear and tack shop called the Country Dresser. We bought a number of items from him; talked about riding, learned some local gossip, and a number of years later, Richard and I rode to the hounds together with the County Limerick Foxhounds.

We also sent many a postcard back to the States, each time going to Adare's post office, where we met and became friendly with the postmistress, Liz Twomey. Each post office has the right to sell whatever goods it desires, in addition to stamps, so they're their own little businesses. Because Adare's post office building isn't much bigger than a postage stamp, Liz didn't have much room to sell other products, but you could top off your cell phone and buy gift certificates. There's always a queue and no local transacts their business without first saying "Hi, Liz," and exchanging a few pleasantries. In later years, we came to thanking Liz for saving one of our dinners—literally.

We did all our grocery shopping at Lohan's Centra Market. Centra is a franchise of food markets throughout Ireland, each bearing the name of the individual franchisee, in Adare, Sean Lohan. In our first years "living" in Adare, we went to the centra every other day and saw Sean and his brother Andrew. Sean, like Joe O'Dwyer, did a good job of not looking you in the eye until one day I broke the taboo and spoke to him directly. From that day forward, every time we were in the store, Sean mysteriously appeared at our side while we were in one of the aisles to ask something important like, "Where are ye staying?"

"The cottages."

He'd usually say something profound like, "Oh." Occasionally, he'd offer a tidbit of information: "Have ye tried the tatched pub on the outskirts of the village?"

"No, we haven't, Sean."

"You should now. It's better than anything in town. And did I tell ye about the apartments we're building?"

"No Sean, you didn't."

"Well, they'll be to the rear of the store, and they'll be just grand."

We developed a friendship over the years with Sean. One time I damaged my glasses from taking a fall while riding at Clonshire. Karen and I went to an eyeglass shop in Limerick, but they didn't handle repairs. I asked Sean if he knew where I could get my glasses fixed. He said, "No problem. I know just the man to fix 'em, a blacksmith he is. Let me have 'em and I'll have 'em back to ye shortly."

"A *blacksmith*? Are your sure this is something he can do?"

"Just as sure as I am that it'll rain today."

"Okay. Here they are."

Karen looked at me like the loon I was as I handed them over. Each time we returned to the centra, Sean continued to tell us they'd be ready soon. Then one day he said to me, "Well, I'm afraid I've a bit of bad news."

"What's that?"

"You know the blacksmith who had yer glasses?"

I didn't like the "had."

"Well now, he has a dog that loves to bury t'ings in the backyard, and it seems he got your glasses, so they're now out there somewhere."

"A dog buried my glasses in the blacksmith's backyard?"

"Appears so."

"So they won't be found until some archaeological dig?" I said, joining in the joke.

"Don't know about any such digs planned."

I thought his reply was good craic, as he'd hand me my repaired glasses. It wasn't and he didn't. I never saw my glasses again.

That winter, Sean's centra burned to the ground. When we returned to Adare the following year and went to the new, bigger, and better centra for the first time, I saw Sean. I stopped about five feet from him. Before saying a word, for about five seconds, I stroked the bottom of my chin in an upward motion with the fingers from one hand. Then I hunched my shoulders slightly and in my best Brando imitation, I said, "You know my business, Sean? I do people favors. In return, if I need a favor, they do it for me. Sometimes it's a small favor, sometimes it's a big one."

I shrugged my shoulders again. "Where I live, people call me Godfather." I was looking right at Sean. I wasn't smiling. Neither was he. "All that I ever ask for is respect. Is that too much to ask for, Sean? I don't think so."

I hunched my shoulders again. "When people disrespect me, other people I know get upset and they try to set the record straight. You understand, Sean? You know that fire you had? I can't say for sure how it happened, and believe me, from the bottom of my heart, it hurt me when that happened. But do you remember my glasses that you never returned to me? You remember, don't you Sean?"

He nodded.

I took two steps closer to him, bent over, put one hand on each of his shoulders, and in a whisper said, "Next time I give you a pair of glasses, return them to me, Sean. Is that fair?"

I continued to look at him for another five seconds with a deadpan stare. He looked away from me. Then he looked back. I started to crack up. He broke into a grin, then a hearty laugh and soon, everyone within sight of us, not knowing why, had joined in rollicking laughter.

I never gave Sean another pair of glasses to fix and his store never burned down again.

Our first year at the cottages, we split our dinner locations, eating in one night and going to a local restaurant or pub the next. One of our favorite pubs was the Collins, not to be confused with the *other* Collins just up the block. *Our* Collins was owned and run by Pat Collins, and in later years, by his son Michael.

In 2004, the Irish government banned smoking in pubs, restaurants, and other enclosed workplaces. In the years before the no-smoking ban, it wasn't easy staying in a pub without becoming quickly poisoned. When the ban began, we didn't believe it would be enforced, because smoking in pubs in Ireland was something akin to a religious right, but the government imposed a few three thousand-euro-per-infraction fines on some smokers and pub owners in Dublin, and word got around the country quickly that the ban was for real. For us, it was a blessing; it became possible to eat and drink in these places without choking to death and without your clothes smelling of smoke.

We came to learn that a pub like Collins had damn good food. The seafood platter was, and remains, one of our favorites; with a couple pints of Guinness, it puts me close to heaven. It took longer to figure out that only the locals knew to ask for the specials. The pub never offered information about them; you had to know to ask and even then, unless you were *really* a local, they'd be out of the specials until, suspiciously, you'd see one served to a regular. Some years later, when we asked about the specials, without hesitation, we were told what they were and if we wanted one we got it—another important marker that we were accepted as honorary locals by returning year after year, becoming known to many villagers, and by accepting local customs and norms.

Another thing we learned about the pubs was that you never knew what zaniness might pop up of an evening. One night, we were having dinner next to a table with four couples, ranging in age from fifty to sixty. While Karen and I were eating our dinner, they were drinking theirs and having a few drinks to go along with it.

John, clearly the instigator, spent scant time sitting. Mostly, he was at the bar ordering rounds for the group, and though he drank enough to sink a ship, his wit got sharper as the evening wore on. He told us that the whole group lived in and was returning that night to Cork (easily a two-hour drive). I hoped it wasn't true. If it was, we probably should have taken away the keys of the drivers and had all of them sleep at our cottage.

John asked us the usual questions: Where we were from in the States. Whether this was our first time in Ireland. What we thought of the weather, and in an indirect and polite kind of way, our opinion of President Bush. A Yank's view of *W* was a litmus test as to how you'd be treated. If you let it be known that you liked him, you generally became a nonperson, disregarded, if not shunned. If you let it be known that you disliked him, you were embraced as a long-lost cousin. (More on this later.)

At any rate, once we answered the usual questions and passed the *W* test, John turned to one of the other men in the group and said, "How about 'Song For Ireland,' Sean?" Sean needed no prompting. He immediately belted out the song a cappella, and I'll be damned if he wasn't grand. When he finished, he took a long swig of his pint as those at the table applauded. And so it went. John sang a ditty. Mary took some cajoling, but eventually she launched into a number. Martin unleashed an improvised song, a wee bit off color, but hilarious. The evening wore on as John continued to return to the table laden with enough wine and Guinness to open his own brewery. As each member of the group sang a traditional Irish song, Karen joined in as she had some years earlier at the bar in Dromoland, since she knew the true Irish tunes. I joined in on the few I knew and faked it on the rest.

Eventually, John turned to Karen and me and said, "It's time for the Yanks to do a song." I'm not bashful. But bashful or not wouldn't have made a difference. Once you're accepted into a group in a pub in Ireland, demurring is out of the question. You can try all the excuses you want—you can't sing, you have a scratchy throat, the dog ate the music—but nothing works. You're part of the clan now; you've been invited to participate and they'll wait till Christmas for you to comply.

Still, I didn't really know any Irish songs and even if I did, what was left of my brain was swimming in Guinness. I glanced over at Karen, furrowing my brow, looking for help on what to sing. I probably know a thousand songs, but at that moment I couldn't think of one. Finally, what came into my mind was "Sixteen Tons."

So there I was, in an Irish pub, surrounded by a group that for the last hour had been singing every traditional Irish song ever written, belting out a Tennessee Ernie Ford song about a US coal miner and the company store. Grand. What is it with me and singing in Irish pubs? Last time at Dromoland, it was "House of the Rising Sun" and now it was "Sixteen Tons"?

Oh well. The key in Ireland is just to do what you're doing with gusto and we did, in a hearty duet. As we were wrapping up, I went into a thirty second finish with "I ooooooowe my soooooouuuuulllll [pause, pause, pause, pause] to the company stooooooorrrrrrrrre" and snapped my fingers as I hummed the final music. Our new best friends immediately broke into wild applause, as though we'd just finished a set at a packed house at Carnegie Hall. We may have sung a stupid song for being in an Irish pub, but we'd joined in and been good sports. The willingness and the effort were all that mattered.

But just like the false finish of the foxhunt, it wasn't over. John told a joke. No people have a better sense of humor than the Irish, and when they tell a joke, they do it with relish and impeccable timing—lubricated with a few swigs of their pint.

Some years later, I thought back on the humor shared that evening when reading the liner notes in Tommy Makem's (of the Clancy Brothers) album, *The Tommy Makem Songbag*. On the album, he sings a beautiful love song he wrote, titled "Gentle Annie." In his liner notes, he explains, "I wrote this song for my wife whose name is Mary, but I had written so many songs that included the name Mary that I thought I needed a different name. She understands." That's Irish humor. Understated. Unbeatable.

Meanwhile, back at Collins, John passed the joke-telling mantle to Mary and so on around the table. Some of the jokes were bawdy and all were funny, and there's nothing like hearty drinking, singing, and laughing to get you good and high in several different ways. Then John turned to us and said, "Your turn."

We've all, at one time or another, gone through that sense of having a word, a name, or a joke "on the tip of my tongue," but you can't quite reach it. I'm not a bad joke teller. It's just that generally I hear them, enjoy them, and forget them.

Finally, I remembered one. The joke goes something like this: a guy goes into a pub and orders three pints. After finishing all of them, he thanks the barkeep and leaves. He returns a week later and repeats his three-pint order, drinks them all, and departs. When he places the same order a week later, the barkeep asks why he always orders three pints at a time. The guy says, "Oh, I drink one to the good health of me brother in Australia, one to the good health of me brother in Amerikay, and the third one's for me."

The barkeep says, "Well, here's to the good health of all of ye."

"Why, thank ye kindly."

Then the customer disappears for a month. When he shows up, he orders two pints. The barkeep, feeling badly that apparently one of his brothers had died, says, "I'm sorry fer yer trouble," to which the customer replies, "Trouble? What trouble?"

"Oh, I tawt that because you were havin' only two pints, one of yer brothers had passed."

"No. No, man. My brothers are jest fine, but 'tanks very much fer yer kind toughts. It's just me. I've given up the drink."

Except I botched the joke halfway through and forgot the punch line. I looked to Karen, started all over again, and never got it right. I ended up saying something witty like, "Anyway, the point is that neither of the guy's brothers was dead." Blowing a joke is like letting air out of a tire. It always leaves people staring at their shoes, and then voting with their feet. Not with this group. I was now a member of the club, and they applauded as though Robin Williams had just finished one of his nonstop twenty-minute riffs that leave you laughing so hard your sides hurt.

"Good try, lad!"

"That's just grand!"

"Just grand!"

They covered my failed effort and then one person in the group immediately launched into a raucous joke to fill the dead space. I wanted to adopt the lot of them. And Karen and I did something we'd never done before; we closed down a pub in Ireland.

Sometime later, we learned of another incident at the Collins Pub. As background, whether you loved him or hated him, all Irish knew that Michael Collins had been assassinated during the Irish Civil War (1921–1922) by those who thought he'd been a sellout to the British following his negotiation of the treaty with England that created the two states of Northern Ireland and the Republic.

Some seventy years or so later, one of the locals in Adare routinely got drunk and obnoxious at the Collins Pub. Pat Collins was bartending one night when he'd finally had it. He threw his towel on the bar, pointed to the door, and in disgust yelled at the customer, "That's it! I've had enough of you! You've gone too far. Out with you now, and I never want to see you in here again. Never! Now be gone, man!"

Everyone acknowledges that the man who got the toss deserved it and that he was so drunk that night he could barely stand. That didn't stop him from finishing his drink, wiping his mouth on his sleeve, and leaving in a huff. As soon as he was out the door, the room was abuzz with what had just happened. Moments later, the room got dead quiet as the man stumbled back into the pub. Pat Collins was still behind the bar.

The drunk said, "Can I shay, say, shay jest one t'ing?"

You could hear a pin drop. Pat, wiping the bar, said, "Have yer say, man, and then be gone with you for good."

"I jesht, jest, jesssht want evvvvveryone here to know one t'ing."

The room remained quiet as a tomb. He looked around, found Pat, extended his arm toward him, and pointing a finger, blurted out, "They shot the wrong Collins!"

With that he turned, walked into a wall, backed up a few steps, stumbled to the front door, but pushed instead of pulled it, thus walking into it; then pulled it open, fell onto the sidewalk, got up, dusted himself off, and stumbled into the night, never to return.

Staying at the cottages, we got to know Bernie Lohan, who owns the dry cleaning store in town and is one of Sean and Andrew Lohan's sisters. We knew the manager of the local hardware store, the same one who served us drinks when he moonlighted as a bartender at Collins. We ate at every restaurant in town and got to know the owners. One of our favorites for lunch was the Dovecot, though we tried to avoid being there when the loads of tourists arrived in buses. At those times, the Dovecot filled up like water being poured into a jar. It happened in reverse, too, when the tourists were reloaded into their buses and carted off to their next destination.

We also got to know Maeve, who owns a gift shop in the village's Heritage Tourist Center where the Dovecot is also located. We knew John, the maître d' at the Maigue, and Jack, the headwaiter. Jack's picture is on a Dunraven brochure (pronounced BROsher); he's in a tuxedo with a white towel carefully tucked into his slacks as he serves champagne from a silver tray to a group of riders mounted in front of the hotel—all in full formal dress about to start a hunt. We sometimes shopped at the local butcher, Costello's (pronounced, as we were once corrected, COStello's, not CosTELLo's).

In short, we got to know many of the local merchants and others who were owners and operators in the village so that, more and more, we began to feel like we belonged there. It just remained for us to get friendly with some of the residents themselves, because that would really get us inside life there. This seemed a daunting challenge, but we were in for a big and wonderful surprise.

Chapter 12

⁓

Dan Flaxman, Sarah, Dingle,
and Mrs. Murphy

Our friend Dan Flaxman is one-of-a-kind, very much his own person. Dressing up to Dan is jeans instead of shorts. He always wears a baseball cap and it takes some doing to get him to take it off, even in a restaurant. He's usually wearing the same old blue sweatshirt; in it, he sweats and always comments on how warm the room is.

He doesn't drink alcohol. He just doesn't like it, even though for about twenty-five years he was a waiter at Perry's, one of San Francisco's popular restaurants. Since then, he's made his living doing tax returns. Meanwhile, having spent so many years as a waiter, you might think he developed a good palette. But this is Dan Flaxman. The first time he ate dinner at our house, he took a mouthful of salad, frowned, and spit the lettuce into his hand.

"What's on there?"

"Oil and vinegar."

"I like mine dry."

And so, from then on, dry it was and that became a metaphor for what he'd eat.

Dan never married. And like anyone who lives alone for many decades, he became unique. He's beholden to no one. He never needed to make adjustments for the benefit of someone else. He thinks many traditional social conventions are silly. He says what's on his mind without first filtering it through that part of the brain that asks, *Is this proper? Does it sound weird? Can it be taken wrong?*

Dan speaks quietly, he's a deep thinker, and he's bright. He's an avid reader. He's traveled extensively, takes detailed notes of each place he visits, and is generous in sharing the benefit of his observations so others can have prime travel experiences.

He loves London and used to go for ten days at a time, seeing twenty plays, a matinee, and an evening performance daily. We first met him when the three of us served as directors for a local theater group.

Dan was extremely devoted to his mother Sarah who, well into her eighties, was active, spry, an avid reader, and traveled occasionally with her son. It wasn't until she was nearly ninety that she moved into the Jewish Home for the Aged in San Francisco. She remained sharp as a tack until the end of her life.

While she was in the Jewish Home, Dan saw her every day. Yep. Every day—tax season, rain, hail, earthquake, whatever—every day until she died. At her memorial service Dan spoke, wearing his baseball cap, of course.

It takes awhile to understand and accept Dan. His social skills certainly wouldn't qualify him for a position in the state department, but when you figure him out and more importantly, when you accept him and vice versa, he's your friend for life, and he'll give you his right arm without once hesitating about the consequences.

One night in early 1998, when Dan was at our house for dinner, we mentioned that some months later, we were going to Ireland and we asked if he'd like to join us for about a week. Dan said "I'd love to." And without missing a beat he asked, "Can my mother come?"

"Sure."

"Can I use your phone to call her right now and ask her?"

"Sure."

So before we'd even had a chance to process what had just happened, Dan was on the phone talking to Sarah.

"Hi, Mom. Listen, would you like to go to Ireland? We can stay with Karen and Harvey. No, no, Mom, I'll pay. Yes, you'll need a passport.

You don't have one? Oh, when did it expire? That's okay. We can fix that. What do you say? Yeah, we'll go for a week. Don't worry; I'll make all the arrangements. Good. Do you want to say a word to Karen and Harvey?"

In something of a daze, we took the phone to tell Sarah how excited we were that she and her "Danny" would be joining us for a week. We assured her it was no inconvenience and that it would be "fun," which is a great word to use as filler when you're suffering from a mild case of shock.

After Dan left that evening, we each had an extra glass of wine and kept repeating to each other, "It'll be fine. Right? It'll be fine." Then we each had another glass of wine.

As it turned out, it was more than fine. It was great; actually, it was grand. They arrived about a week after we did, so we had a chance to get over our jet lag and were ready for guests. With layover time, they'd traveled for twenty-four hours straight, but amazingly, Sarah looked terrific, although at eighty-eight, a bit dazed, and exhausted. Not amazingly, Dan was wearing a baseball cap and shorts. Shorts? In Ireland? Oh well, this was Dan.

Within a day or so, Sarah was in great shape and ready, willing, and able to do just about anything, except horseback ride. We saw some sights, taking her to places that were comparatively accessible on foot. Then Dan said he really wanted to go to Dingle Town. He'd stayed there thirty-five years earlier and felt a strong tug to return. We'd not yet been to Dingle, so we were up for a visit.

To get there, you have two choices. One is via a regular highway that takes you through some towns and villages, but is mostly a straight shot. The other is the way we chose, via Conor Pass, the highest mountain pass in Ireland. I don't know the top elevation of the pass, but at one point, it crosses the top of Brandon Mountain, which is slightly higher than thirty-one hundred feet. As you descend, eventually you reach a *real* road, still about fifteen hundred feet above Dingle Town. From there, it's a winding ride of about four-and-a-half miles, heading down toward Brandon Bay, cliffs, a waterfall, and lakes.

Near the top of the pass, in places, there's room for only one vehicle. So when you encounter one coming in the opposite direction, one has to back up to a tiny indentation in the road to make room for the other to pass. As luck (of the Irish) would have it, on the day we took the pass, it was socked in with fog so thick that we had trouble seeing our hand when we stuck it out the window. This made for great fun when encountering another car coming in the opposite direction and trying to figure out how to back up without going over the edge. After enduring this nerve-racking exercise a number of times and grumbling about the stupidity of taking the pass, the fog suddenly broke. The sun shined in all its splendor, and laid beneath us on a virtual silver platter was a breathtakingly beautiful valley.

Conor Pass
(Courtesy Jeremy Weiss)

At that moment, our near-death experiences were distant memories and well worth the effort. This was like flying our own plane into Brigadoon, with the added advantage of getting to see from on high the bay, the cliffs, and Dingle Town laid below in all their scenic glory.

Dingle is in County Kerry, on the Dingle Peninsula south of the River Shannon and north of the Ring of Kerry. The westernmost part of the island was the first land Lindberg saw on his historic flight after leaving New York for Paris. It was, and remains, a hot tourist spot. Although its population is slightly less than two thousand, during high season the number can swell to twenty thousand. There are some gorgeous sights, fishing for those inclined, great traditional Irish music, and did I mention, pubs?

Once we got into Dingle Town, we blundered along until we found our way to Doyle's Restaurant and Townhouse where we ate a fabulous seafood dinner and settled in for a few nights. The next afternoon we drove to Slea Head (pronounced Shlayhead), a beautiful ride along the water's edge with rolling hills and bracing cliffs. We passed stone houses, stopped for sheep and goats on the road, and had views of a countryside that looked like a chessboard with patches of Ireland's forty shades of green dotting the hillsides, a sight we never tire of seeing, especially as we're flying into Shannon, a reminder that we're home again.

From the parking lot at the top of a bluff at Slea Head, Dan, Karen, and I walked down a winding road etched by a stone wall to a beach cove from which we felt the raw beauty and power of the place. From Slea Head you have a direct view of the Blasket Islands. The Great Blasket is roughly eleven hundred acres of wild, meandering, mountainous terrain about four miles long by a half-mile wide, situated at a spot where its ancient inhabitants saw some of the Spanish Armada ships wrecked. Into the twentieth century, one hundred and fifty families still lived on it, but the population dwindled due to the hard life. In 1953, the island was abandoned. Boats take tourists to rentals in four restored houses at the top of what had been the village.

When we returned to Dingle, Dan wanted to find the B&B where he'd stayed thirty-five years earlier and had fallen in love with the rugged southwest coast of Ireland. He'd come for a week and stayed for three months. We knew his attempt to locate the place was a fool's errand, but we went along with him. As it turned out, we were the fools. He found the inn, knocked on the door, and lo and behold, the same Mrs. Murphy who'd owned and run the B&B when Dan had stayed there answered it.

Somewhat tenuously, she invited us into the drawing room where Dan launched into a history of the time he'd spent there. He wanted to know if Mrs. Murphy remembered the soup and sandwich she'd prepared for him the night of a ferocious storm when he couldn't go out to eat. Mrs. Murphy quietly demurred. She'd only made about thirty-seven thousand meals since then and weathered as many storms.

During our visit, each of us disclosed to Mrs. Murphy just about everything about ourselves except our Social Security numbers. On the other side, we managed to learn she had one son living in San Francisco, but when we asked for his telephone number, she couldn't "recall" it. She "wasn't sure" of his address either. In short, she gave up nothing. I'd always thought of the Irish as ready and willing to tell you their life histories. But over time, I came to realize that though they love the craic and talk a blue streak with stories, viewpoints, and political opinions, when it comes to divulging the real inside information, they get far more than they give—unless and until you've earned the right to personal details. With Mrs. Murphy, we hadn't come close.

That night we went to a local restaurant and then to a pub where we happened onto some musicians doing what's done all over Ireland: playing for the love of playing for hours on end (and having a few pints in the process). Listening to the music that night struck us how much crossover you find between traditional Irish music and American country and western—not all of it, of course, but plenty. I'd say the odds are reasonably strong that Irish music affects American music and not the other way around. After all, they have us by more than a two thousand year head start.

On the way back to Adare, but before leaving Dingle, we found a by then, much decayed part of a movie set that had been built for *Ryan's Daughter*, a 1970 film set in 1916, the year of the Easter Rising. Intertwined in the story is an Irish woman married to a local schoolteacher. After the wife has an affair with a British officer, she's accorded rough treatment at the hands of the townspeople who are livid at a local being a whore to a Brit.

The movie wasn't well received in Ireland. One criticism was it gave an unfair portrayal of the Irish underclass as uncivilized compared to the British soldiers (never a favorite comparison for the Irish). Worse, the film was seen by many Irish as roughing up the legacy of the 1916 Easter Rising and the ensuing War of Independence against England. This was particularly disturbing since the Troubles had started unfolding in Northern Ireland shortly before the release of the film, and anti-British sentiment was again at a boil.

I'd seen the film years before I knew anything about Irish history or sensibilities. I thought it was a hard, but interesting story, and magnificently acted, but when I learned of Irish sentiment toward the film I was smart enough to keep my thoughts to myself. Anyway, it was a kick walking on the abandoned set and recalling scenes that had been shot there. Pretty much hanging off a cliff, the front was the schoolhouse, while the back doubled as the house in which the teacher and his wife lived.

We also stopped at Inch Beach, so named because on a typical map, it's roughly an inch long. Another dramatic scene in *Ryan's Daughter* was filmed on Inch when the town comes to the waterside in a grueling storm to gather arms being brought in on a ship for the IRA.

The next day, we settled Sarah in with a good book and the three of us drove to Nenagh in North Tipperary to attend point-to-point horse races sponsored by the North Tipperary Foxhounds. A large part of hunt revenues comes from these race events, organized and run by the clubs in conjunction with a jockey club, the horses both from within and outside the club.

The point-to-point horse race is different than American racing. First, as was true at Nenagh, the race is often in an open field. (The brochure for these races noted: "[b]y kind permission of Peter McCutcheon, Esq.," meaning they were on his land, and he no doubt was a club member of the North Tipperary Foxhounds.) There are no grandstands. For the price of admission, you can wander around anywhere in the infield; the racetrack is on the outside perimeter. Second, the race is not just on the flat, but also involves jumps with wide spreads. On some, there are bushes at the top of the jump with a landing in water, so in addition to being strong, the horses also must have heart so they're not spooked by foliage and water. Third, because you can walk around the infield area, you can go to different jumps to watch how the riders handle them. You stand right on the side of a jump where you can focus on the thundering herd heading toward it, or train your eye over the jump to see a blur of horses and riders. Each way of watching gives you a different sensation; the latter lets you know just how fast the pack is traveling when they take these jumps. How fast? Damn fast.

The jockeys are bigger than in the States. These races aren't just about speed, but also about jumping and endurance. Initially, it was striking to see the jockeys riding differently than we're accustomed. In the States, the stirrups are pulled up as high as possible, and the jockeys literally stand up in the stirrups the entire race. In a point-to-point, the stirrups are much longer. To take the jumps, because they often end at a downward angle and into water, the rider often sits back in his saddle to avoid tumbling over the horse's head. Then, as soon as the horse makes the jump and is back at a gallop, the rider leans forward. It's a beautiful sight to watch, especially when it's done with such apparent effortlessness.

During the course of the race, though, both Karen and I noticed that some of the horses seemed to be laboring. We learned later that many horses start their racing lives at point-to-points, and the better ones graduate to the highest echelons of national hunt racing in Ireland and England. But it seemed that some of the steeds at this point-to-point weren't strong enough for the nationals and were running out of gas as the races wore on. During one, some distance from us, a horse took a bad spill over a jump. The rider, though roughed up, was okay, but the horse broke a leg and was put down right on the track. We couldn't watch. We also decided we'd seen our last point-to-point race.

The ephemeral nature of the whole setup was brought home when the betting booths and food stands disappeared. Before the races start, the booths are hoisted onto the infield grass next to the food stands, which are trucks with side panels. When the race is over, the betting booths are collapsed, tossed onto trucks, and the food booths are driven off the premises. Within minutes, you'd never know any event had gone on in this stray field.

As Dan and Sarah's week with us ended, we waved good-bye at Shannon. At the same time, Sheila, my cousin from London, flew over to join us. Before she came, she said she'd only stay three days. At the time we didn't question her, although she was welcome to stay longer. Karen said to me, "Perhaps she has other plans."

We told her of the wonderful week we'd had with Dan and Sarah and what a joy it had been to share some of our experiences in Ireland with them. She listened, nodding her head the whole time. "It's lovely that you feel that way; I'm sure they had a wonderful time and you're good friends to them."

That sounded like there was a big "but" coming.

I said, "We're certain they enjoyed themselves, and who knows if Sarah will ever again be able to make such an arduous trip."

"You just need to protect yourselves a bit."

"What do you mean?" Karen asked, knowing the "but" was on its way.

"Well, for many years our family entertained quite a bit. Often that meant having guests stay at our house. Let me share with you what I learned the hard way."

"Okay," I said, "What's that?"

"If you don't impose some limitation on who can stay with you and for how long, you'll be inundated with visitors and freeloaders. That's exactly what happened to our family years ago."

"But," I said, "This is Dan and Sarah—"

"Obviously they fall under the category of close friends. I'm just telling you to beware of fish and visitors. Both get old after three days, and then you want to get rid of them."

We don't exactly live by Sheila's three-day rule. We always want my kids, close relatives, and some special friends to spend as much time with us as possible. But ironically, they're the ones who always impose their own time limits, knowing that Karen and I enjoy special company, but also value our time alone together. What we've found is that those with whom we're not so close have been the most imposing. So, on the rare occasion when people we aren't interested in spending a few weeks with ask when we're returning to Ireland so they can stay at the cottage, I tell them they can't come because the Great Plague is again sweeping through Europe. Okay, so I usually find a slightly more diplomatic way to say it, but it's at times like these that I remember the joke about the Jew who says, "God, you know how honored we are to be the Chosen People. But could you do us a favor and share the honor with someone else for a while?"

Hmm. Fish and visitors. We've modified your rule a bit, Sheila, but the principle remains sound.

Chapter 13

How Long Can We Stay?

All of our working years, Karen could take a vacation for no more than a week at a time. I could take off two at the most. Karen handled endless business details in a nearly constant crisis mode. There was never a slow period in her business, and this was in the era of telexes, not computers, and e-mails. Often, she returned to her office after dinner to review telexes from her Philippine customers whose day was just starting, so she could organize the schedule for her next day. I'd worked my way up the ladder to become a senior partner and head of the trial department of a midsize San Francisco law firm. As the lawyer responsible for a wide range of civil lawsuits, it was difficult to find even a two-week spot when something major wasn't happening in at least one of my cases. It's one of the great ironies in any business or profession. The more successful you become, the less time you can take off. Though there's wisdom in the adage to be careful what you pray for, I'm not complaining. What the hell. I took the money.

Two things changed our lives dramatically. In 1994, five years after we were married, Karen's company shut down. She and her partner had had a good long run, but after they'd been in business for thirty years, its primary customer, a Philippine copper mine, wanted to absorb the operation ending its autonomy as an independent supplier. Karen and her partner didn't want to end their careers as employees. They wanted to end as their own bosses, so they retired.

After closing down the business, Karen was petrified. All of a sudden, she faced a life in which she feared she'd sit all day long and watch the pendulum on our grandfather clock swing slowly to the left and then, in what would seem an eternity, slowly to the right. As I suspected, it took her roughly ten minutes to start enjoying being out of the work world. For her first time as an adult, she could *really* enjoy the simple pleasures. She could cook, shop at her leisure, not during the aftermath of rush hours, one among the crush of people anxious to get home and throw their meals together. She could read voraciously and horseback ride more.

Then the clincher. Shortly after she retired, Ashley, my youngest, called to announce that she'd decided to go to law school and wanted to know if she could live with us while she did. This turned out perfectly for all of us. Many years earlier, Karen had resisted being forced into the role of homemaker before she'd forged her own life. Now, with her business success behind her and Ashley no longer a child, Karen had the time and desire, and she created a household for us.

The three of us had dinner together nightly and for me it was magical. I was able to "talk law" with my daughter, challenge her, have her challenge me, and watch her analytical and writing skills grow by leaps and bounds. At the same time, it was a godsend for Karen, who had no time to think of boredom from retirement.

As a bonus, Karen and Ashley developed a bond made possible only by living together. This was exactly what Karen had always wanted: no confusion about her role. She wasn't raising a child in competition with Ashley's mother; she was dealing with a young woman and was capable and interested in being a sounding board for Ashley's never-ending questions to Kar, a woman she came to love and respect, as also became true for my other two daughters.

As the icing on the lifestyle cake, for the first time in her life, Karen could take as much vacation time as she wanted.

That left me.

For some years after Karen retired, I worked hard trying to arrange my schedule so that we could take two weeks off together. It was tough, but I managed. Then, in early 2000, I started feeling unusually tired. I gave myself good talking's-to: *Quit being a namby-pamby, you slacker. Most people who work hard get tired. Nothing new in that. Besides, you're making damn good money, so prove you deserve it, you ungrateful worm. Get up, go to work, and quit making excuses.*

One day in March of that year, while sitting in my office, suddenly the room was spinning. I felt horribly nauseated and had such a strong sense of vertigo that I couldn't discern the ceiling from the floor. I desperately wanted to lie down because I felt about to fall out of my chair, but I was afraid if I tried, I'd smack my head against the end of my desk. I had no sense of up or down and had almost no control over my body.

As paramedics removed me from my office to take me to a hospital, I asked my longtime secretary Kathie to phone Karen and tell her I wouldn't be able to meet her and her mom for dinner and a play that night. When she got Karen, in her usual understated manner, Kathie said, "Hi, Karen. Listen, Harvey asked me to call to tell you he won't be able to make it to dinner or the play tonight."

"I knew he didn't want to see this play, Kath, but what's his excuse?"

"Unfortunately, it's a good one. He's on his way to UCSF, by ambulance."

"Oh my God! What happened?"

"They don't know, but his blood pressure was over two-thirty, and he was looking pretty gray when they took him out of here."

I stayed overnight for observation. The working diagnosis was that I'd had a TIA, or transient ischemic attack, essentially a baby stroke, a temporary blockage of blood flow in the brain that lasts long enough to screw things up, but then blows through, leaving no obvious traces except for the temporary havoc it wrought. Sort of like a small tornado touching down for a brief time, stirring up matters and scaring the hell out of you, but not causing lasting damage.

Still, even after my discharge from the hospital, my blood counts all remained abnormally low, and I couldn't shake the persistent exhaustion.

My internist ordered test after test, but the results all came back negative. Finally, he sent me to Dr. Jahan. It wasn't until we walked into the suite where his office was that we realized we were in the hospital's hematology/oncology clinic. Not comforting.

After a series of tests, in July 2000, Dr. Jahan told us that I had a disease within the family of myeloproliferative disorders. He named them. Karen asked which we least wanted it to be. He said "chronic idiopathic myelofibrosis." (The "idiopathic" is fancy doctor-speak for "we don't know what the hell causes this.") He told us that treatment for this category of blood cancers was beyond even his expertise. He referred me to a team of specialists at UCSF who were not only hematologists/oncologists, but also who routinely handled bone marrow transplants (now commonly called stem cell transplants). It's hard to forget his parting words: "Good luck."

On July 20, 2000, we met Lloyd Damon, one of the specialists. Before we met him we did some web research about myeloproliferative disorders (now known as myeloproliferative neoplasms in recognition that these diseases are blood cancers) and learned why we least wanted me to have myelofibrosis, a rare (perhaps fifteen out of a million people) and a deadly disease in which the bone marrow becomes filled with scar tissue, leading to a host of chronic and eventually lethal complications.

Although Dr. Damon still had a few tests to perform, he started by saying, "I have no doubt about the fact that you have myelofibrosis."

This was not a good beginning.

"This is a really rare disease."

We knew that.

"You're tired all the time, right?"

"Right."

"That's because you have anemia, which will get worse."

"Why worse?"

"Bone marrow produces red blood cells and related proteins. With your disease, your marrow will produce less and less red blood cells, because it'll continue to fill with scar tissue. The lower those blood counts, the less oxygen you'll get to your organs and muscles and the more exhausted you'll become."

Karen asked, "Can other organs help to produce the cells?"

"Yes, his liver and spleen will kick in, but his spleen will act as a sink, because it won't know how to get rid of the blood it will produce."

I asked, "What's the consequence?"

"Your spleen will grow larger and larger. Eventually, it can cause you great distress and press on other organs, which can cause a whole host of problems."

"So what do we do then?"

"We'll try drugs to reduce it. If they fail and it's threatening to burst, or causing other problems, we'll have to remove it. You can live without a spleen, but there are a number of reasons why we want to avoid that, if possible, one being that you can't live without a liver and with a splenectomy, your liver then would be your primary backup."

"Back to the anemia," I asked, "what about blood transfusions?"

"They can help, but you can't afford to become dependent on them."

"Why not?"

"Because over time, you'd gain iron, which will harm your liver, your heart, and possibly other organs."

"Is there more?"

"Unfortunately, lots more. Blood clotting is typical, but paradoxically, so is a tendency to bleed. Blood clots, strokes, TIAs, and heart attacks are all manifestations of this disease. Often in the late stages, the white counts drop and you start getting infections that become increasingly difficult to control."

"We've read about stem cell transplants as a cure," Karen said.

"A stem cell transplant is a cure for many diseases. For myelofibrosis patients, it provides only a slim possibility as a cure, and the median survival from diagnosis is five years. Not great."

Not great? I was stunned, thinking, *He just told me I'll likely be dead in five years.*

Karen took over as I was recovering from the doctor's startling revelation. She asked, "Why is a stem cell transplant only a *possible* cure?"

"Because no one with your husband's disease who's undergone a stem cell transplant has lived more than five years, and a five-year survival is a general marker to establish the procedure as a probable cure. So, his disease is viewed as chronic and terminal."

I stared at him. He'd just announced my death warrant a second time.

I sat there, drained, as the shock washed over me. Karen stepped in again. "Does it make a difference if a full sibling is a donor?"

"Yes, he has one, correct?"

"Yes, his sister."

"If she's a match, the odds that he'll survive the procedure improve."

"If Harvey's sister is a match, will she have to come to San Francisco for the transplant?"

"Yes."

Slowly emerging from my fog and needing to cut the tension of the calm but deadly news we were hearing if even just for a moment, I asked, "Why, don't you have tubes that long?"

Unfazed by my feeble attempt at gallows humor, the doctor explained the high mortality just surviving these transplants (reduced somewhat by matching sibling donors) and the agony often suffered by patients because of deadly infections from what's called graft-versus-host disease.

We felt like a Mack truck had clobbered us. As we sat there, dazed and attempting to be stoic, the doctor said, "Look, you have a life-threatening disease. It's insidious, in part, because it follows no specific pattern. It affects different people in different ways, so we never know exactly how it will attack you, but at least it tends to move slowly, so you'll never fall off a cliff. Still, what's clear is that it'll limit your life expectancy."

That was just to cheer us up from all the bad stuff we'd heard. Because of all of his upbeat information that day, Karen and I dubbed him Dr. Demon.

We went to Stanford for a second and third opinion. The two doctors we saw confirmed the diagnosis, but modified the prognosis from five years to between three to five years. Was there no good news? Yes! One of the doctors told me, "Except for the fact that you're dying, you're actually fairly healthy." That certainly made me feel better. At least I'd be a comparatively salubrious corpse.

In that early phase of consultations, one of the doctors confirmed what we already knew, that though my liver was fine, it could be assaulted by complications from the disease, so I should stop drinking. As we left, Karen said, "Do you understand the doctor just said you may be dead in three years, but you should stop drinking?"

"Yep. I heard him."

"Screw it. Let's go home, have dinner, and have a drink."

We did—and still do.

After going through bouts of grief and depression, including the "why-me" and the "woe-is-me" syndromes and visualizing my own funeral (not that I'm a drama queen or anything), I came to terms that whining aside, my disease wouldn't just magically disappear. I tried to continue practicing on a fairly regular basis. But because of the relentless exhaustion and other symptoms that are a part of my illness, I could no longer work the kind of hours I had for the last thirty years.

Only trial lawyers know how physical trial work is and eventually, I came to terms that I could no longer try cases. I withdrew from the partnership and came to an arrangement with my firm to work almost exclusively from home when and for how long I was able to do so. Although my earnings were a fraction of what they'd been, I was grateful to continue any kind of practice.

* * * * * * * * * * * * * * * * * *

Some believe that with serious diseases come blessings. Count me as one of the believers.

All of us, of course, live under a death threat. Still, it makes a difference when doctors tell you they can see the end of your life and that it won't be pretty. Ultimately, however, I realized that I had a choice. I could choose Door Number One and hide in a cave with a neon sign at the entrance flashing "Pity Me" and retreat deeper and deeper into the darkness, or I could choose Door Number Two and allow my senses, never so focused as by the verdict of a terminal disease, to shout that I now had a reason like never before to be thankful for every day that I could see, smell, hear, taste, and touch. I chose Door Number Two. You never *really* smell a rose until you've been told you'll likely die within the foreseeable future. So I began to marvel at the gift of life, which up till then, I admit, I'd taken for granted.

At the same time, I began to reorganize my priorities, much as I had while saying Kaddish for my dad. I started placing all the hitherto "urgent" matters at the bottom of the pile, replaced by matters like "do something kind for your wife at least once daily." I fully recognize that I'm unusually lucky that my wife and I are best friends, and it's extraordinary how easily we slipped into our postretirement, post-diagnosis life, just as we'd adjusted so naturally to living together after we were married.

The one we're living now we spend virtually all of our time together. We have an enormous capacity for enjoying each other's company. Sometimes we do so by talking, sometimes just by quietly being in each other's presence, perhaps one reading a book and the other being on the computer. The warning of one of the doctor's notwithstanding, we love having a drink together. As the sun sets, we toast each other by clinking glasses and saying, "Sláinte." Especially now, I always add, "To your good health."

Sometimes, we enjoy making a meal together, going to ride our horses, or just watching a movie. And sometimes after a visit to the doctor with news that my numbers are worse again, or years later, learning that the time had come to remove my spleen even with all the attendant risks, the weight of it all bears down on us. We sit together awhile, hold each other, and Karen says, "What will I do when you're gone? I want to die when you do."

I hold her tighter and say, "You know you'll go on, and you'll be stronger for it. You know I'll love you and be with you even when I'm no longer here." It doesn't comfort her, and we just hold each other and cry.

One night I was outside at the barbecue grill at our house in Sonoma County about an hour north of San Francisco. It was a starry, starry night. I knew that Vincent would have loved to paint that sky. I gazed at the heavens, knowing I was viewing millions of light-years away. Then I looked into the kitchen and saw Karen setting the table. I took a sip of some single malt scotch, a customary companion when I grill. I raised my glass to the heavens, looked up, and with tears welling in my eyes, softly said, "God, I know the beauty and vastness of what you've created, and I am in awe of it. But all that I want is thirty feet from me. I'm not ready to leave Karen yet. She doesn't want me to leave yet. Let us grow old together."

God didn't answer. I took another sip of my dram and let the warmth course through me. When I went inside, not knowing God's answer, I kissed my wife.

Finally, what at the time was crushing turned out a blessing. My sister wasn't a match, so there was no rush for the transplant.

For her part, Carol was devastated. She cried saying, "I was positive I'd be a match, and I'd be able to save you."

I said, "Look, darling, there's good news here."

"What is possibly good news about this?"

"Well, for one thing, I don't have to be nice to you anymore."

She didn't laugh, but Karen and I are convinced that had Carol been a match, I'd have had the transplant years ago and become very sick from it. In fact, we believe I'd probably be dead now from the graft-versus-host disease complications.

A few years ago, I met someone at the clinic I knew. He'd had a stem cell transplant for a different disease. He said, "Don't do it unless you have absolutely no choice, Harvey. You're never the same. Where others catch a cold, you go down for a month and fight for your life. Your immune system is shot. Don't do it."

Dr. Damon introduced us to his only other myelofibrosis patient. He had the transplant and from a matching sibling. He died, free of the disease, but his system overcome by infections.

I've been fortunate. So far, I've avoided the transplant. Eventually, I did have to have my spleen removed and I've endured many unpleasant symptoms, but essentially by forcing me to stop work, Karen and I are free to spend as much time away from home as we can afford, without the crush of business that until then had minimized the length of our vacations.

The year I was diagnosed, we'd already booked the Adare Cottages for a few weeks starting in late August. We asked Dr. Damon if he thought it okay for us to keep our travel plans. "It will be, for the time being, the best medicine available." So we kept our date with the Emerald Isle.

And from then on, we've spent five to six weeks in Ireland almost every summer, long enough in a small village to get to know the butcher, the baker, and the candlestick maker. We came to view our trips, not just vacationing in Eire, but also returning to live there for a month or more and in doing so, gaining an appreciation of the country and its people far deeper than otherwise would have been possible.

Who would have thought that being diagnosed with a terminal disease could be a blessing? It might sound eerie, but my disease has brought a peace and tranquility that Karen and I would not have otherwise known. Don't get me wrong; it's not that I recommend terminal illness as a prescription for my family and friends, but I do say that it can give you a renewed appreciation about life.

Oh, yes. I'm now in the twelfth year since my diagnosis, and without apology, still throwing off the medical community's mortality statistics for my disease.

Chapter 14

∼⌒∼

Thoor Ballylee and a Few Miracles at Knock

In 2001, Karen prevailed on me to go to Knock in County Mayo, one of Europe's major Catholic Marian shrines. Knock's notability dates back to 1879 when fifteen locals, ranging in age from five to seventy-five, all reported an apparition of the Virgin Mary, St. Joseph, St. John the Evangelist, and a lamb standing next to a cross, a traditional image of Jesus as the Lamb of God, offering himself as a sacrificial offering for the salvation of humanity, a central tenet of Christianity.

Understandably much of Christian imagery derives from Judaism. During ancient times, Jewish law required the sacrificial offering to God of a first born, unblemished male lamb during Passover. (To this day, every Passover Seder has a ceremonial plate including on it a burned lamb shank reminiscent of this ancient custom.) Jesus and his disciples grew up with that tradition. The crucifixion occurred during the Passover season. It's logical that the deification of Jesus uses that image, but radicalizes it by portraying Jesus as the sacrificial Paschal Lamb.

We also know that the origins of Mass emanate from the recounting of what Jesus said at the Last Supper. If the Last Supper was a Passover Seder the bread that would have been present would have been matzo, unleavened bread eaten during Passover. Jews say a prayer over bread, thanking God for bringing it forth from the earth, then offering a piece to all present. However, as Jesus offered portions of the bread that night to his disciples, he transformed the tradition into a part of the Eucharist by saying, "This is my body." If that bread was matzo, this may explain why the host for communion is unleavened.

In any event, two ecclesiastical commissions sanctioned the trustworthiness of the apparitions and in 1976 Knock became a recognized shrine. It joined the ranks of Lourdes and Fatima in 1979 when Pope John Paul II, a strong supporter of devotion to the Virgin Mary, came to Ireland for the primary purpose of visiting the shrine and commemorating the centenary of the apparitions. While there, he presented a Golden Rose, a rarely used token of papal honor and recognition.

Getting the church dedicated as a shrine is largely credited to Monsignor James Horan, who transferred to the parish in 1963 and became its priest in 1969. The monsignor is also largely credited with getting the pope to come to Knock, and having the site elevated to the status of a basilica, a large and important church given special ceremonial rites by a pope. (There are only about fifteen hundred in the world.) Only some basilicas, including Knock, are notable shrines with pilgrimages sanctioned by the Holy See. As the number of pilgrims increased exponentially, the monsignor also oversaw construction of a new church, Our Lady of Knock, Queen of Ireland, which can seat ten thousand people. And he pushed through construction of the Ireland-West Airport in Knock, which opened on a foggy boggy hillside in 1985 over great local objection. But the good monsignor knew what he was doing. The papal visit, elevating the site to international status, the building of Our Lady of Ireland, and the construction of the Ireland-West Airport, all combined to put Knock on the radar to the point that it receives a million and a half visitors/pilgrims annually, and the airport is now acknowledged as used not just for those visiting the shrine, but as a general boon to the economy of the region.

Karen was anxious to visit Knock so she could light a candle for me in her never-ending quest to burn down the country. I didn't argue, since with my diagnosis a year earlier, we were living under the belief that I had two to four years to live.

As we were heading to Knock, with no particular arrival time in mind, we stopped at Thoor Ballylee, one of our favorite spots in Ireland. A short distance outside Gort in County Galway, it's a sixteenth century tower that W. B. Yeats, perhaps Ireland's greatest twentieth century poet, bought and lived in during the 1920s with his wife George (Georgie) and their family. He was prolific there, and a number of his poems mention the tower.

Inscribed in stone on its exterior is:

> I the poet, William Yeats,
> With common sedge and broken slates
> And smithy work from the Gort forge,
> Restored this tower for my wife George;
> And on my heirs I lay a curse
> If they should alter for the worse
> From fashion or an empty mind,
> What Rafferty built and Scott designed.

Apparently, his curse was taken seriously. Thoor Ballylee is still much as it was when Yeats lived there with his family, next to two mellow streams with the sound of running water casting a peaceful spell. Once we toured the tower, ducking our heads as we wended our way up the winding stairs, struck by the raw beauty of it, but wondering how in God's name anyone actually lived there. When we got to the top, we had a commanding view of the countryside, including Coole Park with its own literary history, often frequented in the early twentieth century by Yeats, Sean O'Casey, George Bernard Shaw, and other towering writers.

On this day, we ate a picnic lunch at one of the tables across from the tower, and then sat quietly reflecting on our innermost thoughts and enjoying the tranquil surroundings as we imagined Yeats had. Then, it was on to Knock at a leisurely pace.

Though the origins of Knock are holy, a carnival-like atmosphere greets you as you enter the perimeter of the shrine. To me, it stirred this ironic reminder of the story in the New Testament of Jesus pulling down the stalls of the moneylenders when he goes to the temple as a youngster, angry at the defiling of its holy purpose. At Knock, as you approach the church and its grounds, you walk through extensive stalls of hawkers of every stripe selling food, Bibles, cheap statues of the Virgin, other faux holy relics, postcards of the church, and pretty much anything that anyone with poor taste could possibly want.

We pressed on. Karen said, "I just want to go to the chapel, light a candle, say a prayer, and then we can decide what we want to do." I'm convinced she's a pyromaniac.

So we pushed through the hawkers and arrived at the church grounds. At almost exactly that moment, we heard an announcement on the public address system: Mass for the Blessing of the Sick would begin in ten minutes. We looked at each other. In answer to my questioning stare, Karen said, "I swear I had no idea."

This was weird. Karen had talked me into coming to this holy site; we hadn't set a particular day or planned on arriving at any predetermined time. We'd dillydallied at Thoor Ballylee, leisurely made our way to Knock, and then arrived within minutes of Mass for the sick, a Mass, we later learned, that's said only once a month.

"Okay," I said. "I admit this is surreal, so let's go to the Mass and count it as one small miracle."

As we turned to enter the basilica, I noticed it was one of the ugliest buildings I'd ever seen. It looked like a bunch of irregular shaped boxes of varying heights, glued together, and mounted on stilts. The interior is no better. Much of it, including the altar, is dominated by turquoise beams. Large sections of the walls are covered in light pink square tiles; other portions are whitewashed, and still others have broad areas of what look like thin redwood slats. But hey, we weren't there to be taking notes for architectural digests or designer magazines and by the time we left, we were mesmerized by the experience.

The church, constructed in the round, had perhaps seven or eight triangular shaped seating areas, the pinnacle of each emanating from the circular altar. We seated ourselves in one of the regular pews. Many in wheelchairs were rolled to the front with no pews. For the Mass, all the stops were pulled out. Six priests participated, all but the head priest swinging lit incense holders in this direction and that, sending the scent throughout the church. As my mother would have said, they were doing the whole *megillah*.

The priest leading Mass delivered a touching homily about how being sick can bring those afflicted to better understand the beauty of life and the gift of each moment of each day. What he said struck home: we knew exactly what he was saying. And just as it seemed that he was talking to Karen and me, no doubt, all the other sick people felt he was talking to them. Then he announced that the priests assisting him were going into the congregation to anoint the sick with holy oil by placing the sign of the cross on their forehead. Karen looked at me. She said nothing, but I tilted my head, planted a mild smirk on my face and whispered, "Don't press your luck." She smiled.

As the priests started into the congregation to do the anointing, the boss priest said something that typified so much of what I love about Ireland, a combination of seriousness and wit. "Now, this is for those truly sick," he said. He paused, and with perfect comedic timing and a twinkle in his eye, he finished, "Just being old doesn't qualify."

In the States, you just know there would have been a five-minute explanation of the qualifying criteria of being "sick" enough to receive anointing oil. In Ireland, it was, "Just being old doesn't qualify." *How perfectly Talmudic,* I thought.

As the priest covering our area neared our pew and looked down the row, I looked straight ahead and let him pass. Karen said nothing.

The Mass ended. We left the church, both of us quiet, overawed at the simplicity, yet the complexity of the confluence of circumstances that had brought us to be at this holy place at the precise day and time when a Mass was being said for the sick. It was downright mystical.

We walked to the car in silence, neither of us willing to break the mood. Both of us remained quiet as I pulled out of the car park, and just as I did, the most perfect rainbow we'd ever seen crossed the road. I looked at Karen, only to find her looking at me, shrugging her shoulders, both of us asking, without saying the words, whether this second miracle also had been directed by some Hollywood filmmaker or by the Great Director in the Sky. I thought, *Look, I'm not converting, so why are you doing this to me?* Just as I'd asked God a question much earlier on a starry, starry night at our house in Sonoma County, so too, on this evening, I heard no answer. In peace, we drove to our next destination.

Chapter 15

The O'Conor Don and a Muddy Carracastle Grave

With the vision of the rainbow still deeply embedded in us, we left for Clonalis House in Castlerea, County Roscommon. From there, we intended to try to find Karen's relatives' farmhouse again, where she had stood decades earlier. By the time we arrived at Clonalis, we had regained our composure enough to enjoy the beautiful grounds and the long entryway to the house, run by Marguerite, the wife of Pyers O'Conor Nash.

Pyers claimed to be a descendant of the O'Conor Don, the high king of one of the provinces of ancient Ireland. He purported to trace his heritage back fifteen hundred years, which, if true, would have made his unbroken royal heritage the oldest in Europe. The site of the house and its surroundings had been in the family for eight hundred years. The house, though old, wasn't that old, but it was old enough to have a great deal of its own history, and really creaky stairs.

Pyers' uncle on his mother's side had held the title of the O'Conor Don before Pyers, but he'd been a bishop and had no children to whom to vest the land and title. Thus, had Pyers not been willing to assume the title, and had his wife not been willing to assume the burden of maintaining the house and grounds, the property likely would have reverted to the state, and the title of the "O'Conor Don" would have ended.

Pyers' mother asked her son to take over the title and the operation of the house to avoid ending the line. Marguerite and Pyers gave up whatever other life they'd been living to fulfill this request. But it's perhaps a temporary fix: they have two daughters. Since the title must be passed to a male, the only way the line can continue after Pyers, is if some other male relative assumes the task of living in and operating Clonalis House.

Clonalis is operated as a quasi-public facility, "quasi," because to qualify for the accompanying tax incentives, since the house and lands are part of a national trust, the property must be open to the public for a certain number of days annually. That's why we were able to stay there. For the period that it's open to the public, it's operated like any other inn.

The house is filled with paintings of descendants who go back hundreds of years, and who appear to stare at you as you go up and down the long creaky staircase and into the library and dining room. In the library is a book purporting to trace back the family roots for more than fifteen hundred years. The claim that the O'Conor Don family is the longest uninterrupted royal line in all of Europe is met by many an Irishman with a wink and a smile. Me? I love a good old royal dynasty, so I'm ready to give the O'Conor Don the benefit of the doubt.

Marguerite told us on arrival that drinks would be served at seven in the library with dinner to follow. We didn't realize that we were the only guests until we went to the library where Pyers joined us. We learned he was an investment banker and running Clonalis House didn't generate enough income to earn a living. He was also a historian, not surprisingly specializing in the history of the O'Conor Dons and events surrounding their rule; he traveled to various places to lecture on the topic, most recently to Chicago. At dinner, the O'Conor Don's small staff (one in the kitchen and another in the dining room) served us.

After breakfast the next morning, with some of the eighteenth century family members peering at us again from the surrounding walls, Karen and I got ready to try to find the two homesteads of her grandparents that she'd found more than thirty years earlier. Marguerite gave us a prepared lunch and we were off.

Our first stop was Ballaghaderreen (pronounced Balladureen), the market town for the surrounding villages. From there we got directions to her grandparents' villages of Cloontia and Derrinacartha. We arrived at the general area, but finding specific spots in that section of the country is no easy trick. Many parts there are wild and wooly. Off the main road, you take a single narrow lane with potholes so big they're guaranteed to break any axle that hits them square-on at a speed more than fifteen miles an hour, so you're constantly weaving back and forth. I remember thinking; *I bet it'd be tough for me to get AAA out here to give us a tow.* Though the surrounding countryside is rocky and the earth is hard and gray, and doesn't look like it will grow anything except rocks, tall grass crowds the edges of the road, so it's hard to see anything even a short distance away without stopping the car, getting out, and peering over the grass.

One of Karen's cousins, Larraine, had located what she thought was the Duffy homestead about five years earlier, and she'd described getting to the site as best she could. For a landmark, Larraine gave us a photograph of a church near their grandfather's homestead. We found the church, but it was locked. With no one to talk to there, Karen tried to get her bearings. We drove up and down the single lane road a number of times in search of her cousin's farmhouse, and Karen spotted what she thought might have been the site, but the building had been abandoned long ago and either torn down or fully gone to seed. Likewise, we couldn't find the farmhouse where her grandmother had lived and where Karen had received a chilly reception from the woman from Tipperary who'd married into the family. We did notice that in some of the driveways were BMWs and a few Mercedes', not carts and donkeys. All things change. After spending an hour and a half or so, we gave up the hunt and took off on a new quest, searching for the area's cemetery.

We found the graveyard at the St. James Church in Carracastle. The church was open, but no one was there. An engraving on a stained glass window told the tale: the church had been funded, in part, by donations from those forced to leave Ireland due to the hard times, but who still wanted to help support the church where they'd once worshiped—poignant stuff.

I was ready for our picnic in a spot on the church grounds, but Karen first wanted to go into the graveyard. Just as we entered, as though on cue from Alfred Hitchcock, the heavens opened up and we were in a lashin' rain. We were wearing our horseback riding coats, which are rainproof—sort of—and have hoods. We opened the gate. It creaked. We started slogging through the mud and there they were. The Towey's (Karen's grandmother's maiden name) and the Duffy's—rows of them. They weren't the only ones who'd taken up permanent residence, but they certainly occupied a good portion of the real estate.

Graveyards, especially in small towns, tell a firsthand history. You can see when some disease tore through the area, taking babies and elders in its wake, all within a short span of time. You can identify the big shots, buried closest to the church with the fancy headstones. You can virtually get a whole family's history, from when the first of a named family member was buried three hundred years ago to the one buried six months ago, and based on what's inscribed on the gravestones, a bit of information, "Loving Wife of ..." and so on. You can determine when a family left either the area or the country, because all of a sudden, say a hundred years earlier, no more members with that family name are buried there.

The skies were getting darker. The rain was getting heavier. The mud was getting deeper. The ground was getting more slippery. Hitchcock was definitely directing this scene. I could almost hear him saying, "I want it to look really macabre. Two people with hooded jackets walk slowly in the mud through the graves, one of them occasionally placing a hand on a headstone to keep from slipping. Make it darker. Add more rain. Whip up the wind. Slap their jackets around so they have to hold their hoods. Good. More rain, more wind. There now; that's good."

Just as I hollered over the rain and wind that I thought it might be a good time to return to the car, Karen found Bernard. Then she found his son, Ned, one of the children who'd been in Bernard's cottage when Karen had been there. He'd died before his father. So, Bernard had come home from Liverpool. Was his body sent to Ireland from England? Did he know he was sick and return to die? Did he come home because his son had died?

We'll never know, but at the time I was so wet and frozen I thought that within the next fifteen minutes they'd be digging a grave for me.

"I'm going to the car!" I yelled, trying to be heard over the winds. Karen was transfixed, staring at the headstones. This was her family. This was where someday she might have been buried, had her grandparents not had the guts to leave their homeland.

Dripping wet and shivering, I turned on the engine to get some heat. Another car pulled up. Five minutes later, the sun came out. This was Ireland after all, where you get spring, summer, fall, and winter all in the same day. After the sun had remained out for another five minutes, a foursome got out of the other car carrying baskets of food. They, too, were determined to enjoy a picnic, but in the outdoors, not in a cramped car. I was amazed at the number of baskets that just kept coming; it took them a good ten minutes to get all the food onto the picnic table.

At that moment, however, Hitchcock intervened again. "Okay, overcast skies. Darker. Good. Cue the rain. Now! We still have one actress tromping around in the muddy graveyard. Sun won't do for the final shot as she exits."

This time, however, it was what the Irish call a soft rain, like what you get from a hose nozzle set on fine, and the folks started their picnic unfazed. Then Hitchcock got serious, turning to a hard drenching, the hose nozzle set to stream. Winds kicked up from nowhere. The rain seemed to be coming up from the ground and straight into your face, rather than down from the sky and onto your head. Next, it came down in sheets, as though water collected on a large roof, was then dumped over the side. But the other party refused to be beaten by the elements. Out came umbrellas, raincoats, rain hats. One held an umbrella while another one ate. By God, they'd have their picnic and enjoy themselves, even if it meant spending two weeks in a hospital with pneumonia and ending up across the road where Karen was still tromping around in the graveyard.

I turned and looked at the cemetery. Karen was finished visiting her relatives. Holding her hood with one hand and reaching for the gate with the other, she seemed frozen by the wind. She leaned into it, pushed forward, stretched her arm, reached the gate, and opened it. It creaked. Hitchcock smiled. "Perfect touch," he said.

As Karen got into the car, she said, "Poor Bernard. Somehow, I think he didn't have a happy life, and I know he didn't have an easy one." Then we had our picnic—in the car.

Chapter 16

⌒

The Stolen Painting Caper

After Karen and I returned from our trek through the muddy graveyard at Carracastle, we did what we'd often do: stand outside Castleroberts and enjoy the view of the church all lit up. One evening afterward, we strolled through the village and ate at one of the restaurants, and then went to the Dunraven for a nightcap. We hadn't yet immersed ourselves in the real life of Adare and drinking at the Dunraven, we hung out with tourists and wealthy locals, many of whom had their wedding receptions there. Almost all of them started with a ceremony at the church, about two hundred yards down Main Street, followed by a limousine driving the blissful couple the half block to the hotel entrance. It was almost a parody of the beginning of a wedding party.

So, while being at the Dunraven's pub wasn't exactly a slice out of the daily life of a local, it was still comfortable. We knew some staff there. The Guinness and the white wine were every bit as good as in any other pub. And it had a painting to die for.

We could never enter the Dunraven's pub without pausing for a good long look at a watercolor on the wall, a stunningly perfect portrayal of a hunt. It depicted one hunter jumping a ditch while holding up an elbow to avoid being scraped by the branch of a tree. You can feel the stress in his body as he legs on his horse. Steam is snorting from the horse's nostrils and coming off his body from the mix of the physical exertion and the chill of the winter air. The horse is midstride, kicking up dirt that hangs in midair. You feel that if you wait a moment you'll hear the clump of it falling back to the earth, almost smelling its wetness. He's riding hard and staring straight ahead, so you know he's heading toward another jump just out of view.

Two riders have pulled up. You see one in a side view: she's at a halt; her horse's ears are straight up, a sign he's attentive; she and her horse are staring straight ahead at the horse and rider jumping the ditch. You see another rider from the rear as he's pulled up perpendicular to the first one, but with his head turned to the left, also viewing the action in jumping the ditch. Both horses are also snorting and throwing off steam. From the splotches of mud on their jackets and on their horses, you know that they've traversed some open fields behind a galloping herd that kicked mud up at them. If you listen quietly, you can almost hear the horses breathing heavily. You swear you can feel the heat coming off the riders and their horses from the physical exertion.

Other riders are in the field coming from the opposite side. The closest has his head turned slightly to the right as he, too, watches the jump over the ditch. A bit behind him, another, already in the open field, also is glancing at the jumping, but he seems more intent on catching up. Yet another one, farther back from the others, is coming through an opening in some bushes. He's too far away to see what's going on in the foreground; he's just concentrating on getting through the undergrowth, into the field, and pulling up to the small group.

Sometimes we'd get a table next to it, where we could be drawn into the painting. It encapsulated in such real and beautiful terms so much of the feeling of a hunt: the formal dress of the riders mixed with the immense physical exertion of both the horses and humans, the bite of the winter chill and the riders' obliviousness to it; the attention from the riders close enough to the action to watch the one in the midst of a jump; and the jumper straining at what he's doing, while intently looking ahead to decide how best to take the jump ahead of him. Those watching are willing on the jumper, but also are studying for clues about how they should take that ditch and the follow-up jump when, in moments, it'll be their turn to tackle them.

While lost in the painting one night, Louis Murphy walked in, as always in his tuxedo, and said, "It is gorgeous, isn't it?"

"Gorgeous? It's captivating," I said. "Who painted it?"

"Peter Curling, a well-known Irish artist who himself often rides in hunts. In fact, I think the rider you see pulling up to the woman who's staring at the jumper is a self-portrait. His work is so well respected in Ireland that he was commissioned by the Irish postal service to do some paintings that have been used on stamps. He also does cartoons, but his horse paintings are what set him apart."

Karen asked, "Does he work in mediums other than watercolor?"

"He also does lithographs. We have some in one of the sitting rooms. Would you like to see them?"

I said, "Lead on, Louis, we'd love to."

We followed him to the room. The lithos were nice, also hunt scenes, but nowhere near as enthralling as the painting.

As we were walking back to the pub, Louis said, "You know, we don't own that painting. We just have it on loan from Peter."

I stopped walking. "You mean we could possibly buy it?"

"Possibly," said Louis, "but if you did, I might have to set some hounds on you." Undaunted by the threat of a pack of hounds tearing me apart, before we left, we obtained Peter Curling's telephone number.

I called the following morning. Peter Curling lived in Tipperary, about a two-hour car drive from Adare. He was able to see us that day. He confirmed that the painting at the Dunraven was indeed for sale; he said he'd show us other paintings in his studio, which was a part of his house. When I asked for his address, he laughed. "We don't have addresses in the countryside. Come to Tipperary and find Goold's Cross, and then ask anyone where my house is."

"Goold's Cross, did you say?"

"Yes, Goold's Cross."

"We'll see you this afternoon." As I hung up the phone, I stared at Karen like a blithering eejit. "Peter Curling lives in Goold's Cross."

"That does it," said Karen. "We're buying the painting."

Before we got to his house, we stopped a woman walking her baby. She gave us the kind of directions we'd come to love. "Go over the bridge and three, maybe four fields past it; go up a road with a sort of smallish tree nearby. Take that road till you see a drive with a bunch of cows in front."

After getting lost a second time, I stopped a farmer on his tractor who gave me enough information so that we actually found the place, which, of course, I'd passed. Never trust cows. Apparently, they'd moved into a rear pasture. Bastards.

Peter Curling's house turned out to be on a beautiful sprawling estate surrounded by stone walls. We parked on a crushed limestone driveway and got out of the car. As there was no door in the front, we walked to the rear of the house. Rounding a corner of the rear garden, we froze. Perhaps forty feet in front of us were a horse and rider, the horse halfway over a stone wall, his front legs tightly tucked underneath him, and his hind legs fully stretched from the exertion of pushing off against the ground. They were heading into a field. The rider was standing in his stirrups, leaning forward, well out of his saddle, his hands up onto the horse's neck. Their position was perfect. After standing there a few seconds, we realized neither the horse nor rider had moved, and for good reason. They were a life-size statue made out of black wire. This was a damn good introduction to talk about the painting of the hunt scene.

After we met Peter, he told us that the statue of the horse and rider was the work of another local artist and we could possibly buy one, but it proved much too expensive, although we dearly would have loved one. He showed us his studio, which had a number of beautiful paintings, some depicting polo scenes, one with the Sultan of Brunei, whom he knew, caught in midswing. But none of them captivated us like the one hanging on the Dunraven's wall.

When we got around to discussing that painting, Karen and I realized how much we wanted it. We didn't haggle. He told us the price. We said, "Okay." We checked a newspaper to see that day's exchange rate, and wrote him a check.

He said, "I'll arrange to have the painting properly packed and shipped to you."

Some months later, it arrived in perfect shape. It now sits proudly in a place of honor over the fireplace at our house in Sonoma County. Every rider who comes into the house is drawn to it, and those who aren't riders, I bore silly, explaining why and how it so perfectly depicts a hunt.

Before we left Peter Curling's house that day, he gave us a gift of some of his commissioned stamps, which we also treasure.

Meanwhile, while we were in County Tipperary, we visited the Rock of Cashel, the seat of Irish kings for hundreds of years before the Norman Invasion. Although most of the original structures were destroyed long ago, what remains, dates back to the twelfth and thirteenth centuries.

As we were driving toward the rock, but still many miles away, we saw what appeared to be a castle floating in the sky. (What's with this sense of floating castles and me? First, I'd seen one when we'd ridden on the beaches of Sligo and now another in Tipperary.) I know this is almost sacrilegious, but once again, what we saw looked like it was created by the hand of Walt Disney. In fact, it's one of the most remarkable vestiges of Celtic architecture in all of Europe.

A round tower standing some ninety feet high on top of the Rock of Cashel appears as though it's vaulting into the heavens. On the rock, among other things, is Cormac's Chapel started in 1127 and consecrated in 1134. Fast work for those days.

Once we arrived, we were put off by a bunch of gift shops at the base of the rock and hundreds of tourists milling the grounds. I know. We're snobs. We drove up as far as we could, but decided this wasn't for us. We hadn't been interested in buying faux items at Knock, and we weren't interested in buying a three-inch likeness of the Rock of Cashel. Before we descended from the parking area at the top, however, we caught a glimpse of a graveyard with many Celtic-styled high crosses. Karen had already seen many Towey's and Duffy's in the muddy graveyard at Carracastle and her father's musings that he was descended from the Irish kings notwithstanding, she didn't expect to see any Duffy's buried at the rock, so we pushed on without looking.

It had been a good day. We'd bought a painting that we had lusted over for some time and we'd seen this floating ethereal visage.

Back at the village, after dinner we stopped again at the Dunraven, this time to toast "our" painting still hanging on the wall of the pub. As we were doing so, Louis Murphy walked in, saw us, stopped in his tracks, turned to us, and said, "I just got a call to advise me that you've been on a caper, and you've stolen that painting right off my wall."

We smiled, lifted our glasses, and I said, "We promise to give it a good home, Louis. Sláinte."

"In that case," said Louis, "I guess I'll call off the hounds."

Chapter 17

Muckross House and Ballymaloe

All countries have their tourist attractions, some worthwhile, others, like the area at the base of the Rock of Cashel, a bit schlocky. Muckross House in Killarney is among the better attractions. It's in what is now Killarney National Park. One-horse buggy rides galore around the park make people feel as though they're going back in time. For me, I wouldn't sully myself by getting into one of those things. For God's sake, those are for tourists.

Muckross House is in County Kerry on the Muckross Peninsula between two of the Lakes of Killarney. From the dining room, the view of the lakes is stunning. The Tudor-style house was built between 1839 and 1843 for Colonel Henry Herbert, completed just two years before the Great Irish Famine. It has sixty-five rooms, but a large number are closed to the public, probably because they haven't been maintained. The dining room, though spacious, isn't overwhelming. The table is set for twenty-six or so people, obviously big, but hardly of the state-dinner variety. You don't feel lost in the drawing room; you can imagine four or five couples sitting beside the fireplace, having after-dinner drinks.

The Herbert's made extensive improvements to the house and grounds in the 1850s in anticipation of a visit by Queen Victoria. Apparently, they spent a bundle in expectation of some royal grant thereafter, a not uncommon act by the queen after spending time at some locale where she knew an extra effort had been made for her comfort and pleasure or after she'd enjoyed something particularly pleasing. So, for example, after she and Prince Albert savored a dram of scotch, she granted a royal license to the distiller in Scotland; this is why, to this day, Royal Lochnagar bears that name. Had the Herbert's received what they were hoping for, not only would it have paid for the renovations, but also likely would have given them a title and a grant of lands that would have more than set them up for life. Alas, such was not to be their luck.

Although the queen did stay at Muckross in 1861 (you can go into the room where she slept), in December of that year, her beloved Prince Albert died. The queen spent most of the rest of her life in mourning. Of the many items that got lost in the wake of her inconsolable grief, one was making some royal reward to the Herbert's for their extensive improvements for her brief visit.

The Herbert's never recovered from the financial setback caused primarily by the cost of the renovations. Refused further loans, the house and lands were forfeited to the lender. In 1910, the house and lands were leased to William Bowers Bourn, the owner of the Empire Gold Mine and Spring Water Company in northern California. Shortly afterward, Mr. Bourn's only daughter Maud married Mr. Arthur Rose Vincent of County Clare. Her daddy purchased Muckross House and its lands as a wedding gift for them. (I'm a piker. Karen and I gave my kids silver and china for their weddings.) Maud and Arthur lived at Muckross until Maud's death in 1929.

During the years of the Bourn/Vincent ownership, major improvements were made to the property, including the development of rock, sunken, and stream gardens, in all costing more than one hundred and ten thousand pounds sterling, an astronomical sum in its day.

The Bourns owned stately mansions in San Francisco, Hillsborough, and their masterpiece in San Mateo, called Filoli. (The name derives from the first two letters of Bourn's motto: Fight, Love, Live.) They decorated their San Mateo ballroom with ceiling murals depicting scenes from around Muckross, and parts of the gardens at Filoli were from clippings of a variety of plants from the Irish estate. In 1975, Filoli was deeded to the National Trust for Historic Preservation. It is now open to the public as a historic landmark.

In 1932, three years after Maud's death, her husband stated his and his in-laws' intention to bestow the property to the Irish nation. The Irish Parliament passed an act requiring Muckross to be made into a park (now Killarney National Park), maintained, and managed for the recreation of the public. The park and gardens opened to the public as soon as Ireland became its owner in trust. The house wasn't opened until 1964.

On the tour that Karen and I took, we were told, apocryphal or not, that Mr. Vincent's son still has dinner in the dining room every Christmas Eve. I've not checked out that story, but it sounds so lovely that I hope it's true. Another story is that one of the conditions was that the peace and tranquility of the eleven-thousand-acre estate not be disturbed by the sound of cars. Although you can drive in Killarney Park, if you're visiting the house, you must park in a distant lot, and as noted, a major method of travel is by one-horse buggies or jaunty cars.

What was an unfortunate loss for the Herbert's proved an incalculable gain for all who visit Muckross today.

Muckross you can only tour. At Ballymaloe House, you can dine at its restaurant and stay at its hotel.

Before one of our trips, through mutual acquaintances, Bill Niman (of Niman Ranch, a respected brand name in the Bay Area of beef, pork, and lamb) recommended Ballymaloe House for dining and coming from him, we took it seriously and made our plans.

Ballymaloe is about twenty miles east of Cork City and only a few miles from a small fishing village, Ballycotton, where you can take walks that provide stunning views of Ballycotton Bay.

Ballymaloe is a beautiful large family farmhouse on its own four-hundred-acre farm. The buildings date back to a fifteenth-century castle. They include a hotel, restaurant, and a related craft and kitchenware shop. In the back of the hotel, you can cross a bridge over a creek to an idyllic island with wild ducks and other animals.

The originators, Ivan and Myrtle Allen moved into Ballymaloe in 1948 where Ivan ran the farm. In 1964, Myrtle opened a restaurant on the premises. Later, they added the hotel. And as their children and grandchildren grew, many took part in the business. Myrtle had her own cooking show on the BBC. Eventually, her daughter-in-law, Darina Allen, took over the cooking and opened the Ballymaloe Cookery School, a short drive from Ballymaloe House. There, she and her staff, along with tutors and guest chefs, give cooking classes, including a twelve-week certificate course that's highly regarded within the world of cooking.

Rory Allen, one of Ivan and Myrtle's children, now owns and runs the farm, but after its work modernized, he was able to spend more time pursuing his real passion—music. He has two CDs out, one appropriately titled, *Follow Your Passion*. Two or three nights a week, he comes to the large sitting room in Ballymaloe House with guitar in hand, and after dinner, starts singing. Guests sit on sofas and chairs around a fireplace and get drinks from an open bar in an adjacent room. Of the three times we've dined and stayed at the hotel, Rory came with at least one other musician.

He usually knows people in the audience and cajoles them into coming up to sing a song or two. After folks are relaxed, assisted by a third after-dinner drink and the ongoing merriment, an uninvited singer from the audience may also step up and try their hand at starting their new career.

This wasn't the first time we'd experienced singing in Ireland, but it was the first time we'd done it in a family setting. Luckily, I've not been snared into singing "House of the Rising Sun," "Sixteen Tons," or anything else. I've just sat back, enjoyed the music, the peat scented fire, and the relaxed mood that comes with a third after-dinner drink. The food, the rooms, the setting and the singing all combined to make Ballymaloe a part of our Irish landscape.

Chapter 18

Donagh and Picasso

During our trip to Adare in the late summer of 2000, we wanted to ride at a facility other than at Clonshire to experience something different.

We knew about an equestrian center at the Adare Manor, the former digs of the Earl of Dunraven, and by then, a pricey hotel, fancy private golf club (also with a public course), and tony townhouses and condos.

We decided to give it a try and that year we rode at the Manor Equestrian Center several times. During one session, I mentioned to the instructor that I'd love to own an Irish Thoroughbred. We ended the lesson and scheduled another one with her for a few days later.

During the next lesson, a man stood outside the ring and watched us. I thought he was one of the workers with some downtime. At the following lesson, there he was again, saying nothing, just watching. At the end of that session, after we'd paid and were heading to our car, he followed us and asked, "Would ye like to see a video of me daughter winning a jump competition?"

Never ones to turn down good film of winning rides, we said, "Sure."

Mary was about sixteen, and her winning ride was recorded for posterity on her dad's handheld camera.

"Gorgeous," we said.

"Yes, she won it by that short turn at the sixth jump."

"Yes, we can see that. Well, thanks for showing that to us," I said. We turned back toward our car.

"So, I understand ye'd like an Irish Thoroughbred."

Aha. The Irish shoe had dropped.

"I happen to have one that would be perfect for ye, and if that doesn't work, I can show ye some others in the area."

And so we met John O'Hara.

Eventually, we went to John's house where Mary showed us Donagh (pronounced Dunuh), the horse John wanted to sell me. The bottom line was that Donagh was too green for me. He would've required thousands of dollars of training and even then, it was unknown whether he'd be worthwhile. John told me that he intended to have Donagh hunt the upcoming winter, after which he'd be worth much more than he was currently asking.

"I'll take my chances, John."

While John was showing us his barn, a beautiful structure and meticulously maintained, Mary asked if we'd like to come into the house for tea. John looked at her. She didn't blink. Ten seconds passed. Somewhat hesitatingly, John finally broke the silence, "Yes, please do come in for tea." As we entered the house, John said, "Just move a few of those t'ings around. I haven't quite got to the cleaning."

That was a gross understatement. In the chaos that was the interior of John's house, saying he hadn't quite got to the cleaning was a bit like saying the street cleaners hadn't quite got to cleaning up Dresden a day after the last Allied bombing run.

I'd never seen anything quite like it: empty food packages on the floor, on the counters, in the fireplace, and enough dirt and dust to fill the Sahara. Mary's bedroom was a small space off the kitchen.

As John put on water to make tea, I almost asked him if he had a shot or two of penicillin. There was no table, so we sat on a few folding chairs brought out for us. After he served the tea, before each sip I looked in the cup, searching for something that shouldn't be swimming in it. I figured if I were Catholic this would probably be as good a time as any to have a priest give me extreme unction. Happily, we survived and John continued to try to locate a horse for me. He called several times to try to get us to go see this horse or that, but with other matters occupying our time, we left Ireland that year with no Donagh, and no other Irish Thoroughbred to bring home, but there was always another year.

When we returned to the Adare Cottages in 2001, we went back to the Adare Equestrian Center. That year, Michael Cusak, the manager of the facility, gave us lessons.

In the course of one, I mentioned to Michael that the previous year I'd tried unsuccessfully to buy an Irish Thoroughbred. He said, "I've got one you'll love."

"What's his breed and what's his name?"

"We call him a paint, what you call a pinto. His name is Picasso."

"Picasso?"

"Yes, and he's worthy of the name."

"Is he green or is he trained?"

"Oh, he's trained all right."

He brought out Picasso. He was gorgeous, and as Michael rode him for me in the ring, it was also obvious that he was well trained. In fact, he was one of the most beautiful movers I'd ever seen. First, Michael warmed him up by riding him around a bit. Then he started jumping—two-and-a-half feet, then three, then three-and-a-half, then four, and then four-and-a-half.

Extraordinary about Picasso was that not once when he came to a jump did he show any anxiety. Nor, though in a fairly confined space, did he significantly increase his speed as the jumps got higher and broader. If you haven't jumped, you'll have to take it on faith that few horses can jump four-and-a-half feet and even less can do so effortlessly. Jumps also get more difficult as you add spreads, or broaden the jumps with extra posts and crossbars to widen the barriers. The horse isn't just jumping up; he also has to clear broader and broader spreads, a bit like Evel Knievel jumping five, ten, fifteen, and then twenty cars on a motorcycle. Picasso took these increasingly broader spreads in stride with no show of strain.

Michael asked if I'd like to jump Picasso. By that time, that was a bit like asking Pavlov's dogs if they'd like to salivate when they heard a bell. As coolly as possible, I said, "That would be lovely, and I'd like you to give me a lesson on him."

I knew from what I'd just seen that this horse was capable of masterful jumping, so my job was not to screw it up. Picasso was so skilled that he made my ride look effortless and gorgeous. I paid for the lesson and told Michael that, depending on the price, I'd seriously consider buying Picasso.

I arranged with Michael to ride the horse again, not in a lesson, but as a prospective buyer. In the interim, Michael told me his price, which was fairly high. He wasn't interested in negotiating, and when I learned the considerable shipping cost to bring him home, I couldn't afford to buy Picasso, so I canceled my next ride.

He said, "Well, you owe me for the time you reserved."

"Excuse me? This second ride wasn't a lesson. This was a test ride from a possible buyer. No one buys a horse without riding him as many times as he wants—without a charge for the riding."

Michael insisted. "Well, you owe me."

I was grown up about it. I said something like, "Piss up a rope. Hell will freeze over before I'll pay you for a ride I didn't take on a horse I might've bought. Not only have you lost a sale, but you just lost two steady riders at your facility."

This was a rare bad experience with a local, an aberration. Maybe he'd just had a bad day. Maybe he was a cranky sort. Whatever. It takes all kinds to make the world go round, and I didn't let this one experience get in the way of my love of the village. But we never again rode at the Adare Manor.

Chapter 19

9/11

My daughter Ashley, Karen, and I were at the Adare Cottages on September 11, 2001. That day of living nightmares is forever seared in the consciousness of most Americans and many others throughout the world. Just as many of us know exactly where we were and what we were doing when we heard that President Kennedy had been shot, the same is true of 9/11.

On that day, I stayed back at Castleroberts while Karen and Ashley went to work out at a local gym. They were due to return midafternoon. I got up in the late morning and saw them slowly walking back to our cottage. It wasn't just that they were so early that set off alarm bells in my head, but there was something fugue-like about the way they were walking. I remember thinking, *Something's wrong.*

Karen came in and told me that she'd been on a treadmill watching TV when she saw a plane fly into a building in New York. At first she thought it was a tragic accident. (Ironically, five years later, in what was indeed a tragic accident, a small private plane did crash into a high rise in Manhattan.) Then, she said as she'd remained glued to the television, she saw a second plane come into view, and in that horrible piece of footage that has been replayed so many thousands of times, she saw the second plane crash into the second World Trade Center building.

Watching the two planes hit the World Trade Center, Karen and Ashley had seen enough to know this was an orchestrated terrorist attack that had to take a devastating toll in lost lives.

At that point, they left the gym and walked back to our cottage. We turned on the television. For hours, without saying a word to one another, we watched more and more of the horrifying unfolding story. We were numb. We couldn't eat. We couldn't speak. We couldn't move.

As the three of us watched hour on end, we heard news of a third commercial plane hitting the Pentagon, and a fourth going down in an open field in Pennsylvania.

Eventually, and ever so quietly, Karen said, "You know that most of my cousins work at financial companies in downtown Manhattan."

I knew.

Like a zombie, she got up and called Eileen, the wife of Jim Duffy, one of her cousin's who lives in New York. The preliminary news was that though badly traumatized, all family members were accounted for, except one, Michael Duffy. Eileen's daughter worked in a building next to the Twin Towers. She'd escaped from that building to see bodies free falling from the adjacent one. Michael worked in the towers, having started a position as a bond sales representative just two weeks earlier. Eileen promised to call back as soon as she heard any news about Michael.

All day we watched the coverage. When the towers collapsed, we gasped. Karen called Eileen again. No news. She told us that Jim was going to every hospital and makeshift morgue in the area trying to get word about his nephew. The next day passed. We remained glued to the television. Karen called Eileen again. No news. All of us knew what that meant, but none of us would say it.

On September 11, 2001, Michael was one week shy of turning thirty.

In 2002, the *New York Times* published a book, *Portraits 9/11/01*, containing memories and reminiscences of all those lost in that horrific day. Unfortunately, Michael is in the book.

Of the memories and reminiscences about him, his brother and sister wrote that this had been the time of his life. He was young and handsome, regularly breaking girls' hearts. Many of his friends were getting married, but he was holding out, having too good a time as a bachelor. His brother and sister joked that Michael should have slept in a tuxedo, since he'd been in five weddings the year before his death. Karen and I had attended Michael's brother John's wedding, where Michael was best man. We all lapped up Michael's toast to his brother and his new sister-in-law, in which he asked, "Who's got it better than us?" That phrase kept echoing in my brain as I fought the lump in my throat.

We now know that while Michael was evacuating the building, in a stairwell heading down, he told a friend on his cell phone that he'd just heard an all clear announcement and everyone was instructed to return to work. He got back to the eighty-seventh floor where he worked. He was on the phone with another friend when he said that he thought he saw what looked like a plane flying in the direction of the building.

It was John Donne who wrote, "For Whom the Bell Tolls":

Nunc Lento Sonitu Dicunt, Morieris: Now, this bell
tolling softly for another, says to me, 'Thou must die.'

… No man is an island, entire of itself; every man is a piece of the continent, a part of the main. If a clod be washed away by the sea, Europe is the less, as well as if a promontory were, as well as if a manor of thy friend's or of thine own were: any man's death diminishes me, because I am involved in mankind and therefore never send to know for whom the bell tolls; it tolls for thee. Neither can we call this a begging of misery, or a borrowing of misery, as though we were not miserable enough ourselves, but must fetch in more from the next house, in taking upon us the misery of neighbors.

In 2001, three hundred and seventy-eight years after Donne wrote those words, I knew exactly what he meant. The pain of loss is universal and timeless. I know how much Michael was a piece of the continent, how much he was a part of the main. I know how much Michael's death diminishes me. I know, by taking in the sorrow and mourning of all he left behind, what it means to take "upon us the misery of neighbors." I no longer bleed from the wound of his death, but it has left me with a scar that I will bear the rest of my life.

On September 13, based on an order of the Taoiseach (pronounced Teashuck), the Irish prime minister, essentially all of Ireland, paused in its normal routine. Schools, businesses, and banks all closed, as the country mourned the devastation of the 9/11 attacks. In Adare, as all throughout Ireland, the Holy Trinity Church held a special Mass for those killed. The place was packed. A local businessman, born in the States, spoke. The priest gave a homily about grieving. Karen, Ashley, and I were in a fog, but even then, we realized how extraordinary it was for a nation to shut down for a day in solidarity with those who'd died in an event that had occurred in another country.

It's true that Ireland had been far from pitch perfect on its stance toward minorities. Its position toward Jews during World War II is impossible to fairly defend. Officially, it remained neutral and based on that political stance, did nothing to take in Jews who attempted to flee Nazi Germany.

In contemporary times, it has displayed some xenophobic signs against growing minorities, largely from Eastern Europe and upper Africa. As Ireland's economy grew into the Celtic Tiger, economically and/or politically repressed people from other countries arrived in Ireland for refuge, but many were not welcomed with warm and open arms. I remember thinking at times, *Shame on you. You, of all people, the object of discrimination for centuries, should open your door to others.* Still, who in the hell were we, as Americans, to criticize other countries for dealing poorly with minorities? Our record is hardly spotless. Annihilation of American Indians, slavery and then Jim Crow laws, turning our back on Jews trying to escape Hitler, internment of Japanese Americans, and in more recent times, in the wake of 9/11, discrimination against Muslims, comprise but a partial unhappy list of all those we've targeted for racial and ethnic mistreatment.

On the day that Ireland closed down, though, I saw its capacity for compassion and greatness. I still have my qualms about some of its stands on ethical issues. However, its stance on September 13, 2001, was enough to calm the waters of skepticism coursing through me.

Although scheduled to fly home on September 15, no flights had yet been permitted into the US, and it was unclear when the ban would be lifted. We thought about delaying our return, but felt an urgent need to be back on US soil. So, without knowing if, after arriving at Heathrow, we'd be permitted to fly from there to San Francisco, Karen, Ashley, and I left Ireland with heavy hearts.

When we arrived at Heathrow, British troops met the flight and all passengers were escorted to a ground level parking lot that had been transformed into a holding area surrounded by police and military. No one could leave the lot until the flight was called. Food stalls were set up to feed all who were herded into the area; portable toilets were also available. We still had no idea if our flight would be allowed to depart, or when.

After a number of hours, our flight was called. We were instructed to queue up. Then we were escorted by the British military to the departure gate where security was as tight as I've ever seen it in anywhere other than the airport at Tel Aviv.

At takeoff, the captain announced that ours was one of the first flights permitted to fly to the United States since the attack. For many hours, I looked around me, convinced that each person who got up from his seat was a terrorist, out to commandeer the plane, turn it around, and use it as a missile to slam into some London landmark. This was a frightening and somber flight home.

As the plane taxied down the runway in San Francisco, we looked out the windows and there, standing on trucks, tractors, and cars, were fifty to sixty airport workers, all waving American flags, some holding up signs, Welcome Home. I've always been proud to be an American. I've always been grateful to my grandparents for having the guts and wisdom to emigrate, thus allowing me to be born in the United States rather than in rugged circumstances in Russia or Poland. But I'd never been a flag waver. That day, seeing those American flags as welcome signs after the terror that had just struck our country, I did what everyone else on the plane did. I applauded and cheered with tears in my eyes.

Months later, after Michael's parents finally accepted that he was gone, Karen and I flew to New York for his funeral Mass. A card was distributed to all who attended. One side reads, "Michael J. Duffy, September 18, 1971, to September 11, 2001: loving son, loving brother, loving grandson, loving friend." On the opposite side is the image of a Celtic cross. The inscription next to it is, "Grieve not nor speak of me with tears but laugh and talk of me as though I were beside you. I loved you so. 'Twas heaven here with you." That card remains on my desk. But the poem's admonition notwithstanding, I still can't read that card, or speak of Michael, without crying.

Chapter 20

❧

Purtill Cottage

As it turned out, 2001 was the last time we stayed at the Adare Cottages. We didn't return to Ireland in 2002, a combination of one of my daughters getting married and my need for some ongoing medical tests. When we tried to book time for our stay in 2003, we learned that the Dunraven had turned the cottages into long-term rentals; a year or so later, they started to sell the units.

Karen and I were sad, but as often happens when one window closes, another opens. We didn't know it then, but we were about to embark on a whole new experience in Adare. We would move on from knowing the librarian, the postmistress, and grocer on a first name, but still casual basis, to developing a real friendship with a couple living in Ireland. They, in turn, would afford us an insider's view of the country—not as visitors, even frequent ones, but as people who could mingle with and become a part of the lives of many of the villagers and get to be comfortable with our status, not just as outsiders, but as people who belonged in Adare. We were to become what the Irish call "fierce locals."

In the fall of 2002, knowing that the cottages were no longer an option, Karen got online and started to work her magic. After viewing a number of possible places to stay, she found a site for Purtill Cottage. At first, we thought its location, a few miles outside Adare, was a negative; at the cottages, we'd always been able to "walk the village."

Outweighing that, Purtill was a thatched cottage and had the same amenities as the Adare Cottages: three bedrooms, two bathrooms, one en suite with the master, a kitchen, and a dining room/sitting room combination with a fireplace, a dishwasher, and a washer and dryer. The website featured a sixty-second video showing a brief sweep of the interior, but then came the killer, a twenty-second shot of two horseback riders riding up a lane next to the cottage and walking their horses' right in front. That did it. Within minutes, Karen was booking the rental.

Soon, the owners, Victoria and Tony Treacy, would be not just the folks from whom we rented their cottage. They and their family would embrace us as lifelong friends, and we would love them right back. I don't count many people truly as friends. I count the Treacy's as friends, a friendship strong enough so that when Ashley was married in 2004, Victoria and Tony came to the wedding in San Francisco and stayed at our house while in the city.

Of course, back in 2002, we knew Purtill only as what looked like an adorable cottage, thatched roof and all. We also knew about spin, whether in a political campaign or selling a vacation rental. But in the end, we took a chance and booked the cottage for five weeks the following summer.

Prior to our departure in 2003, Tony sent us a map of how to get to Purtill after driving through Adare. It had markers on it, including an arrow to a line named Crossroads. I knew this meant an unnamed intersection, perhaps a mile and a half out of the village; and just to make it trickier, trees and other foliage surrounding the intersection are as thick as the corn is as high as an elephant's eye.

However, he also gave us written directions: "Take Askeaton Road at Village Hall." (There are two roads at Village Hall. Askeaton Road bears no road sign. Only locals know it by that name.) "At crossroads turn right." This would be the crossroads on the map with the arrow pointing to it and hidden from view by vegetation. Ah, the countryside of Ireland where the markers often are not unlike describing the location of an object as being three cows past the second midsize tree that's not all that far out of the village. "Follow road, pass school, and sign for cul-de-sac. Entrance is first left after cul-de-sac just prior to a pink house. Drive in private road approximately one quarter mile." I suspected I was in trouble when I noticed Tony had typed on it: "If you get lost, call Tony Treacy or Victoria Treacy" with their telephone numbers. I *knew* I was in trouble when I asked a clarifying question or two and he e-mailed back the same dreaded words I'd heard some years earlier from Louis Murphy when he'd described to me on an eighteenth century map how to get to Ruan: "You can't miss it."

Our flight connections brought us into Shannon late in an evening. We landed tired, but definitely apprehensive as to whether we'd find a ramshackle building with rain pouring through the roof in bucket loads. The first order of business, of course, was to get to the cottage. We made it to Adare just fine and were locals enough to know to turn onto the unmarked Askeaton Road at the Village Hall. I still don't know how, but we even managed to find the crossroads. No doubt Tony's advice that it was "not far past the truck stop/dairy farm on the left" helped. We passed the school feeling good, but that's when the fun began in earnest. A thick fog settled onto the road, so I was driving with two or three feet of visibility.

We couldn't see a cul-de-sac sign (although later in this misadventure we drove into the cul-de-sac several times). It was damn quiet in the car as we both intently looked, but couldn't find the pink house, on the far side of the driveway that led to the cottage.

The road at this point was narrow and the fog so thick that no two cars could safely pass each other without one pulling over to the side. That was no easy trick, as you couldn't be sure whether, in pulling over, you'd drop into a ditch or (as I remembered coming out of Ellen's Pub some years earlier), a bog and never be seen or heard from again. I knew we'd gone way too far, but literally there was no turning back. I pulled into every driveway we passed, but either they were gated, or didn't lead us to a thatched cottage.

After roughly thirty minutes of this agony, I thought I'd found the place and pulled into a driveway that left us both quieter than quiet. This was a rundown farm with walls crumbling, cow shit all over the drive, and broken windows. Uh oh, what had we gotten ourselves into? After sitting in the car for a full minute without saying one word to each other, I backed out, simply willing this not to be the place where we were staying and that we had to continue our quest.

Of course, the simple thing would have been to call the Treacy's, as Tony's own map had invited, but they'd left on a holiday in France earlier that day, due to return to Ireland two or three days later. So we were on our own.

Soon, I discovered the landmarks were looking quite familiar, and I realized we were driving in a big loop. Still no pink house. Then, through the fog, I saw coming at us what looked like a spaceship, but I guessed was another car. *Great,* I thought. *I've got to back up into what's probably a damn bog.* As I did, I started saying the *Sh'ma* to myself (the most important prayer in Judaism), hoping this wasn't the end. Ever so slowly I pulled over far enough to let the spaceship pass. I sat there for a moment, drained of hope and energy, but knowing we really didn't want to sleep in a car on a chilly night on the side of a country road, so we continued our search. We found all the same locations we'd already passed four or five times by then, and not once, but twice, entering the damn cul-de-sac.

Finally, I saw a dirt road. It had neither a sign nor a pink house next to it. The adjacent house was mustard colored. I turned into the road.

"What are you doing?" Karen asked a bit panicky.

I said, "This is it" with a hell of a lot more conviction than I was feeling.

She said something comforting like, "Are you crazy?"

I well understood her sentiment. This was definitely too narrow for two cars to pass under any circumstance. Once you entered, you had no choice but to continue going forward. With four-foot bushes on each side, you couldn't see what you were passing, though in the pea soup fog, that didn't really make much difference, because you could barely see the bushes. Did I mention that the driveway was winding and muddy? I wasn't about to confess to Karen that it looked possible the car could be stuck, so I just drove ahead slowly.

For the next quarter mile, Karen kept mumbling, "I can't believe we're doing this."

We rounded yet another turn. My hopes were going from a wishy-washy three down to a shaky two when suddenly, up ahead, was a light. I headed straight toward it.

The light was on a cottage; it had a thatched roof.

I pulled the car to the side near an old water pump and switched off the engine. For the first time in an hour both of us breathed, but the final test was still ahead of us. The key was to be under one of the flowerpots. There it was. It worked! We *were* at Purtill. There was a God and he was a good God. I thanked him for not sending us into a bog, and I promised to be a good Jew and to follow all the laws (except the ones about keeping kosher, observing and going to services every Sabbath, and not marrying a *shiksa*).

We schlepped our suitcases inside the cottage, and as exhausted as we were, gave the place a good viewing. We were thoroughly delighted with what we found, although for the life of us, we couldn't locate the washer and dryer. Never mind. Right then we were too tired to figure that out, and if that was the only misrepresentation, we'd work around it somehow. For now, we decided to go to bed for our usual first night's sleep after landing in Europe of two, maybe three hours. Before turning in, though, we took a quick tour. We went into the kitchen, starving and yet not hungry, a sensation only weary travelers can fully understand. I flicked on the light and we had our first introduction to Victoria Treacy: a fully baked lasagna that just needed reheating in the microwave, home baked scones, and a fresh tossed salad with salad dressing already made. We loved this woman. And we hadn't even met her yet. Okay, we decided, we're hungry after all. And so we had our first meal at Purtill courtesy of Victoria, who herself had left for France earlier that same day, but took the time to cook and deliver a full meal for first time guests.

Purtill had a photo album chronicling the ramshackle cottage when the Treacy's acquired it, and the changes they wrought in stages. Not only had they fully restored what had been there, but had added a few minor touches including electricity, indoor plumbing, showers, a modern kitchen, a second bathroom, and two bedrooms. The next day when we explored Purtill and its grounds more fully, we found a small thatched building outside the rear of the cottage, which housed the washer and dryer, ending that mystery. Also, twenty feet away, was one large building containing empty horse stables, a storage area, and a tack room.

The front entrance to the cottage was a red Dutch door, one in which the top half opens. (To this day, Tony insists it's an Irish door.) Outside, maybe twenty feet to the right was a fence where a herd of some thirty cows came up to us. We learned later that these cows and the land they were on belonged to someone else. Twenty feet straight ahead from the front door was an iron gate opening onto a large grassy area that was part of the Treacy's property. The gate had stone columns on each side. Starting that year, Karen would put enough birdseed on the columns to feed every bird in Ireland, and every one of them comes when they know she's there. Inside the gate and on the broad grassy area was a bench for resting your weary bones or just contemplating.

It wasn't until I was deep into this memoir and told Karen I was writing about Purtill Cottage that she confessed her secret about that bench where, over the summers and on many evenings, she sat for solitude. As darkness started to fall around 10:00 p.m. or later, she'd stare at the riding ring down a slight slope, the distant hills, and Ireland's mythical and mystical forty shades of green. What she was really seeing, though, was not so much the green as the future, wondering whether we would ever return again, thinking that the very moment she was enjoying was filled with quiet, peace, and tranquility, but also touched with traces of sadness due to my diagnosis. She wondered if this was the last season she would ever sit in that spot and look at the majestic view. Above all else, Karen is Irish, which means, in part, possessing dark places no one can reach.

I know why I love her so deeply. She offers me so much: intellect, beauty inside and out, shared beliefs in ethical and political matters, an abiding love for animals, a deep love and sense of responsibility for her family, and above all her parents. She has a passion for books, respect for tradition but an openness to change, a fervor against injustice, a deep and abiding love for me, a willingness to accept into her life my children and all the obligations they entail, and so much more. Still, there has always been this part of Karen inaccessible even to me. That's the part of her that sits on the Treacy's bench alone on summer evenings, awakens at 3:00 a.m., watching to see if I'm still breathing, and thinks black thoughts. The part that rarely shows me her fear of life after my disease has finally killed me, but is deathly afraid of how she'll survive that time. The part that fights darkness and often loses, but always comes back for more.

I wrote a song when we were married, years before I was diagnosed with a terminal illness, but which, even then, included the line, "After death, I choose not to part from you." Our love affair was meant to be.

Even after more than ten years of living with this disease, at times when alone, I still cry, not out of self-pity, but thinking how blessed I've been to have this woman in my life and how much I don't want to leave her. (I guess I have more Irish in me than I'd known.) It's not so much death that scares me. It's being separated from her. If I fervently believed at some point we'd be reunited, I could relax more. I haven't quite gotten there yet, though I'm still working on it.

Enough mush.

Our first day we took a short walk downhill from the grassy area and saw the riding ring up close; next to it were two more horse stables. Past them were two large pastures, as we'd learn, including thirty acres, all the Treacy's land, containing their own cross-country course, designed by none other than John O'Hara.

This wasn't just a cottage; it was part of an idyllic setting. Seeing where we'd landed, especially after the ordeal of getting there, we slowly took it all in. We walked through one of the pastures where Karen picked heather growing wild in the large fields undulating like waves. Then we came to a stream, which included some manmade obstacles, a part of the Treacy's cross-country course, crushed gravel taking you into the stream and a series of giant steps up the opposite side. We crossed the stream and emerged into yet another field, still part of their property, with built-in small knolls and another jump.

From then on, Purtill wasn't just our vacation spot in Ireland. It wasn't even just our house when we stayed in Ireland. It was our home where we lived while in Ireland.

Chapter 21

"Where Are The Pretty Pubs?"

When I was in college, I read *The Ugly American* for one of my political science classes. The book, set in a fictional country, imparted the message that Americans do great damage abroad, whether acting as actual ambassadors or just as civilian representatives of their country. At the time of its publication (1958), the novel focused on what the authors viewed as a fight the United States was losing against communism. Oops. Got that one wrong. Anyway, the critical message remains true: Americans continue to lose the struggle for what later became known as "the hearts and minds" of those living in other countries. Our arrogance, our pompous disinterest, and our unwillingness to accept the local culture in the countries in which we serve in an official capacity or are just tourists, make us targets of animosity around the world. Ancient history? How about Iraq?

In the novel, one of the characters, a journalist, notes, "A mysterious change seems to come over Americans when they go to a foreign land. They isolate themselves socially. They live pretentiously. They're loud and ostentatious. Perhaps they're frightened and defensive, or maybe they're not properly trained and make mistakes out of ignorance." Over time, the phrase ugly American came to refer to the arrogant, thoughtless, and demeaning behavior of Americans abroad, a portrait that in the novel takes on greater importance than just being disliked, because of the political implications.

The central thesis was that Americans, whether in formal positions or as civilians, could foster a positive influence abroad if they were willing to learn, respect, and accept local norms. Instead, almost unfailingly, they isolate themselves, insist on their own customs, lack respect or show disdain for local ways, and are generally hated for their boorish insistence on being ugly Americans.

I enjoyed the book and found it even more compelling as I got older and traveled a bit outside of the States. I saw many ugly Americans for myself who, rather than when in Rome doing as the Romans did, expected things to be as they are in the good old US of A and when they weren't, complained about it, loudly and obnoxiously.

"Harry, why can't they have nice showers in Ireland like we do in Columbus? Why do they have these dinky showerheads you have to hold in your hand?"

"Sandy, why can't I get a meal without all of these vegetables and potatoes? We don't have that at our restaurants in Detroit."

"Peter, is it always so cold here? I can't believe we left our lovely hundred-degree weather in Boca. Will it warm up soon?"

"Why does it rain so much, Martha? We don't have that in Phoenix."

Once, in the pub in the Dunraven, an American man asked for a glass of Sauvignon Blanc. The Dunraven has a trained staff; many of them have been there twenty years or more. But, like Cashel House in Galway County, it also has a staff in training, typically college students taking courses in hotel and restaurant management and apprenticing at various hotels and restaurants throughout Ireland. Maybe the young woman behind the bar should have known Sauvignon Blanc, but it was obvious by her blank stare that she knew no more what he was asking for than had he requested a pink elephant in a candy box. Finally, she said, "We have white wine and red wine, sir."

"I *know* you have white wine. I want *Sauvignon Blanc*. *Not* Chardonnay, *not* Pinot Gris, but *Sauvignon Blanc*."

I'd seen this guy around the hotel, generally endearing himself to various staff members on other issues, but this was his most obnoxious performance. I wanted to slap him. Luckily, one of the senior bartenders unobtrusively stepped in and helped the woman without punching out this ugly American.

It's not just the Yanks who are assholes. Once Karen and I were at a horseback riding facility where we'd never ridden before. We went for a nice relaxing trail ride. As is customary, the owner asked each rider for his or her comparative level of experience. Most people, even those with years of riding experience, normally claim to be average riders. Not this young Englishwoman in the group that day. "I'm an excellent rider, skilled at three-day eventing. I want a horse that will be challenging and up to my ability."

I turned my head toward Karen, raised my eyebrows, and said quietly, "Oh boy. This should be interesting."

The woman running the facility said nothing; she just slowly nodded her head. Then, she gave orders as to which horses to tack up for the ride. The horses were brought out, one at a time, and each rider mounted. The Englishwoman was the last one to get her steed. She stood there impatiently, till finally a pony with probably the only Western saddle in all of Ireland, arrived. The rest of us did all we could to avoid cracking up as the "excellent" rider mounted her pony and sat in her Western saddle. It didn't exactly pay back for the eight hundred years or so of English domination, discrimination, and cruelty toward the Irish, but at least it was a start. Meanwhile, I doubt that woman ever again told an Irish riding establishment that she was an excellent rider. If she did, she's even more of a gobshite than I thought.

Americans share a penchant for wanting Disneyland wherever they travel. They know Ireland. They've seen *The Quiet Man*. Barry Fitzgerald's character is supposed to take them down the Main Street in a jaunty cart. A woman looking like twenty-year-old Maureen O'Hara should be greeting them in town, wearing an adorable apron, preferably with shamrocks on it, and asking them to join her and her husband at their thatched cottage for tea. Someone looking like Ward Bond should be the local priest, fishing in the local river and there to answer parishioners' most intimate questions.

And a big bruiser, looking like Victor McLaughlin should be either at work in the fields bare-chested, or better yet, at a local bar bellowing out jokes or ready to get into a fistfight that will spill into the cobbled streets. Ireland is a land where everyone is poor but happy and living the simple farmer's life. God fearing. The children dance the jig on their way to school. And the entire population is perpetually drunk.

Since that's Ireland, in Adare, tourists of all stripes, whether Americans, Germans, Japanese, Aussies, or those from some other country, climb all over the town with their cameras to snap pictures and prove to their friends back home that the Ireland of their fantasies really does exist. They want the photos in front of the cute church, the quaint thatched cottage, or the colorful pub. Of course, the reason tourist buses pour into this village is precisely because Adare bills itself (rightly so) as the prettiest in Ireland, so in fairness, it is complicit in massing tourists to itself. But tourists, and especially Americans, take matters over the edge. Hello. In the latter years that we were there, Ireland was at the height of the Celtic Tiger economy. It had become one of the most successful countries in contemporary Europe, so try as they might, tourists couldn't force Ireland into being the quaint backward place of their imagination.

Sometimes Karen and I happen to be in the village when a busload of Americans has just been dropped off at the Heritage Center, where the Dovecot Restaurant is well equipped to handle a sudden load of fifty or so tourists, hungry for lunch. Occasionally, Karen and I get caught among the hordes. When we're finished eating, we sit outside on a bench that surrounds an oak tree, waiting for the adjacent Adare Library to open.

"Joan, where are the pretty pubs? I just went to that place across the street called Lena's and it's not pretty. Everyone says there are pretty pubs in Ireland. I want a picture of a pretty pub. Maybe we can get a picture with a cute Irish person standing in front of a pretty pub. Wouldn't that just be adorable?"

Karen and I slide a little farther to the opposite side of the tree, bury our heads deeper into our books, and quietly wait for the library to open so we can dash in to safety. If I speak to Karen, I put on a brogue: "Darlin', when do ye t'ink the library will open, so?"

Frequently, in front of the center, catering to tourist fantasies is a little man dressed in green, including his plastic top hat, playing an accordion with all the tunes the noninitiated think are Irish ditties. In front of him is a donation bowl, often filled by his marks, primarily the American tourists. Daily, he gets picked up by someone driving a Mercedes. No doubt, they laugh all the way to the bank.

You don't have to be abroad to be an ugly American. Tony Treacy worked for Texas Instruments for some years before forming his own company in Ireland. While in the States, he was often asked to "say something" so people could hear his "cute" Irish brogue. Then, they'd ask what he most admired about America. He told us he'd always pause, drop his head a bit, put a thumb under his chin, tap a finger against his lip, as he'd appear to reflect deeply, and then say, "Indoor plumbing."

All listening would say to one another, "Can you imagine? Poor man. Such a shame. But isn't his brogue just adorable?"

He'd turn his head, roll his eyes, and mutter to himself, "Eejits."

Chapter 22

⌒

Donal and Patsy

The first year we stayed at Purtill, we were surprised one day to see a small, beat-up car come up the drive and pull in next to the cottage. If it had ever been washed, it was a long time ago. Out came a man and a dog. Later, we learned they were named Donal and Prince. In all the years we've seen Donal, only twice was he wearing anything other than his torn pants, a raggedy sweater, the same frayed gray hat, his wellies, and a suit jacket that was about forty-three years old, worn at the elbows and with splotches of paint all over it.

In addition, only twice did he have less than a combination of two-day, five-day, and two-week facial hair growth over various parts of his face. I don't know how he manages it. No one could plan this. It could only come from the most extraordinary benign neglect. For some time after we'd first spotted him, we hid behind the curtains, because it was obvious he was loony, maybe harmless, but we weren't sure.

After he'd pull up and turn off his engine, he wouldn't get out of his car for five minutes or so. Then, his car door creaked; Prince jumped out, and slowly Donal emerged, opened the boot, and removed his pitchfork and a pail. He took his sweet time ambling toward the pasture next to the cottage where the cows milled about. Slowly, he opened the iron gate, and as the cows turned away from him, he entered. His routine never varied:

he'd disappear over the hill, be gone for thirty to forty minutes, and then slowly come shuffling back with his pitchfork over a shoulder, carrying his pail. He'd put them back in the boot, Prince and he would get into the car, and unhurriedly he'd drive off.

For a few years, he never even looked toward the cottage, although he parked his car next to ours, so he knew someone was there and we knew he knew someone was there.

In our early years at Purtill, and after we'd seen him go through his routine a number of times, I decided he was harmless and considered offering him some money, so he could get a decent meal, a roof over his head at least for a few nights, some clothes, and a shave. It was obvious that he was some poor worker barely eking out a living.

Finally, I asked Tony if he knew the old guy who frequented the field. "Is it okay with you that this funny little fella keeps coming onto your property?"

Tony laughed. "Yes, it's okay," he said. "That's Donal Cagney, probably the richest man in the county. He sold us these thirty acres, including the cottage you're staying in, and I had to beg him to sell. Where he goes walking into the cow pasture is but a tiny part of his land. He never married, and he lives on the road into the village. I'll point out his house the next time we drive past it. It's the one that looks like a castle. His brother Michael lives right across the road from him."

I said to myself, *Hmm, I guess I should pay heed to the adage about not judging a book by its cover.* Patting myself on the back for not being a hundred percent ugly American, I thought, *At least I hadn't told him to scram off the Treacy's land.*

After that, I sometimes wandered outside when Donal came by. I'd kick the dirt letting him get the sight of me, but he wouldn't look me in the eye to save his life. Finally, I said, "Good day." He nodded.

Eventually, he actually said, "Good day" back. I was elated. It was similar to my breakthrough years earlier with Joe O'Dwyer at the Adare Cottages.

After we'd been there a few years, I went for broke. I approached him and said, "Lovely day."

"Not sure," he said. "Looks like rain's comin' in from the west, I'd say."

From that point forward, I wasn't a threat, and before he'd head into the pasture, he looked toward the cottage and seeing us, he tipped his hat. We were in.

The next time we were there, he approached me to say he'd received a letter from a Purtill family member. The relative was coming to Ireland from the States and Donal asked if we'd let the Purtill and him inside the cottage. This was my first real conversation with Donal, and it was only then when he looked at me that I saw he had eyes so deep blue you could float boats on them. I was delighted he'd asked, and Karen and I looked forward to the upcoming visit and making Donal as comfortable as possible.

During this discussion, Donal told me he'd worked for years with the Purtill family. As far as he knew, no relatives ever communicated with them. One day while working in the fields, one of them collapsed, apparently of a stroke. Donal brought him back to his cottage and cared for him until he died. After his death, Donal learned that he'd left Purtill Cottage and the land on which it was situated to Donal, forming but a small part of Donal's eventual holdings.

Many decades later, Tony convinced Donal to sell the thirty acres with the broken down cottage, which Victoria and Tony turned into the place we now considered our Irish home.

One day that same year, Donal arrived excitedly at the cottage. He wasn't wearing his hat, and he had on different pants, one of the two times we've seen him not wearing his regular uniform. Donal had the young Purtill and his wife in tow. Karen answered the door. He asked "the Missus" if they could come in.

Karen and I welcomed Donal and the Purtill's like long-lost royalty, but the young man was as friendly as an iceberg, acting the brief time he with us as though we were squatters and Donal a thief. He refused tea, in and of itself a slap in the face, making Donal uncomfortable that someone he'd invited was refusing a simple gesture of civility. I was glad when he and his wife left. Donal never again spoke of them. Neither did we.

I know how excited Donal had been to have a Purtill back on the land, and he wanted to show him what life had been like way back then. But, the young Purtill was completely disinterested in hearing anything of the history, made clear he wanted to leave quickly, the short time he was with us acting like a stiff piece of leather. I could have throttled him for the disrespect he showed Donal who, by that time, we'd come to know as a shy old bachelor, but a man with a work ethic as long as your arm and a civility and decency that few could exemplify.

For example, by this time, Prince had died. We asked why he didn't get a new dog.

"There was only one Prince."

We knew that Donal missed Prince's companionship, so we asked, "Wouldn't another dog be a comfort to you?"

"It wouldn't be right. It would feel, I don't know, I guess, disloyal."

Wow. So he chose to deal with the loneliness of the loss rather than replace Prince, which, in his mind, would have been dishonorable.

Donal told us fascinating stories. He told us that "in the old days," what's now Purtill's tack room was used as an underground Catholic church. When the British outlawed the practice of Catholicism in Ireland (again), word of a scheduled Mass in the tack room was quietly spread and attended by locals at the appointed time on the designated day.

He told us of fairy mounds. "Never interfere with a fairy mound, even if it's in the middle of a field and its location is inconvenient. The fairies can be nasty creatures, aye that's the truth, and they can do you much mischief if you disturb their domain."

He told us of the years before Ireland became a Free State (prior to 1923), when the British had a police garrison down the road and used prisoners as an excuse to build a second floor. "They had no prisoners. It was just to make their living easier."

He told us about the real Ireland, not the Ireland of the pretty pubs. It had been a hard place to live, though far from breaking him, it'd made him tough as iron.

Now that Donal trusts us, we play this game. As he starts heading for the field, if we don't come to the front door, he coughs, we appear, and we say hello. He shuffles forward and offers some homily, sometimes about a fifty-year-old issue, sometimes about one in yesterday's news. So it could be about the Brits in the old days or about contemporary drug abuse by young ones. We don't understand much of what he says, because he speaks with a heavy brogue, ever so softly, and even then, he tends to talk to the ground, but we always get the drift, certainly enough to say, "Terrible" or "Something should be done about that."

"Yes," inevitably he says. "'Tis the truth." Then he doffs his hat, gives a slight bow of the head and says, "Well now, good day to ye, and to ye, Missus," puts his hat back on and shuffles off toward the pasture in his ratty old uniform, pitchfork and pail in hand.

In 2006, I ended up spending time at the Limerick Regional Hospital, the first night in the accident and emergency wing. That was the second time we saw Donal out of uniform. In fact, he was wearing a suit. His flyaway hair was slicked back, and he was as close to clean-shaven as I've seen him before or since. Apparently on his way to visit a sick friend or relative, Donal walked past me. I was sitting on a bench outside the hospital, catching some fresh air. I saw him walk by, but didn't have the energy to say hello. He entered the waiting room, briefly glanced at Karen, but walked past her too.

A few days later, Donal asked Karen if that had been her at hospital. "Yes, Donal. Harvey wasn't feeling well, and we were waiting for him to be admitted. I thought I saw you, but you disappeared before I had a chance to greet you."

"Yes, 'twas me, and I did see ye, Missus."

"Why didn't you come up to me?"

"Why, unless a man is absolutely certain that he knows a woman, it's just not proper to approach her."

"Why not, Donal?"

"Well, she could get the wrong idea now, couldn't she?"

For the rest of our time there, Karen and I were back and forth to the hospital. You didn't have to be a raging genius after seeing me with my gray pallor but to know I was sick. Each time Donal came by for his ritual walk into the pasture, he stopped by the front door. "Good day, Missus. How is Himself doing today?"

"Why, he's doing better, Donal. Thank you for asking."

"Please give him my regards."

"I'll do that."

He'd tip his hat and say, "Well, I'm off now," then he'd head to the field, pitchfork and pail in hand.

When speaking *to* Victoria or Karen he'd always call them "Missus," but when speaking *about* them, he'd refer to them differently. One holiday Karen's mother, sister, and my nephew stayed with us for a while. When he met Karen's mom he said, "Oh, yes, you're the mother of the gaerl." On the other hand, as a generational distinction, when referring to a teenager, such as Victoria's daughter Rebecca, he'd refer to her as the "gaerlie."

To this day, Donal continues to come to the property unshaven, in his frayed gray hat, torn pants, paint-splattered sweater, wellies, and worn suit coat. Although he always doffs his hat and often stops by to tell us about the weather, or depending on his mood, some story, he never accepts an invitation to come inside. Other than the time he entered with the cold young Purtill, coming into a cottage is simply too familiar. After his brief chat with us, he disappears into his field for thirty to forty-five minutes, perhaps to see if the gold bricks he hid there long ago are still in place. I hope they are and that they're nowhere near a fairy mound.

* * * * * * * * * * * * * * * * *

While staying at Purtill we also had the great pleasure of meeting and getting to know Patsy Noonan, an Irish force of nature. Tony had hired Patsy to do some patching on Purtill's thatched roof. Since few houses in Ireland now have thatched roofs, patching, or constructing them from scratch, is a dying art and Patsy is an artist.

Each morning when we walked out of the cottage, he was standing on a ladder shoving fistfuls of strengthened straw, sharply pointed at the ends, into the roof to build up the worn spots. When he'd spot us, he'd come down and greet us each day, "Good morning, Hervey. Good morning, Missus. You're as welcome as the flowers in May."

Mornings in Ireland often have a chill and each day we'd bring him hot tea and scones, which he was happy to receive.

Patsy was an original—midheight, barrel-chested, and a ruddy complexion. His hands looked so tough that they appeared as though he could have driven nails into a board with them. His hair, graying a bit, was always askew; he also had twelve hundred bits and pieces of straw in his hair, his sweater, sticking out of his pockets, and poking out of his wellies. He always had a wonderful smile and never did we see him that he wasn't singing to himself or listening to his radio.

One day, Karen and I ran some errands. By the time we returned, Patsy was gone for the day. His ladder was still propped against the cottage, as usual, enough straw around it to feed a pasture of horses. We got to thinking of the area surrounding his ladder as something akin to a Jackson Pollock painting, except that instead of throwing paint onto a canvas, Patsy's medium was straw, strewn on the ground in unusual swirls and overlays.

That day when we returned to the cottage, we not only saw his "painting," but also heard music. When I climbed to the roof, I found Patsy's radio still on. It hadn't slid off, thanks to his simple but ingenious method of anchoring it. He'd tied one end of a piece of string around the radio and the opposite end around a spike that he stuck into the roof. I pulled out the spike, brought down the radio, and the next morning when Patsy showed up, I brought him his tea and scones, and his radio, string, and spike. When he spotted the radio, he smiled, but before he had a chance to say anything, I said, "Why, Patsy, you're as welcome as the flowers in May."

He laughed heartily, patted me on the shoulder and said, "Now, there's a good lad," then reached for his tea and scones.

A few weeks later, we heard about a demonstration in the village of fixing thatched roofs. When we got there, Patsy was mounted on his trusty ladder, hair blowing in the wind, fistfuls of pointy straw in each hand and more sticking out of his pockets and his sweater. He was putting on a show for the tourists who, of course, were taking pictures of the cute Irishman. As he was getting down from his ladder to get more material, he spotted us standing across the road. He waved to us. "Hervey! Missus! You're as welcome as the flowers in May!"

We waved back and smiled. "Hello, Patsy. How's your good self?" I asked.

"Why, jest fine, Hervey, Missus, jest fine!"

His audience looked at us a bit strangely, wondering how a couple of Yanks knew a local. We turned and walked away saying to ourselves, *Damn, are we fierce, by god locals or what?*

While we were standing there, we saw a black kitten dart into Main Street. Adare, though a small village, has no bypass, so all traffic heading in either direction must rumble through and this includes some massive trucks. As we looked up, we saw one of the monster rigs bearing down on the kitten. Karen panicked and stepped into the street, but before she had a chance to kill herself, the driver stopped, got out of his truck, picked up the kitten, put it on the sidewalk, and patted it on the head. The kitten meowed; the driver got back into his rig and took off.

We crossed the street to the kitten, fearing it would try its luck again on the busy road. Karen picked it up and was stroking its head when we saw its mother in a nearby garden. Karen put the kitten down in the garden; its mother quickly came forward, grabbed it by the nape of its neck, and took off. As she did, Karen said to the mother, "You're as welcome as the flowers in May."

Purtill Cottage

Karen's Bench with Purtill Cottage in the Background

Patsy Noonan

Patsy Noonan's Work Area at Purtill Cottage

Chapter 23

Margaret

The first time we stayed at Purtill, we asked Victoria if she could recommend someone who could clean the cottage. She suggested Margaret. Victoria told us that Margaret was dear to their family. She'd known the Treacy's forever and had cleaned house for them during the years when both Tony and Victoria were working at Tony's new business. Many was the day Victoria returned home, only to find Margaret nursing one or more of the "poor darlings" who seemed to have a fever, a tummy ache, or whatever. If ever a Treacy child was the slightest in distress, Margaret dropped mop, rag, and broom to tend to him or her. In return, the children adored her. She was Mary Poppins without the singing.

Four things were distinguishable about Margaret. First, she came over on a Rolls Royce, the name for her bicycle. I asked repeatedly if she wanted me to pick her up and drive her home, but she loved riding her Rolls on the back roads of Adare where we saw her many times and where she lived, near the crossroads. Second, by the time she came to us, she was retired. She was helping us only because Victoria had asked her. Third, she was a master at building the makings of our next fire. She'd go all over the property, find kindling lying here and there and build a structure in the fireplace worthy of an architect's drawings. Without fail, when it came time to light the next fire, with one match the flames danced into being as though Margaret were in the background concocting some sort of ongoing spell. Maybe she did have some of Mary Poppins's powers? And fourth, she loved to talk the craic, and since I do, too, the combination was deadly.

"So Margaret, have you seen Donal lately?"

"Well now, isn't that the funniest t'ing you happen to ask. Why just yesterday ..."

"So Margaret, do you know how the Mustard Seed is doing these days?"

"Isn't that interesting? I just saw Dan Mullane last week and he happened to mention ..."

"So Margaret, is it true that Liz Twomey got her job as the postmistress after apprenticing for Tony's mother for a number of years?"

"My my, you are getting to know about the locals. Well, the full story is ..."

"So Margaret, is it Brian or Louis Murphy's parents who live on Main Street?"

"Well now, the talk is that Brian bought the house between the chemist and the Treacy's place on Main and ..."

Margaret's best friend Josie is married to Donal's brother Michael. As Tony had told me, Donal and Michael live across the road from each other. Margaret added that every afternoon Donal is over for lunch prepared by Josie. Josie's only apparent escape is on Tuesdays and Sundays: on Tuesdays, Josie and Margaret travel to the Tesco supermarket at a shopping mall in Limerick and each Sunday they go to church. The Tesco outings are something of a ritual and Josie's chance to kick up her heels for a few hours.

Once, Margaret confided that Donal had asked her to lunch.

"Why, Margaret. When will Donal be popping the question?"

"Bollocks on popping any question. Donal is an old goat, at seventy-something about as confirmed a bachelor as one can be. I'm an old widow and have no interest in replacing Josie as a routine lunch maker."

Alas, she was right and the budding romance never got to bloom, although I did enjoy teasing Margaret about her "boyfriend" every time she came to clean.

Margaret continued to regale us with vignettes about many of the village residents. She also was a virtual *Yellow Pages* (in Ireland, the *Golden Pages*). When we told her we wanted to buy some ewes as a gift for Tony and Victoria, she put us in touch with Michael Power, a local sheep farmer whom she identified by having her son get us the contact information.

At any rate, eventually Karen got used to the idea that when Margaret came to clean, she'd do so in whatever time remained after she'd built our next fire and we'd had a fine round of craic. Karen would just shake her head at me and roll her eyes as I'd pour Margaret another cuppa and ask, "So Margaret, is it true that ...?"

Chapter 24

Oirish Time

We learned that for any function scheduled in Ireland, you never arrived at the announced time. In fact, if you showed up at a private dinner less than at least thirty minutes late, it was deemed impolite, and you'd likely find the host and hostess partially dressed and still scampering around to put finishing touches here and there. For certain publicly scheduled functions in the countryside areas, you were to arrive at least sixty or ninety minutes late, sometimes a good deal more.

Our lesson started one day when we saw signs for a feis (pronounced fesh) at seven o'clock at the Five Sisters Pub in Kildimo. Karen grew up watching many a feis, or Irish step dancing. Through her and especially after we saw *Riverdance* in London before coming to Ireland together one year, I loved it too. So the decision was easy. We were going to see a feis in the Old Sod, and we wanted to be on time.

When we arrived at seven, we were directed to a hall at the rear of the pub. No one was there except a few little girls carrying around their dancing outfits. We managed to find a woman who took our entrance fee. She looked at us with a furrowed brow as though asking, *What're you doing here so early?* Undaunted, we sat down at a table, the only patrons in the hall that had its own bar. It's not exactly the norm to see any pub in Ireland empty, makeshift or not.

I ordered drinks.

We nursed our first, and then a second, but by 8:30 and still the only folks in sight, we were beginning to feel like characters in an episode of the "X Files." It seemed that everyone in Ireland had disappeared except the bartender and I thought that any minute, he'd morph into an alien and whisk us away on his spaceship, which he had hidden in the adjoining field with the cows. It might have been the same one we passed the first night we'd struggled to find Purtill Cottage.

I sauntered up to the bar. "So, has the feis been canceled?"

"Not a' tall, sir. Quite the opposite. There'll be quite a crowd."

"But the notices said seven o'clock."

He laughed. "That's seven o'clock Oirish time, sir. Oirish time. People won't start showing up till between nine and half-nine."

Silly Americans. Sure enough, the dancing started at about 9:30 with the young ones and by 10:00 the room was so full we couldn't see any of the dancers without standing, because everyone else was on their feet and the smoke in the room was enough to choke a horse. By 11:00 or so the dancing was getting really good, but our eyes were burning from exhaustion and smoke, so we gave up the ghost and left, missing some of the later performances from *Riverdance* step dancers.

We'd seen enough to know that these folks could *dance* and that the Irish took their step dancing dead seriously—everyone dolled up in their costumes, young girls wearing blonde curly wigs, all dancers with hands held straight down at their sides, eyes straight ahead, no smiling, and feet flying at the speed of light—just as we'd seen at Ellen's pub, but here dressed in full regalia.

When Victoria and Tony invited us to our first dinner at their house, by then we knew better than to show up exactly at the appointed time. We weren't impolite heathens. We weren't even silly Americans any more. We were Oirish. Even so, we arrived on time, but parked outside their house and waited in the car awhile. Then, being mature, we peeked through the dining room window and saw that the table was set for a number of people. Now we knew others were invited so we could gauge the proper time to enter by when they did. We hid in the car till we saw guests knock at their door. Then we counted to two hundred before making our seemingly casual entrance roughly forty minutes after we'd been told to arrive. Thank God others had been invited. Otherwise, we might still be in the car waiting for the right moment to knock. Thus, we learned that generally, the time to arrive for Oirish occasions had a laxity. Still, there were times even in Ireland when punctuality was required, a lesson we learned the hard way—at the Mustard Seed.

First, are you thinking Ireland is stuck in the Stone Age when it comes to food? All you can get is boiled-to-death vegetables and three kinds of potatoes? It makes no difference where you eat in Ireland, because it's all mediocre? Get over it. That was true when we started going to Ireland in the late eighties. Since then, as we'd learned at Ballymaloe and a number of restaurants all over the country, the food, and the cooking have made leaps and bounds changes for the better.

What's true in Ireland, as in most places, is that if you want food and atmosphere at the top of the chain, it's there, but as in most places, for top-of-the-line dining, you'll pay top-of-the-line prices. On the other hand, if you want just plain good food that won't win awards and isn't served in a fancy setting, but also doesn't cost an arm and a leg, it's plentiful throughout the country.

One of Peter Mayle's books is *Acquired Tastes*, in which he samples and reports his views on luxuries at the highest level of shoes, cigars, champagne, London hotels, Parisian bistros, second homes, French truffles, antiques, and more. His thesis is to hold out for the best. If that means passing up the opportunity to spend money on second-rate places or luxuries, pass. Wait until you can afford the best, even if it's only a rarity. Though we don't always practice what Mayle preaches, and we're sure he doesn't either, the Mustard Seed restaurant would likely meet Mayle's criteria. While it doesn't require a second mortgage, it is pricey, but worth every penny. When we first stayed in Adare, it was located on Main Street, and owned and operated by Dan Mullane.

Then one year, upon returning to Adare, we discovered that Dan had moved the restaurant to the village of Ballingarry, maybe ten miles away from Adare. But he'd expanded his operation, which now included a restaurant and a small inn on the site of what had been a convent.

180

The drive from Adare to Ballingarry knocks your socks off. It's picture perfect, including a copse of trees that bends across the road to form a tunnel of green foliage for all passing through. And when you arrive at the Mustard Seed, you drive past stone columns, and then up a long, winding driveway. Walking to the building, you get a stunning view of the surrounding valley, and a lovely church taking a prominent position on top of the tallest hill.

In a series of interviews by Bill Moyers of Joseph Campbell titled "The Power of Myth," one of the many salient points that philosopher, writer, and teacher Campbell made was that throughout time, the high ground was always reserved for what was then the most important symbol of power. At one period, it was Roman temples, then royal castles, then churches, and today, skyscrapers. What we were seeing in Ballingarry as a historical point of reference was the time when religion was top dog.

As you enter the Mustard Seed, sometimes a few cats that live on the grounds meander inside. Within moments of your entry, either Dan or his assistant of many years, John Edward, is there to kiss the women and greet the men, and then usher all into a library off the entry hall. In the cold weather, the fireplace is aglow with a peat fire. In the library, you have drinks and canapés as you peruse the menu. After ordering, you linger there awhile, before being shown to your table with your blood pressure already lowered from the calming effect of it all, except the one time when we pushed the principle of arriving Oirish time beyond its limits.

We had invited Tony and Victoria to the Mustard Seed for a Saturday night dinner to thank them for their mounting kindnesses. When I called to make a reservation for that Saturday, Dan had nothing available. After I used up all my begging rights for the next year, Dan relented. "I can't tell you how tight a squeeze this is, but I'll do it. But pleeeeease be here promptly at eight."

"Dan, I owe you. And I understand. Not Oirish time. See you at eight on Saturday night. And thank you."

Tony and Victoria invited us to their house for drinks at seven. That was tight, but allowing ten minutes for hellos and fifteen minutes for a drink, we could make it with a couple minutes to spare.

I told them we had reservations at eight sharp, and that we'd arrive promptly at their house at seven, hoping to emphasize that we weren't dealing in Oirish time. Tony served drinks in a room with a blazing fire in the fireplace. The fire was a bad sign; it meant a nice relaxed pace. *Uh oh.*

Then Tony took photos, and said he'd serve a second round of drinks. I said, "We really don't have time, Tony. We promised Dan we'd be there spot-on at eight."

"Okay then, just a quick one and off we go."

In Ireland, "a quick one" is the same as any other one. It's just a polite way of avoiding saying, "Sod off, we're having another drink."

Bottom line. We left at nine. I drove fast. We arrived at about 9:15.

The front door opened. Dan was there. No joking. No kisses. No, "You're very welcome." No craic. All bad signs. Worse, instead of being ushered into the cozy library for a drink, canapés, and a relaxed review of menus, we were whisked straightaway to the table. The order was taken quickly. The food came promptly. Then the coup de grâce. Just as we'd finished dinner and were about to order coffee and dessert, Dan reappeared—none too cheery. "I'm going to have to ask you to have your coffee and dessert in the room down the hall. I simply must have the table back."

No smiles from Dan. None from Tony, either. The Cold War had come, but this time within Ireland.

As we walked to the other room, Tony was furious. "Why, do you know how much business we've given him over the years? Doesn't he realize it was the locals who established him?"

"He did accommodate us, Tony, and we were over an hour late."

"Doesn't he realize that in the off-season it's those living in Adare and the surrounding area that keep him going?"

"He did accommodate us, Tony, and we were really late."

"He's stepped way over the line."

Victoria and Tony hadn't returned to the Mustard Seed when, two years later, Tony had his "event," a heart attack, less than a week before we arrived for our summer stay. We were at their house one afternoon when Tony showed us an expensive bottle of wine with a best wishes card that Dan had sent. Tony muttered, "It was nice of Dan to remember me; perhaps it's time to let bygones be bygones."

I pounced and asked if it would be okay if we took them a second time to the Mustard Seed for dinner. Tony pretended to resist a tad, but quickly relented. I called Dan and made reservations for 8:00 p.m. on a Thursday night. I emphasized that this time I was making sure to stay away from his busiest night of the week. He laughed. Good.

Victoria and Tony invited us for a drink. We had one, and then I suggested we have our second drink in the restaurant's sitting room. They agreed. We arrived fifteen minutes early. *Very* unOirish. Dan greeted us in the hallway entrance with hugs and kisses for the women. Better. Graciously, he ushered us into the sitting room for the usual routine there. Dinner was perfect and utterly unrushed. As his final peace offering, Dan bought us all an after-dinner drink. I almost crossed myself. Whew. Now we could take our dear friends back to one of our favorite restaurants in the area. All's well that ends well.

But Oirish time continues to reign in Ireland.

* * * * * * * * * * * * * * * * * *

One of Karen's nephews, David, grew up in San Francisco. He lived in the same pair of flats as his grandparents, Mary and John B., and their relationship became deep and enduring. Every day when he came home from school, David sat at his grandfather's knee, to be regaled with stories of being a cop on the beat in New York, or life during the Depression, or serving as a grunt solider during World War II, or landing on Omaha Beach on D-day. David listened attentively, until Grandma brought him to the table for a "wee snack," essentially a full dinner, before he went upstairs for dinner.

David loved Karen. When he was five or six, he'd hop in her car for a quick spin when she stopped by after work, and he spent many a weekend with her.

When I first came on the scene, David wasn't crazy about me. I was this big hulk, taking up too much of his aunt's time and attention and elbowing his way into her life, thus diminishing his time with her. Though he sort of got used to me, the problem didn't *really* get solved till, when he was about eleven, he spent a weekend with us shortly after we were married. He was watching a movie, all comfy on the bed next to his aunt, wearing my smoking jacket. I walked in and offered him an hour-and-a-half cigar. Peter Mayle would have approved of its quality. David looked at me as though we were entering into a criminal conspiracy. I cut the end, lit a match, and he puffed to get the cigar going. Within five puffs, he turned one of Ireland's forty shades of green and stamped it out, saying he didn't want to smoke up the room. But our bond was sealed: I'd allowed him to commit a forbidden act. Our solemn oath of silence (or, as David would put it in later years, when he had something to tell us in secret, our "circle of trust") was established.

Many years later, David spent his junior year in college at the University of Galway as an exchange student from the University of California at Santa Cruz. We heard about the Swedish, German, and Irish girls David had befriended and the Thanksgiving meal he made for thirty of his closest Irish friends, not the least bit concerned that Thanksgiving wasn't exactly an Irish holiday. We heard the names of the pubs he frequented regularly. We didn't hear too much about the classes he attended, but we did hear that he fell in love with Ireland.

While there, he formed a close friendship with Brendan (Ben), who occasionally showed up in the States. It was never quite clear what Ben did in Ireland, or for that matter what he was doing in the States, or where he planned to stay, or for how long. But like David's Siamese twin, Ben was always there.

In 2004, David and his girlfriend, Maggie, toured Europe, including Ireland, where David wisely left out a few details of some of his activities as a junior.

Of course, they spent time in Dublin with Ben. The plan was that David and Maggie would catch a ride to Adare with Ben, who was on his way to Galway, to do whatever it is that Ben does. David called to say, "It'll just be Maggie and me at your cottage, Uncle Harv. Is it okay if we come tomorrow?"

"That would be grand, David. No problem. What time do you think you'll be here?"

"Ben says we'll leave here tenish, so we should be there by about two. Does that work for you?"

"That's perfect. We'll be going to dinner later that evening, so sometime in the midafternoon will work just fine. Have a safe trip, and we'll see you tomorrow at two."

Karen and I agreed that since Ben was doing the scheduling, like all good Irishmen he'd be working on Oirish time, so arriving at two probably meant at five, but that was still okay.

At noon the next day, David called to say that Ben thought they'd be leaving Dublin about one. We figured that meant leaving by two and arriving by six, a wee bit later than we'd assumed, but still alright.

At three, David called to say they were just getting going, but Ben said it was a straight shot and they'd likely be there by seven.

At seven, David called. Ben was a wee tired from the night before (which meant he'd been falling-down drunk) and needed a break, so they stopped for a quick bite to eat (which meant a couple of drinks); then they'd be right on. He paused a bit on the phone. I knew that pause: David had something to ask.

"What's up, David?"

"Well, they were going to drive straight through to Galway, but Ben may be too tired to do that."

"Who's 'they,' David?"

"Oh, Ben and Meehan. You remember Meehan, don't you, Uncle Harv? She was with me at Santa Cruz and the year in Galway."

"I didn't know she was in Ireland, or that anyone else was coming along for the ride."

"Yeah, well, I guess I forgot to mention it, because they were just going to be driving us, dropping us off, and keep on going, but—"

"But they need a place to sleep tonight, possibly in a village called Adare?"

"Uncle Harv. You're so smart. Would it …?"

"Sure, they can stay at the cottage."

"I love you, man."

"Yes, I know. Ever since the cigar."

Rather than wait until midnight for their arrival, at nine o'clock we headed out for our dinner date. We were walking in the village toward the restaurant when David came storming out of one of the pubs, screaming our names. They'd made it and it was only nine-fifteen or so, actually something of a timely arrival record for Ben, just a bit more than seven hours later than his original ETA. Not bad, and of course, they'd stopped at a pub in Adare before calling to let us know they'd arrived. Why not? Hell, this was Ireland.

Chapter 25

 ~

Tony, Martin, and the Good Stuff

W e whizzed past the landlord-tenant relationship with Tony and
Victoria almost before we'd arrived for our first stay in their
cottage. After Karen booked Purtill, I launched a correspondence with
Tony. I started by asking him if, in lieu of cash, he and Victoria would
accept San Francisco sourdough bread as payment for the rental. Oddly, he
refused, but not before he countered, "I might consider title to the Golden
Gate Bridge." I knew I had a wacko soul mate in Tony.

After Victoria and Tony returned from their holiday in France during
our first stay, and we met in person and clicked, they started to show us
real Irish hospitality. They invited us to dinner at their house in the village.
Years later, they built their dream house on their thirty acres and rented
out their house in town, thinking that someday one of their children might
want to live there. As it turned out, the backyard of their village house was
adjacent to Castleroberts. For years, we'd lived next to each other without
knowing it.

Tony and Victoria are perhaps twelve years younger than we are. Tony
is about five feet ten, has brown hair, is slender, and as much as it kills
me to write it, a good-looking bloke, but his wit exceeds even his looks.
Victoria is a beautiful, blue-eyed, five foot three, blonde twig of a woman,
always in motion, forever bringing us food, and often at Purtill doing

or directing one task or another. As a young woman, she helped run her parents' hotel.

Our first year at Purtill, their oldest, Martin, was fourteen and already a handsome brown-haired lad. He was home for the summer from Clongowes, the private boarding school he attended outside of Dublin. Rebecca was twelve and had no idea what a beauty she'd become. She was on vacation from an all-Irish-speaking private school in Limerick. Gordon was a red-haired, ten-year-old with freckles who was then attending the school that we'd passed on our first fateful night trying to find Purtill. One day during our second stay at Purtill, Victoria asked us to collect Gordy (you collect rather than pick up people) at school and bring him back to Purtill where she'd collect him later. We drove to the school, but there was no Gordy. Anxiously, we waited and watched as all the other kids got into cars and were driven off. Then, Gordy came running along the road, backpack and all, huffing and puffing. "You drove by me coming down the drive; I was in the field."

"Why didn't you yell for us?" I asked.

"I did, but you'd already taken the turn on the drive."

We took him back to Purtill, where as her penance, Karen gave Gordy dinner, as a snack before his dinner—shades of David and his grandmother. During Gordy's meal that day, we learned that it was Rebecca and Gordy riding in the brief film clip that had sold us on renting the cottage.

All our dinners at the Treacy's have been special, but our first one is perhaps the most memorable, partly because we had no idea how it would turn out, and it turned out to cement our friendship and gave me a few stories.

How Victoria could possibly have dinners ready at the end of any of her typical days still amazes me. She'd go for a run every morning at 6:00 a.m. along a footpath next to the Maigue. She managed her household, shopped for food daily, and carted her kids all over kingdom come for riding lessons, music lessons, and playdates. When Tony started his own computer chip business in an industrial park on the outskirts of Limerick, she worked there daily while raising three children. She came to the cottage every day to care for their horses, muck out stalls, cut grass, garden, plant and tend to vegetables, and oversee landscaping, often doing the labor herself. In later years, she tended to the sheep at their house on the thirty acres. And she attended to a myriad of other daily details, such as having a full meal waiting for us on our first night at Purtill, although she and the family had left for France earlier that day. Routinely when we stay there, Victoria delivers to us home-baked scones, pies, and a variety of full meals. Whenever I'd ask how she could do it all, she'd say, "Nothing to it, Harv. I just love it," and I believe her.

She also loves to have dinner parties and thinks nothing of entertaining ten or twelve people with a full sit-down meal, often with no more than a day's notice and more times than not in the middle of the week. She does all the cooking herself, although Tony pitches in, including grilling if it's called for and helping with other parts of the meal. Victoria also serves dinner; her only help comes from Tony and the children and this certainly isn't because they can't afford it. She just prefers to keep her entertaining a family affair.

The first time we went to their house for dinner, they were still living in the village, but Victoria was with us at Purtill in the afternoon after she'd completed some chores there. Suddenly she remembered she'd forgotten to turn off her AGA (an oven, in the old days also used to warm the house) in which our dinner for that night was baking. She called Liz Twomey to ask if she could turn it off for her. "No problem." Liz closed the post office, went to the Treacy's, opened the door with her key, turned off the AGA, removed the roast, and returned to the post office, which was once again open for business. Just like in the States. Every time since then when we go to the post office in Adare, we always thank Liz for saving our roast that would otherwise have been burned to a crisp, and she always blushes and smiles. Meanwhile, the dinner that night was a spread worthy of Ballymaloe.

We came to learn that it was typical of Victoria's dinners to have a dining table graced with beautiful Irish linen and gorgeous crystal glasses, Tony never stopping pouring wine and Victoria serving a four-course meal. All that was followed by Irish coffee and other after-dinner drinks and dessert, and all the while priceless conversation and banter flowing as freely as the wine.

That first dinner, they invited friends from the village, Martin and Kathy O'Farrelly. Victoria and Tony repeatedly introduced us to their friends and family, and the window they opened allowed us to gain a foothold into making Ireland home.

During the years, through Tony and Victoria, we've met June and Bernard Duggan; Tony's brother Declan and his children Ronan and Orla; Victoria's brothers Allen, Robbie, and Pat; Tony's cousin Kate and her husband Andrew, whom Tony insists on calling "George," I'm sure because it annoys him; Tony Clark and his wife Eileen and many others. Knowing so many people who live there has immeasurably increased the pleasure we take staying in Ireland. It's added a deep dimension that simply would not have been possible. The Tracey's made us insiders and we love them for the gift.

Having dinner that evening with Martin and Kathy O'Farrelly, we learned that Tony and Martin had grown up together in Adare where, when they were youngsters, Tony's mother had been the local telephone operator in addition to being the village postmistress. Martin recalled a conversation they had about a fishing outing when they were just lads. Martin had called Tony early that day. Since at that time, all calls went through the local switchboard, Mrs. Treacy answered the phone.

"Hello, Mrs. Treacy. This is Martin. I need to talk to Tony."

"Martin, it's very early. This had better be important."

"Oh, it is, Mrs. Treacy, quite important, in fact."

"I'll put Tony on the line."

"Hello, Tony. Are we going to buy worms or dig them out of the bank by the Maigue?"

"I don't know, Martin. What do you think?"

"I think we should dig them up."

"Okay, I'll see you in an hour."

Before Martin hung up, Mrs. Treacy said, "Martin, that was *not* important." Then he heard a click. Martin stared at the phone still in his hand and thinking, *I'm dead.*

Martin and Tony roared with laughter as Martin recounted this story, both of them remembering it as though it had happened a week ago.

The village house where Victoria served dinner that night for eleven (including the six of us were the Treacy kids, one of my daughters and her husband) was the house in which Tony grew up. When Mrs. Treacy was postmistress, the part that was the post office, cage and all, was walled off from the rest of the house. Years later, Tony removed the wall and they used this area as a downstairs sitting room, that night using the area behind the cage as the bar.

Martin had wine. I had some of Tony's Special Reserve Irish whiskey. I'm not exactly the shy and retiring type and neither is Martin. It took us roughly thirty seconds to warm up to each other, Tony, of course, also right in the thick of it.

When Victoria called us to the table, everyone left the makeshift cocktail room before Martin and me. As we were about to exit, Tony, wanting to start the evening with a prank, locked us in the room.

Martin shrugged, and immediately asked me, "More of Tony's reserve whiskey?"

"Absolutely." Martin plays on an amateur water polo team, and with his seven-foot wingspan, easily reached over the counter into the caged area and got me the whiskey, then reached in again to get more wine for himself. And this is a man who knows how to pour. We sat down, continued talking the craic, and were quite comfortable when suddenly the door burst open and Tony came in yelling, "Lord, what have I done."

Martin and I smiled. We lifted our glasses to Tony, each took a healthy sip, and said "Sláinte" before we got up and slowly sauntered to the dinner table. Tony never again locked Martin or me in the old post office room.

That night at dinner wasn't a fair fight. With Tony, Martin, and me vying to outdo one another, no one else really had a fair chance to speak. And so Tony and Victoria started that evening giving us a special gift, one that continued to grow—the opportunity not only to vacation in the community, but to live in and become a part of it. Eventually, thanks to their gift of bringing us into their inner circle, and because of that, our increasing comfort and familiarity of being in Adare, and because others living and working in the village accepted us as belonging there, I'd earn the moniker of a "fierce local."

Chapter 26

The Treacy Kids

I don't know if it's the living in a quasi-country setting, or the strict but loving rules laid down by their parents, or some combination, but you know how there are some kids you want to eat with a spoon? That's how Karen and I feel about the Treacy kids: Martin, Rebecca, and Gordon. I have general reservations about cloning, but I'd clone these three in a hot second.

At the Treacy dinner parties, the three kids always join in, serving, eating with, and cleaning up after the guests, with no fuss. They know all their parents friends, so there's always a lively interchange, not just robotic and grudging behavior at the table, serving food, and clearing. Occasionally, with some cajoling, we can get Gordon to play a new piece on the piano. If these kids don't love being around their parents' friends and family, they sure do a good job of fooling me.

While we were at the cottage, they frequently came by during the day. Soon we developed this ritual. First, they'd stop in front of the cottage, where the red "Irish" door inevitably had the top half open, and they'd yell, "Hello." Then they'd go about their assigned duties: cleaning up the tack room, mowing part of the large lawns and the grass behind the cottage, giving extra feed to the horses, or mucking out stalls.

After completing their duties, they'd come to the cottage, sometimes before their mom and dad, and they'd go through Cokes like Grant going through Richmond. Karen always had an ample supply of soda and snacks, and extraordinarily, we'd just spend time with them, often with me sitting in a wing chair by the fireplace, Gordon sitting on the edge with one of his arms draped over my shoulder. The kids always gave us a kiss on their coming and their going.

Tony and Victoria would always drop in themselves, sometimes with the children, sometimes a bit later. Whenever they came by in the early evening, it was always after chores and before dinner. They almost always started the same way: "We're just coming by to say hello. We don't want to interfere, but just want to know if you need anything and how your day went. What did you do today?"

In the early stages, I'd ask if they wanted a drink and they'd always say, "No thanks." I always disregarded them and served each their preferred drinks; soon I stopped asking and just served them. Victoria's drink is a glass of white wine. Tony's drink is Bacardi and Coke, Diet Coke for a brief while after the Event. I know to put ice in Tony's glass, but always allow him to pour his own mixture, since I'd screwed up the ratio once and didn't want to repeat the mistake. One of our gifts to Tony one year was a crystal tumbler, etched "Tony's Bacardi and Coke." We also gave him and Victoria a four-sided crystal glass with an etching on each side: on one side a shamrock; on another a horse and rider jumping; on another the Claddagh logo, and on the fourth side, of course, a Magen David. Tony uses both glasses every time we're at their house.

Inevitably, we'd have a peat fire going. They'd settle in for a chat. More times than not, the answer to Tony's question about what we'd done that day was, "Not much." Then, we'd talk about local auctions (mostly antiques), upcoming horse competitions, issues at school for the children, Irish politics, and who knows what else. Tony and I always trade friendly insults. It became its own competition, almost a form of performance art. When the kids wandered outside, we'd talk about them. Often Tony would comment that we were the only Purtill guests who truly lived in the village and didn't just treat it as a vacation spot.

All three of the Treacy kids are fabulous horseback riders—of the point-and-shoot variety. As is true of many Irish riders, they don't have much patience for minor details, like how to turn a horse, or the subtleties of control. They ride. They ride as if they were born to the saddle, which they were, and they point-and-shoot their horses over jumps, figuring since they're out in huge fields, they have plenty of time to get the horse to do what they want.

The kids would come to the property to perform their duties, but also to ride their horses almost daily. They'd all taken riding lessons (as it turned out, some with John O'Hara), but as in any sport, some have a natural ability and others plod. All three of the young Treacy's, however, "got" riding. During many of the summers we were there, they went to a riding camp at Clonshire. We went to some of those classes and to some of their riding competitions at other venues where they always did well. At Purtill, they rode in their riding ring, primarily to warm up and perhaps take a few jumps just to get the feel before heading out to the cross-country course.

I earned my riding stripes at Purtill when one day during our first year, Martin asked if I wanted to ride with him. At the time, they had four horses: Ollie, Honey, Star, and Roger. Martin rode Ollie that day, allowing me to ride the largest of the group, Tony's horse Roger. After a brief time in the ring, we headed out to the cross-country course. Each time Martin took a jump, he asked if I wanted to try. I always said yes.

We jumped large logs tied down in the fields, fences in between pastures, and a "drop," which you got to by riding around the side, turning, and then jumping off a ledge. We also took the drop in reverse, heading straight for it and jumping up. We hand galloped across open fields until we came to the stream on their property. On one bank was gravel sloping to the water; on the opposite side a series of large steps, framed on the perimeter in wood, which led up to another riding field.

Martin said, "We've never tried this before. Are you game?"

"Lead on, Martin."

"Are you sure? If you hurt yourself, Dad'll kill me."

"If I don't die, I'll deal with your dad. Let's do it."

And we did, our horses bounding down the gravel, into the water, and up the steps. As we emerged on the opposite bank, we cantered in an open field, and then up and down a built-up mound of earth. We continued toward the end of one side of the property, but before reaching it, took a big looping arc to our right, and still at the canter, jumped a large tree trunk back into the open field, and then up and down another couple of earth mounds. Then we took the steps in reverse, heading down into the water and up the other side on the gravel, reentering the other field, ending our romp with a race that Martin won.

That night at the cottage Tony said, "Martin tells me you took all the jumps, including the steps into the river, and you did well." (Tony still insists the stream is a river.) "You know I haven't taken those steps yet?"

"Just trying to lead the way for you, Tony. Meanwhile, it was a grand ride. I loved it, and Martin is a terrific teacher."

Tony said, "You know, we're not set up as a horse-riding facility and have no insurance if a rider is injured, but if you're willing to take the risk, you and Karen can ride anytime you'd like."

And so, Purtill now wasn't just our own slice of heaven on earth, but also our slice of horse heaven.

Once, Karen and I rode with Martin and Rebecca to Curraghchase. It was one of our grand rides on the roads of Ireland and arriving at our destination, especially on horseback, was a thrill.

Curraghchase is now a thousand-acre forest park between Adare and Askeaton. John Hunt originally built Curragh House in the latter half of the seventeenth century, but the existing house dates from the eighteenth century. A descendant of John Hunt's, Aubrey Thomas Hunt de Vere, became a famous poet; he recorded his memories of a lake at the bottom of the house, surrounded by a rich meadow divided by a slender stream. They're all still there and still beautiful. Although the main house was accidentally destroyed by fire in 1941 and is boarded up, the lands still comprise a major tourist attraction. Since 1957, it's been owned by the state. Part of the property is used for commercial timber, but the larger part has walking trails, camping, and caravan-park facilities, and it's often used for picnicking. The day we went, many people were sprawled across the vast meadow. I could well understand a young poet being inspired by the sight of it. We were.

All three of the Treacy kids have been on a number of hunts with their dad, ostensibly so that Tony can protect them, but I'm convinced it's the other way around, because these kids have no fear and they're Grade A riders.

When Martin was in his fourth (and last) year at Clongowes, Gordon started his first year there, while Rebecca attended her school in Limerick. (Inspired that Rebecca's classes were all in Irish, Karen and I ourselves mastered Irish to the point that by the end of a few seasons, we could say, "Sláinte" every time we had a drink.) At the end of Gordon's first year at Clongowes, the school held its year-end festivities. The Treacy's invited us to join them and we happily accepted, at least happily at the time.

Victoria packed a picnic lunch. We all went in one car. The drive was about three hours. The school is in County Kildare, perhaps an hour's drive from the center of Dublin. The entry is by way of a long straight driveway from which you see the school directly ahead, possibly half a mile away. The school looks like a castle and for good reason. It was a castle. Clongowes Wood College is one of Ireland's most celebrated boys' prep schools. On the long approach were sheep on one side and cows on the other. As we drove up that entry, I swear I heard the trill of the trumpets that introduce each episode of *Masterpiece Theatre* and I'm sure I'm correct, because the whole feeling is that of a BBC production.

The school, founded in 1814 as a Jesuit school, is still run by the Jesuits. One of its attendees was James Joyce, who studied there from 1888 to 1891. Although Joyce was unable to complete his studies at Clongowes due to his father's financial troubles, he always counted his days there as some of his best. Two of his protagonists attended Clongowes: Stephen Dedalus, in *A Portrait of the Artist as a Young Man* and in *Ulysses*, and Buck Mulligan, in *Ulysses*. Mulligan is supposedly modeled after Oliver St. John Gogarty, who attended the school and whose portrait is on one of its many walls.

The school has cricket pitches, so their sweeping greens provide a dramatic setting for the castle. The day we were there, kids were running riot across the fields.

Inside the school are creaky stairways and cubicle areas for two students each, the cubicles on the side of large hallways, sealed off by pull curtains on a rod. Within each living space are two beds, drawers, and probably a 150-year-old makeshift closet, again with a draw curtain. The Jesuits are less into fancy rooms than creating worthwhile minds. As Gordon took us upstairs to his quarters, I swear I saw Harry Potter peeking around one of the corners and other wizards flying around the ancient halls on their brooms.

You can't compare Ireland's school system to the States', in part, because you can start at a school like Clongowes before what we'd view as high school age. In addition, in Ireland, when you leave a school, you take Leaving Cert Exams (Cert for Certificate), a single series of multiday exams. Regardless of your academic career, athletic accomplishments at a school, comments from teachers, or civic duties performed, your score on the certs is the sole basis for determining to which university, if any, you can be admitted and in what subject. You must attain a preset score for certain universities and areas of study. If you don't get the necessary score, you either go to a university or pursue a course of study that's not your first choice or you take the leaving cert exam again. It may sound rough, but the Irish students were the ones ready to staff the Celtic Tiger when the economy started exploding in the early nineties, and the cert system is still in place.

Martin wasn't pleased with his first Leaving Cert Exam results, so he studied for them again. He did so well the second time that he was admitted to a business school. Rebecca did exceptionally well on her initial Leaving Cert Exams and was offered a position at Trinity College Law School, which she accepted. When Tony wrote to tell us the good news, of course, he threw in, "My only fear is that she could turn out like Harvey."

My response, after chiding him for allowing his daughter to go to a "Prod school," "Let her know a position awaits her at my law firm, where we specialize in suing Irish nationals with operations in Poland." Three guesses where Tony expanded his operations.

Meanwhile, back at Clongowes, we went back outside to the car for the picnic. Just as we got there, it started spitting—not so much raining as spraying water in your face, not enough to stop anything, but enough to be annoying. Victoria, with the help of the kids, started to unload lunch. Karen and I did a lot of blowing to try to keep some feeling in our hands. Then the rain got serious.

As the skies turned menacing, Tony took out a series of metal poles and tarps, and with help from his kids, they quickly put together what looked like a gigantic jigsaw puzzle that was actually an open-sided tent. We needed it. Right when he had it put together and hoisted—Karen and I feverishly pitching in by sliding one pole into another—the heavens opened up. We had another lashin' rain, and we weren't even at the muddy Carracastle graveyard. Do you think it stopped Victoria? Not for a beat. She'd brought a picnic and by god we were going to enjoy ourselves. I kept saying to myself, *Spring. Summer. Not just fall and winter all in the same day.*

Undaunted by the weather, tents popped up all over the place. It makes no difference that a day starts with sunshine. That's just like a head fake by a football player. You can't fall for it. I swear the Irish live by the Boy Scout motto Be Prepared.

We all dug in, same as all the others in their own tents. Victoria handed out sandwiches, barbecued chicken, scones, pickles, and a variety of dips, potato chips, cookies, and even thermoses of hot tea. When she said, "Harv, you're not having enough. Here, have another sandwich," for a flash, I thought I heard my Jewish mother speaking.

About the time we finished wolfing down lunch, the weather broke enough to venture out, and we followed Tony and Victoria to some of the other tents to meet parents and friends they knew. Tony insisted that this had been a "wee rain." I thought it much closer to a Category 3 hurricane.

Finally, and thankfully, it was time to go inside again, this time for the president's welcome and the year-end ceremonies. Among those seated were many of the power brokers of the country. Over here some bigwig banker, over there the owners of McCann's Irish Oatmeal, a few rows ahead some minister in the government, and so on. After introductory speeches by the elders of the school, a few of the students spoke, and they were impressive. You could see the future leaders of the country. All the time, the Treacy kids stuck with us, except when Gordon disappeared to participate in events with his class.

In a nutshell, what makes these kids so special is that they not only help their parents without grumbling, they actually want to be part of the unit.

They enjoy the company of their peers *and* adults. They make themselves at home without being presumptuous. Their affection is genuine. When we're not in Ireland, we still stay in touch, sometimes one of them initiating contact via e-mail. None of them is afraid to hug and kiss. They all have a great sense of humor. They live privileged lives, but never act as though they're entitled to anything. Over a number of summers, Martin worked as a busboy and in the bar of the Dunraven to earn enough money to buy his own used car. He didn't expect his parents to buy him one.

Rebecca is not only kind, smart, and a brilliant rider, but she's also a blooming beauty. I embarrassed her to death one day when, all in their school uniforms, she was with two or three chums on the streets of the village. I went up to her as though we'd never met before and asked, "Miss, can you tell me how to get to Limerick?"

She rolled her eyes, but played along and gave me directions.

"Thank you," I said, and then turned as if to leave. I paused, turned back, and then said, "If you don't mind my saying so, young lady, if you'd like to be in the movies in the States, I could arrange that. You're quite beautiful and I'm a film producer."

At that, she turned as red as the hair of one of her girlfriends, all the while shaking her head and said, "Oh, gawd," and all of them ran away, giggling.

Gordy works hard at both school and play. He willingly helps Mum with her many chores. He's a serious rider. He puts on comic routines using material of some of Ireland's best comedians and sometimes coming up with his own riffs, including his impression of me. "My name is Harvey and that's hiiiilaaaaaarious." He's an accomplished musician on both the guitar and piano. He wrote a piece for the piano, which, as I explain later, saved my butt when I used it as the music for a song I wrote for the upcoming wedding of Karen's nephew David and his fiancée Maggie.

Still, I swear they're not robots. They're great kids who can't fail to accomplish important things in their lives. We love them and critically, they love us back. At one point Tony told us, "You know the kids think of you as their grandparents."

"Couldn't that be an aunt and uncle?" I asked.

Grandparents, aunt and uncle, whatever—Karen and I consider ourselves blessed to be loved by them and considered part of their family. We look forward to watching them grow into the wonderful adults we know they'll become.

Chapter 27

⌒

The Limerick Foxhounds Come Visiting

Training foxhounds is an exhausting, expensive, and time-consuming affair. Puppies are "walked out" in the summer and fall of their first year meaning they're being educated to follow commands of the huntsman, the person with primary responsibility for the hounds in the kennels and on hunts, and they're getting physically fit. The goal is to "enter" the puppies into the pack, which occurs when a hound first hunts. But you don't want that occurring during a real hunt in case they don't work out, so they're entered during cub hunting, or cubbing, informal hunting in the late summer or early fall before the formal hunting season begins.

For the puppies, cubbing is to hunting as Olympic trials are to the Olympics. In both, you've got to pass tests to make it to the big time. So every summer in the early morning, the huntsman sets off on a training exercise, typically with twenty-five to thirty pairs of hounds. (Hounds are always counted in couples.) The huntsman teams a trained hound with a puppy. In this way, the trained one demonstrates proper protocol, and when the huntsman gives a command and all the trained hounds respond correctly, by their conduct they bring the puppies into line—sort of. In fact, some members of the staff carry on hunts several two-strap hound collars connected by a swivel link. Though it's rare for hounds to be coupled, whippers-in—assistants to the huntsman—still carry these straps on hunts in case a puppy needs help.

During summer training, the puppies, full of energy, love to run and play, but the huntsman never lets them feel too free. He starts their training well before he takes them on the morning romps on roads and across pastures, and it's all geared toward his ability, and that of the whippers-in, to control them. Otherwise, you'd have mayhem on a hunt, with the hounds doing whatever they want, rather than participating in an organized manner. You don't want a hound dwelling, or failing to hunt forward, because then he's more likely to be separated from the pack. Even with all the practice, though, it still happens that one will get lost and the huntsman ends up tracking him down sometimes for hours, after the hunt. Once, the huntsman of the County Limerick Foxhounds, Will Bryer, came back with one that a farmer had shot and killed. Control of these animals at all times is paramount.

During the summer training of the Limerick Foxhounds puppies, Will rides his bicycle, always with at least one other person and sometimes two, to help him keep the hounds in order. He takes them on back roads and across fields, all the while running them in pairs and checking to make sure the young ones heed his commands. He's not only training them to obey him, but he's also getting them and himself fit—during a hunt, the physical task is grueling for everyone.

Club members can choose their hunts, the staff rides in all of them, and during the season that can mean two or three times a week. So the huntsman, the staff, and the hounds, like all good athletes, must train hard to be in shape. If they can handle the physical training during the summer when it can be pretty warm, they'll certainly be able to handle hunts during the winter months.

In 2004, our second year at Purtill, one of my law partners, Vicki, and her husband, Michael, visited us as part of their Irish holiday. They owned and loved dogs, so without forewarning them, we asked Tony if he could arrange, if possible, for Will to visit us at Purtill with a few of the hounds.

Several mornings later at about seven, the doorbell rang. Now, it's a gross understatement to say that Karen and I aren't early risers. On the other hand, in the Irish countryside, you don't often have your doorbell rung in error, especially at that time of day. I stumbled out of bed and opened the door, but no one was there. I was still getting the cobwebs out of my brain, trying to figure out what was going on, when I heard barking at the back of the cottage.

Then Vicki screamed, "It's a million dogs!" (Had Tony been there, he'd have corrected her. As he's told me often, "A hound is *always* a hound, *never* a dog.")

I looked out one of the back windows and saw the entire backyard filled with happy animals, yelping and running in circles. "Kar!" I shouted, "It's the hounds!"

All four of us ran out the backdoor in our pajamas. (Vicki was much more proper and bothered to put on a robe.) We found ourselves in a figurative sea of hounds, all excited, yelping, and running around within the confined space in the back of the cottage.

I spotted Will. He smiled and saluted us. Over the whelping pack Will yelled, "Top of the morning to you. Tony said you might want to see a few of the hounds. Is it okay for them to jump up?"

I screamed back, "Yes! It's okay!" I didn't know what I was agreeing to. Soon I thought we were done for, as these meaty animals excitedly jumped on us, and not with the daintiest of paws and claws.

Then I heard Will yelling, "Leave it, Sequin! Git back, Saracen!" as they got a wee bit too playful.

I looked at Will with a somewhat quizzical glance, and then edged close enough to ask, "You know all their names?"

"You have to know them all, so your commands are pointed."

"Yeah, but there have to be thirty pairs here, and I know if I said this about races of people, I'd be called a politically incorrect pig, but they all look alike."

"Not when you get to know them. Artemis! Leave it!"

We offered Will and his helpers' tea and scones, a required bit of Irish hospitality, and they gratefully accepted; they'd already been out for a few hours and were hungry. We joined them outside, eating and drinking tea among the controlled mayhem of a pack of hounds, with one occasionally deciding she wanted a sip, sloshing our tea on us or trying for a bite of a scone. Will, ever at the ready, was always there with a "No, Arnica!"

Arnica, after her sneak attack, slinked down, put her tail between her legs, skulked a foot or two away and five seconds later, was barking, and wagging her tail again.

I'd ridden to the hounds in Ruan, but the sensation of being around them when you're mounted on a horse, as compared to being in the midst of sixty of them while standing on the ground, is an entirely different and humbling experience. When you're in a hunt, the hounds are tearing ahead of you, working the line, and carrying a head (running well together where the scent is wide enough that the whole pack gets it) and in full cry. It's an exhilarating experience and a somewhat blurry adrenaline rush. When you're standing among them, you get a much better idea of their size and see what finely tuned athletes they are. When one of them jumps on you with his hind feet off the ground, his giant front paws are well up the side of your chest. Yet they'll obey even your command to get down, when given firmly and clearly.

I dashed inside for my camera. One of my favorite photos is of Will getting on his bike to leave amid a sea of backsides of hounds.

Before leaving, Will thanked us for the tea and scones and said he hoped to see me on a hunt sometime with the Limerick Foxhounds. We thanked him for the gift of visiting us with his hounds, and he was off, riding his bicycle down Purtill's long back drive with the pack trailing after him, their tails high in the air, Vicki running wildly after them, waving. Within moments, all was quiet.

I stood still in the thrill of the moment and thought, *Wow. Can I do it? How grand would that be if the next time I saw Will and the hounds I was mounted and riding in a hunt with the County Limerick Foxhounds? Do I still have the stamina? Damn, I'd love to experience it again, at least once, if not twice, what the hell. Make that ten times more. We'll see.*

As the four of us reentered the cottage, it took us a good thirty minutes to calm down. We relived the excitement with cup after cup of tea. We'd given Vicki and Michael something to remember for the rest of their lives, and not bad for us either.

By 2005, the Treacy's had built a house on the thirty acres. In the spring of that year, Will and his helpers were back again, this time ringing our doorbell at the cottage before continuing down to Victoria and Tony's house where Karen and I went dashing down to join them.

Will asked Tony if he could take the hounds into the field where the Treacy's had their sheep. When Tony said, "Sure," I asked Will why.

He explained, "During a hunt, as huntsman I don't want the hounds to 'riot,' or go after the wrong quarry. If they do, I'd have to 'rate' them."

"What does that mean?"

"It means giving them a voice command to get them to stop. Then I'd have to regroup them, and then get them to pursue the correct quarry. The time it takes to regain control of a pack disrupts a hunt and that's a bad result."

"So going into Tony and Victoria's field is sort of a test for the puppies?"

"Exactly. It's all part of their training. Many of them will want to go after these sheep. My job is to prevent that. I need to train them to learn the scent, but to disregard it."

With that, Will, one of his helpers, and the hounds entered the field. It was fascinating to watch Will's control and patience and to see the trained hounds keep the younger and wilder ones at bay while the sheep looked like an ink blot, weaving together this way and that across the pasture.

After returning from the field, Victoria put out tea, scones, and toast. She made the mistake, however, of putting some tea on one of the kid's trampolines and quicker than you could say "Saintly," Saintly was up on the trampoline, jumping and sloshing the tea all over the place.

Then, it was off to Harvey Island, a rich local landmark, which, along with Harvey Lake, I explain a bit later. A few of the puppies had already jumped into the lake, while the better trained hounds looked longingly to Will for permission. When he gave it, about thirty of them jumped in and started swimming with the relish of Olympians.

It was a brief treat. Just as when Vicki and Michael were with us, Will had no time to dillydally. He had to be moving his athletes on all too soon and ordered them out of the lake. The hounds obeyed, shook themselves vociferously, barked, ears flopping with each bark, and then they were gone.

Meanwhile, by invitation of the Joint Masters of the County Limerick Foxhounds, Karen and I attended a puppy show that same summer on the Clonshire grounds, where Will put the puppies through a series of exercises in front of judges wearing derbies and formal dress. This show pleased the entire admiring crowd, us included.

Best of all, we were so inspired by the experience of Will's first visit to us with the hounds in the summer of '04, we returned that same winter for me to live the dream I'd dreamed earlier: to ride to the hounds with Will and the County Limerick Foxhounds.

Rebecca, Harvey, Martin, Karen and Gordon Celebrate
Horse Competition Awards Won By All of the Treacy Kids

The Limerick Foxhounds Come Visiting

Will, the Hounds and the Ewes

Will and the Hounds Leaving Purtill for More Exercising

Chapter 28

⌒

President Bush Visits Ireland, Sort of

During the summer of 2004, President George Bush attended a European Union meeting in Ireland on his way to another meeting in Turkey.

Now, to say that President Bush was unpopular with the Irish is a bit like saying King George III was unpopular with the antimonarchist American colonists. Whenever I talked international politics in Ireland, whether with a stranger at a pub or with friends who didn't know my views, they always asked in a roundabout manner what I thought of our president. When I say roundabout, I mean true circumlocution.

"So now, it seems yer country has lots of troops in Eyeraq."

"Yes, we certainly do."

"So it seems yer president thinks he can fix things over there nice 'n' easy."

"Yes, it does seem that way."

"So, do you think that many wars get fixed easy like?"

"No, I don't, which is why most career military officers want to use war as a last, not a first, option."

"Ah, so are you sayin' now maybe things aren't goin' so well for the US of A in Eyeraq?"

"I'd say they're a mess. We had no business invading. We'll probably end up making matters worse, and our president is an eejit."

Shoulders all around relaxed. Smiles broke out. Someone always said, "Sean, buy this man a drink." I got lots of free pints, courtesy of George W.

A number of US presidents visited Ireland previously. Of course, JFK was revered there, Ronald Reagan received a warm welcome, as did Richard Nixon, and the Irish were more than welcoming to Bill Clinton. They were mad for him. He was smart. He was a wonk, but not a geek. He handled difficult situations with seeming agility. They admired him for his winning manner, and because he was the first president to invest substantial energy and prestige on the ongoing problems in Northern Ireland that continued to plague Catholics and Protestants, Irish and British. And probably most of all, he was a fabulous speaker with a wonderful wit. That he'd had sexual escapades and lied under oath about them changed virtually no Irishman's view of him. They were well familiar with scoundrel Irish politicians, many of whom had done far worse. Bottom line: the man would be perfect in a pub.

Not so with President Bush. Smart or not, he was a smirker and the Irish don't like smugness. He had enough difficulty delivering prepared speeches, even when in front of prepackaged, friendly crowds. His performance by most standards, and certainly by an Irish one, was that the man was incapable of verbally thrusting and parrying.

While many disagreed with the president's policies in Iraq, worst of all, he was arrogant. The Irish could never get over the president's dismissive attitude toward any who disagreed with his views. In a way, this was funny coming from the Irish. I've seen many a pigheaded Irishman whose views you couldn't move with a Mack truck. Perhaps the difference was that the pigheaded Irishman still had a wittiness about him that the president simply didn't share, so even though you started by wanting to thrash the pigheaded Irishman for his stubbornness, you ended up charmed by the linguistic agility with which he pulled himself out of a hole that initially he'd dug himself into. With President Bush, most Irishmen saw no wit or charm, just the bullheadedness, so they just wanted to thrash him. The final Irish verdict: guilty of being an ugly American.

My cousin Sheila, the one to offer the advice about fish and visitors, often came from London to spend some time with us (never more than three days) at the cottage. As luck would have it, in 2004 her scheduled departure from Shannon Airport was on June 25, the day the president was due to land. News reports abounded about his impending arrival. There were stories that for up to four months prior to "himself's" arrival, the gardai had gone door to door within a certain distance of the airport to take the names of everyone living there and anyone expected at the time of the imperial visit. Grumbling that had started at a low hum over this intrusion, built in intensity as the time of the visit neared. Reports aired that the entire airport would be closed for up to two hours before the president's arrival and for some unstated time thereafter.

However, on the day Sheila was leaving, it was reported that though the airport wouldn't close entirely, security would be tight. On the way to the airport, I saw perhaps forty tanks on the highway. "Tanks? Are the Russians invading?" Sheila thought not. Then I saw protesters on bridge overpasses. (On the news that night it looked as though they were on the grounds of the airport, but they actually were five miles away.) The Irish government was taking no chances of some horrible incident taking place on its watch especially with the general dislike the Irish held for the president.

When you arrive at Shannon Airport, you stop at a garda station— theoretically. In my experience, the station and its gate were more for show than an actual checkpoint. In my many prior experiences, the officer just waved us through. Not on that day. "Why are you here? Open your boot. Drive slowly. You can't pull up to the airport. You must go into the car park and walk to the departure lounge."

When I pulled up to the car park, again I saw something I'd never seen previously: police at the entry, recording the name and license number of every car entering. "How long will you be here?"

"Well, my wife and I aren't leaving until July seventeenth."

"Not in Ireland! How long will you be in the car park?"

"Oh, well, I'm just dropping off my cousin, so no more than twenty minutes, I'd guess."

The officer wrote down my license number in a book and on a slip of paper, he handed me, noting the time I'd arrived and my estimated time of departure. "Show this slip to an officer when you leave."

After leaving Sheila to her own fates, as I was walking back to the car, I had in my hand the piece of paper on which the officer had recorded the time of my arrival, my estimated departure, and my license plate number. I have this personality quirk, which perhaps I'll try and soften in my next life; often I end up checking things most people wouldn't even consider, let alone, check. It probably comes from my training as a trial lawyer. I was taught to look at prospective jurors' shoes, their books and magazines, the cut of their hair, their jewelry, their clothes—anything to get a clue into who they were, far more telling than their canned answers to such trailblazing questions as, "Can you be fair in this case?" What did I see on the paper? The arrival and departure times were correct, but the license plate number was wrong by one digit. *Uh oh.*

Did you ever hear the joke about the guy going next door to ask his neighbor if he could borrow his lawn mower? On his way over, he says to himself, *I'm sure he'll lend it to me. Why wouldn't he? I've lent him mine. Would he think I'd use his improperly? Maybe he'll think I don't have adequate insurance in case there's an accident. I've seen him be rude before and maybe he will be again, but why? What have I ever done to him?* When the man rings the doorbell and the neighbor opens the door, the guy says, "Keep your damn lawn mower! I don't really need it anyway!"

Well, I was in that state of mind concerning how to deal with the garda who'd check my slip as I exited the lot. I was considering what to say, *It's not my fault, officer, that someone else recorded my license number wrong. I understand it's no joking matter and I'm not being sarcastic. Would you like me to pull over so you can look at my driver's license? Inspect the boot? Call a local who can vouch for me?* As I got closer to the exit, I started getting peeved, thinking, *Why should I have to waste a few hours going through a security check just because of some eejit's mistake in copying numbers?*

When I got to the exit, there was no garda. I just pulled out and was on my way. After all, this was Ireland, where there's often a lot of fanfare about what will happen, and then a bit of a lackadaisical follow-through—unless it has to do with horses, a business deal, or eating. What was the title of that book I'd read? Oh yes, *Don't Sweat the Small Stuff and It's All Small Stuff* by Richard Carlson. I thought it all made sense when I read it. *Yeah, but Richard Carlson would have gotten himself worked up too. I don't care what he says.*

On the highway returning to Adare, every exit for about a ten-mile stretch was sealed to all traffic with tanks, police cars with flashing lights, and about ten officers standing guard. No one was allowed off the highway. According to news reports, some locals who lived as close as a kilometer or so from a particular exit had to make a thirty-kilometer detour to get to their homes if they hadn't previously arranged for special passes. It's funny how for those we love, we'll take just about anything, but for those we don't, every inconvenience becomes monumental.

In all, President Bush remained in Ireland a total of eighteen hours, which cost the Irish government an estimated three million euro in security costs.

According to one Irish blog, titled "Irish Batten Down Hatches for Bush," "Six thousand police and Irish army personnel and nearly one thousand US and private security guards shut down a swath of County Clare, roughly one-third of the entire country's security forces."

A piece in an Irish newspaper noted, "It was the biggest ring of steel ever mounted here …" and "… everywhere you looked there were guys with short haircuts talking up their sleeves." All Irish understood that security for the president was necessary, but I've still not found one Irishman who thought the money was well spent. One fellow in a pub said, "You know how much it cost us to protect yer president when he was in Eire for less than a full day?"

"I do."

"Well, next time you see him, tell him that many of us t'ink the money would have been better spent if our government instead had bought a pint for every Irishman in the country."

"I'll tell him."

A day or two after the imperial visit, news started to circulate that the president had been interviewed at the White House on June 24 by an Irish journalist, Carole Coleman. From the White House perspective, it was good PR to grant an interview to an Irish journalist the day before Bush was to arrive in Ireland, knowing the interview would likely get good airtime there, although probably after he'd already left the country. It got plenty of play all right, but not with the reaction the president had hoped. Instead, it forever cemented the Irish disdain of George W. Bush.

Ms. Coleman started the interview by asking, "Mr. President, you're going to arrive in Ireland in about twenty-four hours time, and no doubt you will be welcomed by our political leaders. Unfortunately, the majority of our public does not welcome your visit, because they're angry over Iraq, they're angry over Abu Ghraib. Are you bothered by what Irish people think?" So, this journalist wasn't leading with powder-puff stuff.

The president gave his usual answer about the necessity of fighting terrorism.

Ms. Coleman said, "But Mr. President, the world is a far more dangerous place today. I don't know whether you can see that or not."

Bush didn't appear to like the challenging nature of the question, but undaunted, Ms. Coleman went for the jugular. "I think there is a feeling that the world has become a more dangerous place because you have taken the focus off al-Qaeda and diverted it into Iraq."

The president dissimulated and talked about how brutal Saddam Hussein had been and had used weapons of mass destruction against his own people.

Ms. Coleman pressed, "Indeed, Mr. President, but you didn't find the weapons of mass destruction."

Bush sputtered with obvious exasperation, "Let me finish. Let me finish! May I finish?"

I've seen the entire interview. In all, it lasted eleven minutes. During that time, the president showed visible irritation when, on occasion, Ms. Coleman wouldn't accept an answer. For Coleman's part, it was irrelevant to her that she was interviewing the President of the United States. She wasn't some sycophantic American reporter without the guts to challenge face-to-face the most powerful person in the world. She was an *Irish* journalist and the Irish had plenty of skepticism about their own politicians and didn't view them, or the president, as untouchable. The president was a guy with power who, in her view, had made serious blunders, and she damn well intended not to let him off the hook with canned and meaningless answers. So she posed and then followed up with challenging questions when he gave what she viewed as evasive responses. In all, five times Bush chastised Coleman for not letting him complete his answer.

Obviously, he and apparently his handlers didn't understand that it's not the Irish way to accept a politician's evasive, nonengaging responses and worse, answers that show no wit and no charm. Ireland is the land of craic, for God's sake; it's a country of oral give and take, back and forth. Out of simple politeness, an Irishman will use an indirect technique of learning a Yank stranger's political views, but when it comes to an interview of a politician, the Irish have no patience for answers that are blather, more blather, and still more blather. They'll just shake their heads and promptly put that person on the gobshite list and once you're on that list, you don't get off.

It's clear that Ms. Coleman didn't buy into the game of allowing the President of the United States carte blanche in an interview. It's also obvious that the president was utterly unprepared for an Irish journalist's propensity to challenge and call to task *any* politician for failing to answer questions on his policies.

Taking the Irish impression of the president from bad to ridiculous, because of Ms. Coleman's "aggressive" interviewing, the White House lodged a formal complaint with the Irish Embassy and canceled Ms. Coleman's scheduled interview for the following day with the First Lady as punishment for her "rude" manner.

If the interview had been intended as some sort of a public relations coup, from the Irish perspective, it should have engendered a coup d'état. The title of one article, published in the *International Herald Tribune*, summed up much of the Irish feeling about the president's performance: "You, Sir, Are No Kennedy, Reagan, or Clinton."

The US invasion of Iraq, and the use of Shannon Airport as a way station for getting US troops to Iraq, were hugely unpopular in Ireland. Beyond the president's high-handedness, a subtlety the White House likely didn't even understand is that from a historical perspective, England isn't exactly Ireland's favorite country, but England was the primary ally of the United States in Iraq. Ireland's neutrality during The Emergency (World

War II) may have been more attributable to its hatred of Great Britain than to its views about Nazi Germany. No doubt, an undercurrent in the Irish anger over the invasion in Iraq had to be understood by its seeing England as complicit in the massive military intrusion into another country, just as it had invaded, occupied, and repressed Ireland going back more than eight hundred years. The use of torture on the US watch, as the British had tortured and executed Irish prisoners over the centuries, also didn't help.

So in fairness, even before the Coleman interview, the president and his policies were much disliked in Ireland. It would have taken a master of language and charm to change many views. However, the interview solidified the opinion of most in Ireland that the president was pompous, inflexible, thin-skinned, and perhaps most inexcusably, incapable of the art of craic.

One paper, quoting a blogger, summarized much of the Irish sentiment about President Bush: "It was the general Irish public that were embarrassed by the antics of their political leaders in the presence of the US President, who many thought should be indicted rather than invited." Ouch.

Still, I heard toasts about the president: "May the wind always be at his back and may it keep blowing him—far away from Ireland."

Chapter 29

Roger the Hammer

Two days before the end of our summer stay at Purtill in 2004 and before my planned upcoming hunt that winter, I decided to have one final ride on Roger. Big mistake.

All of the Treacy's horses stay in large open fields. Karen and I had long since learned that when trying to catch a horse in a pasture the best approach was to speak softly but carry a big carrot. So when we went to fetch Roger, we were well armed with enough carrots to lure Roger, keep the other horses satisfied while I put a halter and lead rope on the big guy, and then lead him out of the field. Roger came for his carrots, and I got on his halter and lead rope. He was happily munching away when I heard Karen yell, "You're letting Ollie get too close to him!" Too late.

When Roger gets nervous, he lifts one of his front legs and stomps. As Ollie crowded him, that's what he did. Unfortunately, the only thing between Roger's leg and the ground was my left foot. With Roger wearing shoes, his piston-like action was like a twelve hundred-pound metal hammer smashing down, in this case, on my large toe.

Ordinarily, I'd use the word exquisite to refer to something beautiful, but I can think of no more perfect word to describe the pain when Roger's foot stomped mine. My grip of the lead rope and the strength of Roger's neck was all that kept me from falling flat on my face. I couldn't speak. I stumbled forward, gulping air.

Karen ran to me. She removed the halter and lead rope. With my arm draped over Karen's neck, I hobbled back to the cottage. By then, some of the shock had worn off and the pain was now constant. I could feel my leg swelling inside my boot (this seems to be a habit of mine). I had to get it off quickly or I might not be able to get if off at all, and the boot would look silly as a permanent fixture. I also knew that the pain of pulling my leg out of the boot would probably not be much fun. I was right, but with Karen as my boot jack, we got it off.

I was hoping I was being a drama queen. Unfortunately, that wasn't the case. What we eventually saw could have been videoed for later use as a segment in some medical training film to demonstrate what some poor eejit looked like after a steamroller ran over his toe. Karen had to cut the leg of my riding pants to get them off because riding pants constrict at the calf and pulling anything tight over my toe was getting less tolerable. An additional challenge was removing the sock, which was essentially matted into my toe with blood. Karen ran water in a bathtub. With her help, I made it to the tub and put my foot into the water. It, too, could have been filmed for later use, this one in some *Jaws* movie, as the tub quickly took on the look of a bloody watery gravesite of some victim of a shark attack. I was having a rough day.

I was in no shape to drive and Karen hadn't driven a standard shift in years. This was a bad time to start again, especially British-style, with the gear shifter and the driving on the left side of the road. Tony and Victoria couldn't help. They were in France. That was the problem with the Celtic Tiger. The Irish could afford to take holidays, so they weren't around when I had a horse stomp on my toe. We considered calling other local friends, but decided no one could help much unless I was going to a hospital.

We considered calling an ambulance, but figured most likely, that would mean being admitted. Scheduled to depart in thirty-six hours, I couldn't be admitted to a hospital and make the flight. On the other hand, I had absolutely no idea how I could possibly drive the car to the airport, anyway. Even the thought of having to use my foot to push in a clutch made me shiver.

The water had relieved some of the matted blood so eventually, Karen got the sock off. To stop the bleeding, she cut some socks into makeshift bandages. Before she tried to wrap one around my toe, she gave me a Tylenol. It did nothing to diminish the pain. I asked for morphine. We had none. I asked for a gun to shoot myself. We had none. But asking for the gun reminded me of the time-honored scene from any number of good old Westerns where the local doctor gives the cowboy a bottle of whiskey to drink before he digs a bullet out of the cowboy's chest. I asked Karen to bring me my single malt scotch. Hey, since I was playing this scene, at least I'd do it with good quality stuff.

I took a swig, and then said, "Little lady, if you're aimin' to wrap this toe, I think I need more than just a girly swig," so I drank up. Not since college had I intentionally drunk too much, but I sure as hell did so that afternoon. After I was feeling good and tipsy, Nurse Nightingale proceeded to wrap my toe.

Sleep isn't exactly the word I'd use for what I did that night, and I kept thinking I should have a bullet to bite on, another time-honored scene in many a Western.

Morning finally arrived just in time to go through another round of dunk the foot in a tub of water to get off the sock bandage and put on a new one. I proved to myself that I'm not an alcoholic. The idea of drinking single malt in the morning was about as appealing as looking at my toe. I spent the rest of that day flat on my back while Karen finished packing.

We were scheduled to catch an 8:00 a.m. flight the next morning—if I could fall sleep, if I could get up at four, if I could walk to the car, if I could drive the car, if I could get through the airport, and if I could handle all the traveling. Even by my standards, there were a hell of a lot of ifs.

Later that afternoon, Karen cut a hole in a slipper so I could move around. I limped out to see Roger. He told me he was sorry and that he hadn't meant it. I told him I knew that, but that he really needed to work on not getting so spooked. Still, over the fence, I gave him a carrot, patted his neck, and told him I knew that he'd just acted naturally and I was the eejit. He shook his head up and down. I also told him that next year

I promised not to put him in a crowded situation. He thanked me and asked for another carrot. I gave him two.

Karen made some calls to the various airlines to arrange for a wheelchair at every necessary point. On our way to Shannon Airport, we stopped at the Heritage Center where Karen bought a Shillelagh walking cane, both as a means of helping me walk, but also to whack anyone over the head if they got too close to my toe. The forty-five minute drive to the airport with a mangled toe was a challenge. I kept thinking, *Where's my whiskey? Where's that damn bullet?* And I'm sure I affected every conceivable facial contortion and uttered a few grunts and epithets here and there, but we made it.

Although I don't recommend traveling with a bloodied foot, I must say that it got us around some bureaucratic corners. Helpers from the two airlines ushered us past lines that otherwise would have been good forty-five minute waits. I kept a long face and a dangling leg for all to see and to quell any prospective riots.

The day after we arrived home, I went to a podiatrist. After X-rays confirmed (to my utter astonishment) that I had no broken bones, I was seated in the doctor's examining room. Karen was lecturing me. "Don't be a macho eejit. What he's going to do will no doubt hurt, so ask him to inject your foot."

"We'll see."

"Don't 'we'll see' me. I know what that means. You're going to be a macho eejit. Ask for the damn injection."

The doctor came into the room and before he removed the bandages, he asked for my medical history. I gave him the short version. His eyes still twirled. He then removed the bandage and said, "Holy shit! Well, we better numb this baby up before I go to work."

The toenail has never been the same beautiful thing it was before Roger used it for batting practice. Even so, it took a year to grow back fully. By the time we returned that winter for my second hunt, I felt no pain from the toe, but I had another problem, a purple one.

Meanwhile, when we returned to Purtill for the hunt, the first time I went into the field to see Roger I had carrots, but Teddy Roosevelt would be happy to know that though I didn't carry a big stick, I did carry a big whip.

Chapter 30

⌒

The Purple People Eater

During our stay at Purtill during the summer of 2004, we managed
to ride, ride, ride. This was our second season at the cottage and
since Victoria and Tony allowed us to use their horses whenever we wanted
to, we routinely rode in the ring, on the cross-country course, and what we
came to learn the Treacy's called the loop. It was a circle that, on our first
time trying to get to Purtill, we'd unwittingly traveled several times.

The long driveway by which we'd entered doesn't end at the cottage,
but continues past it and exits onto another road at the opposite end of
the property. By going down either drive and onto the road and looping
around to the entry point of the opposite end of the drive, you're taking
the loop, a circle of two to three miles. It's a pleasant ride or walk after you
get the hang of hearing cars coming from behind you and pulling yourself,
or your horse, to the side, to allow the cars to pass.

I also continued to have the vision of riding to the hounds that Will
spurred, in part, by his visit and fueled by the considerable riding Karen and
I did that trip. Before we left the States, Karen and I had a serious talk about
the hunt. She worried that with my disease, I wouldn't be able to handle the
physical rigors of another one. I wanted to do at least one more before my
disease stripped me of my ability to endure it. At that point, particularly
after doing some hard riding that trip, I still felt capable of handling another

hunt. I promised Karen that if I participated in one, I'd pull out if I felt disease tired, which is different from normal tired. I know the difference, and I knew that riding in a hunt disease tired, I'd put my horse and myself at an added risk, which I wouldn't do. Reluctantly, she agreed.

So we booked Purtill for that winter and I looked forward to riding in another hunt, this time with the County Limerick Foxhounds, or LFH. Tony said he'd arrange for me to rent a horse for the hunt from Jamesy O'Shea, a member of LFH who owned a number of good horses, and he'd arrange for Jamesy to deliver the steed to the cottage a day before I arrived so that upon our arrival I could ride my mount before I'd ride in the hunt.

Before we left Ireland that summer, we had a very unIrish experience. Early one morning the doorbell rang. This was highly unusual; it's rare for anyone to drop in unexpectedly. I opened the door and two men I didn't know entered. They sat down and started talking, generally about Tony and the County Limerick Foxhounds. I was wondering who the two men were and what they wanted.

Eventually, an Irish shoe dropped. One of them said he understood I wanted a horse for a hunt that winter. Aha. So this was Jamesy. He said Tony had told him that another rider would join me in the hunt (Michael Pacelli with whom we'd ridden at Castle Leslie and Sligo years earlier), and he asked a question or two about his size and riding ability.

I'll call the second man Thomas, to whom I took an instant dislike. He was cocky and overbearing, acting as though he had license when we'd never even met him before. He went into the bedroom where Karen was still in bed, making jokes about tickling her and telling her it was too late not to be up and about. When I went in after him, he quickly rejoined Jamesy who asked a few more questions, and then made his excuses for the two of them to leave. I learned later that Jamesy is shy and didn't want to come alone, but wanted to meet me to get an idea of what size horses to have ready for Michael and me. It was unfortunate that Thomas was his companion that day.

Let's leave it at this. Thomas remains on my short list of Irish assholes, and I say that after I've had a good deal of time to reflect on it—and after an additional experience with him.

A week or so before we were scheduled to return to Ireland for the hunt, I was getting in some final practice tune-ups by taking a jump lesson on a cross-country course. By then, Roger's handiwork on my toe didn't prevent me from riding. Near the end of the lesson, I took one jump, and prepared to take another at a sharp angle. The second jump was a broad, but narrow tree trunk, and I wasn't coming in perpendicular enough. I should have heard J. Michael Plumb's lecture in my head, pulled my horse away, taken him in a circle, and lined him up properly. Instead, I tried to force the narrow jump at a bad angle and my horse refused.

The force of his refusal, strongly pulling out to his right, twisted my body radically. I'm both blessed and cursed with what one instructor dubbed "paralyzingly strong legs." They managed to hold me in the saddle, but the full impact of the twisting motion was extreme. From the pain, I knew instantly I'd hurt myself in the right groin, and I more or less slid off the horse. I've never been one to complain about pain, and I didn't then. My instructor knew about my back surgeries and disease; she also knew how nervous Karen felt whenever I jumped, fearing that a fall could cause injuries more severe than usual. I stayed on the ground for ten seconds or so, catching my breath as my horse took off. Another rider went after him.

My instructor asked, "Are you okay, Harvey? That looked bad."

"I'm okay. It just winded me."

"Do you want to call it a day?"

"No. I can't end without finishing the jump. You know that. You've always taught me, 'never end on a bad jump; always end on a good one'."

"If you *really* think you're up to it."

Karen was standing ten feet from me, knowing at times like these to let me gather myself. But as I slowly got up, she came to me and said, "Don't be foolish about this. Are you sure you don't want to end it here?"

"I'm sure. I need for my horse and me to finish on a good note."

By then someone had returned my horse. Slowly I remounted, took the jump I'd blown, a few more jumps, and ended the lesson.

From there, Karen and I went to lunch. When I got up to go to the bathroom, I knew I was in trouble. I had a pronounced limp and felt swelling from my groin all the way down to my ankle. By the time we got home, I could barely get my boot off. There I go again.

I don't know if you're old enough to remember the song "Purple People Eater," but within a few days, that was me. Neither Karen nor I had ever seen anything like it. Literally, from my waist down to my toes, I was purple and so was everything in between, and I mean everything. I was walking gingerly. A few days later, shortly before our scheduled departure for Ireland and the hunt, I went for regularly scheduled blood tests and a visit with my oncologist.

Usually, only Karen and I see him, and Karen stays in the room when he examines me. That day Ashley was with us, so Karen left the room with her. To avoid alarming his patient, Doctor Damon rarely emotes, especially if what he's viewing is troubling. However, when he saw my injury, he pulled his head back, shook it, hunched his shoulders and said, "Wow! You've lost a good quarter of your blood to internal bleeding. This is bad!"

At that time, of the many medications I was taking, I was self-injecting Aranesp twice monthly, typically used by chemo patients artificially to build up red blood cells before they can take more chemo. In my case, I was taking the injections because even without chemo, my disease caused a decrease in red blood cells.

"I know you took your regular Aranesp injection within the week, but I'm giving you another one today."

You don't give these injections lightly. Each costs a bundle, so I knew the doctor thought this was serious.

"Karen and I are planning on leaving for Ireland within a few days."

"That's okay. I don't have a problem with that."

"Yeah, but I was, uh, planning on going on a foxhunt. What do you think?"

Before answering, Doctor Damon looked at me, sort of cocked his head, and furrowed his brow in a way that left no doubt he was wondering if I was crazy, suicidal, or both. "A foxhunt? Isn't that hard and dangerous riding?"

"Well, it's certainly not easy and to be honest, with these injuries, it may be too painful just to sit in a saddle let alone ride. And if I can start the hunt, but find it too difficult or painful to continue, I'll take myself out of it. So, what do you think? Is it okay for me to try?"

"Look, you know a good deal about your disease."

I knew.

"You know the symptoms."

I knew them.

"You've reported most of them to me: anemia, relentless exhaustion, abdominal discomfort, and night sweats. Also, as you know and as we can see, easy bruising and easy bleeding, plus fevers, frequent infections, bone pain and ..." he paused for dramatic effect, "... a grossly enlarged spleen."

I knew.

"You know the complications: hypertension, ruptured veins, tumors, gastrointestinal bleeding, coughing up blood, compression of the spinal cord, seizures, dropping platelets, and an increased inability to clot, gout, and to wrap-up the partial list, acute leukemia."

I knew.

As Dr. Demon had put it so clearly years earlier, "Not great."

After patiently listening to his uplifting reminder of some of the symptoms and complications of the disease, and needing to prove myself a complete idiot, I asked, "So, can I ride in the hunt?"

"Your spleen is enlarged, because it's engorged with blood."

I knew. He examined and measured it every time I saw him.

"I've followed you for four years now. Your spleen has gotten larger and that's dangerous. We can surgically remove it, but then your only remaining primary line of defense for increased blood-cell production is your liver. You can live without a spleen; you can't live without a liver, so one of the few reasons we do a splenectomy is if your spleen is in danger of bursting. Why?"

I knew, but I also knew he was about to remind me.

"Because if it bursts, it will kill you. So if you fall off a horse and onto your spleen, it will burst, and you'll never even get to a hospital. You'll just bleed out where you fall."

I thought, *Thank God Karen isn't in the room to hear that answer.*

"So what you're saying is that I should be *really* careful."

He gave me the kind of look a frustrated parent gives a recalcitrant child—that "I've-tried-my best" look.

When Karen and Ashley reentered the room, Karen asked, "Well, doctor, how bad are his injuries and how is his spleen?"

"The injury is bad, bad enough that I'm giving him more Aranesp today, and as for his spleen, I've told Harvey …"

Oh, no! He's not going to …

"… that if he falls …"

… rat me out, is he?

"… off his horse and onto his spleen …"

No! No!

"… it likely will kill him."

Bastard, I said to myself.

The silence in the room was palpable. Have you ever noticed how a dead silence can roar like a train? Karen stared at the doctor for a full five seconds absorbing what he'd just said, and then slowly turned toward me. She just tilted her head and said nothing, but her motion and silence spoke volumes. Riding in this hunt would be insane, especially since my odds of coming off my horse increased because of my purple-people-eater injury.

Later that day, I tried to console her by saying that I'd probably not be able to ride at all, so it probably wasn't an issue. Stupidly, I said, "Anyway, if I fall, I'll fall on my right side, not my left."

She looked at me and said slowly, "That is not funny."

She was right. I shut up.

Chapter 31

⌒

Hunting with the
County Limerick Foxhounds

A few days later, we arrived in Ireland. The first day there, we slept. The second day, I figured I might as well find out if I could tolerate sitting on a horse, so Karen and I tacked up Hillman, the horse waiting for me from Jamesy. (*Hillman?* Since he was the size of Turbo, Ben Bulben, One-Eyed Jack, and Roger the Hammer, I'd have named him *Mountainman.*) Using a mounting block, I didn't swing my right leg across the saddle. I inched it over as Karen held the horse steady. Ever so slowly, I sat; I stayed there a full minute allowing my body to sink into the saddle and acclimate to the feel. By the end of the minute, I said, "Maybe I can walk him around."

With Karen following on foot, I went into the riding ring and walked Hillman for five minutes in a big circle, breathing deeply and sinking deeper into the saddle. I hurt, but the longer I sat, the more the pain subsided. Then I put him in a slow posting trot. I had some pain again, but it was endurable. Karen put up a few low jumps, often used as a warm-up for jump classes. If I couldn't take those, I certainly couldn't tolerate real jumps. At a trot, I popped over the jumps a few times—Karen watching like a hawk.

She nodded yes to confirm that my position looked good.

Then we went into one of the pastures. I put Hillman into a trot to see if I could handle him at that gait in an open field. I could. Then

I put him into a canter. At first, I felt a few electric jolts, but soon my legs steadied, and I was able to stand in the stirrups. I took a jump. It felt good. I felt my position was correct, but I looked to Karen. She was nodding her head yes. A no would have ended my ambition to join my second hunt.

I took a few up and down earth banks, and it went well. Karen was still nodding her approval. After a few more good jumps and a long canter in the open field to assure that I could tolerate a bit of hard riding, I took one final jump and called it a day.

The next day was the hunt. I'd satisfied myself, and more importantly, Karen, that I could ride. The remaining question was whether I had the endurance. This time, with no silly jokes about falling on my right side, I promised Karen that if I felt disease tired during the hunt, I'd stop. With that agreement, the hunt was on and I was going to join it.

This time, the meet was at a gas station in the small nearby village of Kildimo. When we arrived, a few others were there, but as the time for the hunt drew near, cars, horse trailers, hounds, and some mounted riders began to congregate. Oirish time doesn't apply to hunts.

I lined up my horse next to a truck trailer, stood on its runner, and using it as a mount, got into the saddle with Karen on the opposite side holding Hillman still, so I didn't have to swing my leg quickly across the saddle. I was still tender, but I put the discomfort out of my head. Hey, it was nearly time to rock and roll.

Every time you mount a horse, you recheck the girth, which often loosens after mounting. Quietly, Karen came up and helped me tighten it. "Stand in your stirrups so I can see if they're even and high enough." We adjusted those as well.

"How do you feel?"

"Fine."

"Liar."

"Is that nice?"

Karen continued to serve as my groom. She even had a cloth with her to give my boots a last-minute wipe. Can't send your man off to a hunt with dirty boots.

As I started walking around, I spotted some riders I knew: Richard, the owner of the Country Dresser in Adare, the local fancy tack shop, and Sue Foley of the Clonshire Equestrian Centre. As we'd learned by that time, LFH owns Clonshire, and its net profits go toward funding the hunt club. Sue and her husband receive a salary for running the centre.

Running a hunt club is expensive. The County Limerick Foxhounds have three Masters of Foxhounds (MFH) who share the responsibilities of hiring and firing the hunt professionals, handling landowner relations, seeking out additional territory over which to hunt, and developing the pack of hounds. As it turns out, they not only donate their time, but they also pay an undisclosed amount to help cover expenses. As huntsman, Will runs the hunt as a paid professional. The club also has one paid, full time whipper-in. Because it's expensive to run a hunt club, its subscribers, or members pay an annual sub (subscription fee), and nonmembers pay a cap. The subscription fee for the LFH members is one thousand euros per season, plus a thirty-euro-per-hunt cap fee. When I rode with the club, the cap for nonmembers was two hundred euros per hunt.

As I was walking my horse around, I also saw Jamesy O'Shea, whose horse I was riding. Jamesy had two hip replacements, but he wouldn't let a small thing like that stop him from hunting. My buddy from California, Michael Pacelli, was mounted on Dolores, also rented from Jamesy. I'd wondered why Dolores was so named, since he was a gelding. I later learned the reason was that Jamesy had bought him from Dolores O'Riordan, the lead singer of the Irish rock group The Cranberries.

This time I knew to pay my cap in advance and avoid the ignominy of having others roll their eyes and shake their heads at the eejit Yank. I scouted around and learned the person to pay was Orla, who, as it turned out, was an LFH member, was going on the hunt herself, and a bit later would have a few choice words for some of the riders.

Will and the whipper-in were mounted. They wore their scarlet livery, a uniform worn only by the MFH and professional staff members. The MFH and the professionals also wore black boots with a three-or four-inch strip of brown leather at the top. Each club also has its own colors. For LFH, it's a black coat with LFH buttons on a green collar.

Only after elected a member can one wear the club's colors and then, only during a hunt.

As in Ruan, an air of excitement built as the starting time neared. This wasn't a drag hunt, so at the time I didn't know whether a fox would be killed, but was praying that wouldn't happen. Karen had allowed me to ride in a real foxhunt only because she knew how desperately I wanted to ride in at least one more, and as hard as she tried before I signed up for this one, she couldn't find a drag hunt this time.

Once again the hounds were mixing with the horses and riders, yapping excitedly, but Will and the whipper-in kept them in check, although there's no way to keep the hounds from feeling the thrill of what was about to start. I was feeling it too. Then we began to walk down the road. I turned and waved to Karen. She waved back. We picked up the trot and headed out to our first pasture. I was apprehensive to be starting a hunt again, this time with the added concern of not knowing how my purpleness would impair my ability to stay the course. Still, I knew I'd give it a hell of a try.

We headed into a pasture and took our first jump, a small ditch. This time I was prepared and didn't bobble. Immediately, the field disappeared from view and we were off, full attention straight ahead.

As soon as we disappeared into the pasture, John approached Karen. He was a Kildimo local, a past hunter, and realizing Karen was a stranger to LFH hunts, he kindly became her guide for much of the day. He took her to the likely spots where the field might again reappear, even if only as a brief and thundering blur. Unfortunately, no church was nearby so she couldn't try again to burn down Ireland by lighting candles for my safe return.

For a brief period, Michael and I tried to stay in contact with each other, but quickly gave up that effort. If you want to decrease the chance of some accident, you need to focus your attention entirely on your riding. We were flying across undulating fields, chasing the hounds, and once again my eyes tearing from the cold, wind ripping at my face, and of course, it was raining lightly.

At different times, the horses rode at different gaits, depending on whether the hounds were in full cry or working the line. At one point after we'd been riding about an hour, we slowed, as Will was looking for a covert (pronounced cover), which can be a wooded area, a copse, thick bushes, or a hedge where a fox may lie for shelter. Although it was cold, I was sweating, more so because I was wearing my jump vest beneath my riding coat to cushion my back or spleen against possibly being thrown from the horse. But I was so focused on the riding that I paid no attention to the cold, the sweat, my own exertion, or the rain, except as it kept sprinkling my eyeglasses.

Then I heard one of the riders ahead of us yell "Tallyho," a word I'd always thought meant something like onward. In fact, tallyho is a cheer raised when the quarry is spotted. But that day the yell was premature. It wasn't a fox, but another animal a member of the field had seen. Sometimes riders get overexcited and give a false alarm. Staff members (four or five spotters also work with the huntsman to help him spot the quarry) don't make the mistake of confusing a fox for some other animal, and they cheer "Tallyho" if they see a fox, or they yell, "Halloa!" (pronounced Holler!), in a high-pitched manner.

Because of the mistaken sighting, some of the hounds became confused and scattered since they'd been alerted that a fox was about. Will was yelling "Hoick," which derives from the Latin *hic haec hoc*, meaning "here," in an effort to regroup them. Some riders drifted to an area where the misguided hounds had headed. We ended near a ditch filled with water. The drop was probably twelve to fourteen feet, and then four or five feet up the opposite bank. It was here that I noticed Thomas who'd come into our cottage with Jamesey that summer. One of the other riders told me, "He's a big shot winner of all-European equestrian events, and today he's the field master for the hunt." The field master is appointed to control the field.

Grand, I said to myself. *An immature asshole is responsible for our safety.*

As I watched Thomas ride around the area near this deep ditch, I could see the ease and beauty with which he rode, but that did nothing to alter my opinion about him. As he was trotting up and down the front of the ditch, he kept up a running commentary. "Come on, take the jump. It looks like the huntsman will call for riders to take up the hunt on the opposite side. Either we get to the opposite bank by going across here as a shortcut, or we'll have to ride miles through pasture after pasture to get to the same place."

All riders hesitated, and with good reason. To take a jump across a broad ditch you have two choices depending on its width. If it's not too wide, you jump the entire open space by coming in at a solid trot or a canter, launching your horse, aiming to land on the opposite side. If your horse doesn't land squarely on the opposite bank, but instead lands high enough up it, you lean way forward, stand in your stirrups to get off his back, and urge him to scamper to the top. If it's too much for him to make it with you in the saddle, to try to avoid having him fall back, perhaps with you still on him, you dismount quickly and scamper up the bank with him. Also possible is that he may slide down or fall over backward with you still in the saddle. But you can only try jumping from side to side if the distance across permits.

If it's too wide to jump across, but not too high to scale the opposite side, the second way is to slowly walk your horse to the edge and urge him forward. A trained horse will take a few steps down the side of the bank until gravity takes over and he slides or jumps into the ditch. Then it's the same routine as if you'd tried a jump from bank to bank, but landed only partway up.

If you can vault across a bank, it's quite a high, because the hounds are at full cry ahead of you, and you and your horse take air, land squarely with a thud, kick up mud and continue to chase them at a gallop.

This bank was so wide and so high that it'd be suicide to attempt to jump straight across. Instead, you had to use the method of bringing your horse slowly to the edge and urging him forward. Because of the height to the water, though, even if your horse slid down partway and then jumped into the ditch, if he came in at an odd angle, he'd take a tumble with you still on him. Dangerous. In addition, because the water wasn't clear, we couldn't tell how deep it was and without knowing that you couldn't know how tough it would be for a horse to get out of the water, so it was impossible to gauge whether you could make it up the opposite bank. Taking this jump was a plain bad idea.

As the riders contemplated what to do, Thomas continued riding up and down urging all, "Come on now! You've got to do it!"

I had in mind the scene from the movie *Braveheart* when the character of William Wallace gallops up and down in front of his troops urging his men into battle. I thought, *Well, though all his men were likely to be slaughtered, at least they had a chance. And wait a minute; Wallace went into battle with his men.* So I piped up as Thomas rode by our group of riders and yelled, "Why don't you show us how to do it?"

He gave me a dirty look, and then rode on and continued to rally the troops. Eventually, with Thomas's continued goading, some riders (including Michael) actually made the jump. It turned out that the water was about three-feet deep. A few actually managed to scramble up the opposite five-foot sloping bank still mounted. A few fell over their horses heads into the ditch and got drenched; then, holding onto the reins, they urged their horses up the bank, themselves scrambling on foot alongside. One rider jumped into the ditch, but his horse then fell backward on top of him. I thought he was a dead man and he would have been had his horse stayed put for a while longer. Luckily, his horse rolled, scrambled to get up, didn't kick the rider in the face, and ran to another part of the ditch. As he did, the rider came up, gasping for air. I don't even want to think what he'd inhaled by taking in some of that water. After he composed himself, he and a few of the others chased his horse up and down the ditch, finally getting ahold of his reins. Eventually, they managed to get themselves and their horses up on the opposite bank.

I actually tried to make the jump, eejit that I am, but Hillman refused. No way was he jumping fourteen feet into water. Thank God at least one of us had some brains. Sue Foley backed away from the edge saying, "No way am I trying that."

At about this point, Thomas the instigator started urging Orla, the cap collector, to take the jump. She kept circling her horse and saying, "No fecking way am I taking that jump."

Other riders joined in: "Come on, Orla! You can do it! Show 'em how it's done!" Finally, grumbling the whole time, she gave it a try. She edged her horse forward, but her horse kept backing away. She persisted. After six or seven go arounds, her horse decided Orla wasn't giving up, and he slid a bit, and then jumped. He hit the water at a slight angle, just enough so he couldn't stay upright, and he dumped her. He fell sideways and totally submerged, among other things, the saddle on his back.

Orla came up for air screaming, "You fecking bastards! I told you this was a stupid jump! First fecking time I've ever used this saddle and now it's drenched in dirty fecking sewer water! Bastards! You're all bastards!"

I guess she was pissed.

Once on the opposite side, one of the riders held her horse while she sat on the ground, took off a boot, and turned it upside down. What appeared to be gallons of water came pouring out. Just seeing the rush of brown liquid started her laughing as if she'd almost single-handedly emptied the ditch of water. She repeated the process with her second boot, still laughing at all the water. As others joined her in laughter, she looked up to our side of the ditch and yelled, "Bastards!"

Just then, the whipper-in rode up behind Orla and announced that those on our side of the bank should ride to a certain spot, exactly the opposite advice that Thomas had been saying to urge the insane jumping. The few daredevils who'd made it to the other side looked across at Thomas in disgust and at the rest of us in despair. Getting back to our side would mean jumping back into the ditch, but this time scampering up a fourteen-foot muddy bank. Impossible.

Without saying a word or missing a beat, the whipper-in scanned the opposite bank and jumped his horse into the ditch. He immediately headed for the one partially dry spot on the opposite fourteen feet of mud he'd identified before jumping in. As his horse started up, he stood in his stirrups, completely out of his saddle, literally leaning over the top of his horse's neck. But he kept his head high enough above the horse's head so that he wouldn't get smacked in the face as the horse bobbed his head up and down from the exertion. The horse lunged forward as his rear feet dug into the mud. He struggled up the slope, but never hesitated. As he got within a few feet of the top, the whipper-in calmly slid his right leg across the saddle, holding both reins in his left hand, standing in his left stirrup, and hopped onto the top of the bank. In the same motion, just as his feet hit the ground, he shifted the reins to his right hand and raised them to avoid interfering with the horse's head. With no rider on his back, the horse made a final lunge and came across the ridge onto the flat without a stumble. As soon as the horse was on the top, he gave his whole body a good shake, as if to say, *No big deal. Where's the hard stuff?* The Scarlet Coat patted him heartily on the neck and remounted.

Everyone watching was silent. No rider stirred in his or her saddle. Not a horse moved. No one spoke, coughed, or made a sound. For a full ten seconds, time stood still in that field. What this horse and rider had just done simply was not possible. Yet, as with all great athletes, they'd made it look as easy as cutting through a stick of butter with a warm knife. I'd never witnessed riding like that before, and I doubt I'll ever see it again: fifteen seconds of sheer balletic beauty, raw power, split-second judgment and timing—fluid movements that required action at exactly the right moment, not the right second, but exactly the right fraction of a second. I remain in awe of what I saw in that fifteen seconds, rendered all the more powerful because the rider neither sought nor received direct praise. Of course, all of us, to one another, continued to say for the rest of the hunt, "Do you believe what that horse and rider did?"

Having seen what we'd just seen, a few riders on the opposite bank were inspired to try it. Bad mistake. No one else made it and all who tried ended up dumped in the water, sometimes along with their horse. One horse reared in the ditch, lost his footing on the muddy bottom, and fell upside down with the rider still in the saddle.

The whipper-in yelled for them to go to a farmer's gate not far from where they were. In turn, those of us on the "right" side of the bank, led by the whipper-in, took a fifteen-to-twenty minute crazy-ass, flat-out hand gallop to reconnect with the jumpin' divils at the designated gate. Sheer heaven.

We arrived at the spot, sweating, but wired. As we pulled up to a halt, I had time to reflect. I understood that unforeseen dangers occur on a hunt. It's inevitable; everyone knows there are serious risks, but all steps are supposed to be taken to protect horse and rider from unnecessary ones. There are enough natural dangers without foolishly adding more, and the job of the field master is to do all he can to assure the safety of horse and rider. Yet, Thomas had egged people on to take a hazardous jump. That was reckless. As I learned later, the regular field master was unavailable that day and since it was known that Thomas was a superb rider, he'd been asked to fill in. All the other masters that day were pros, but I'd never again ride in a hunt if Thomas had any authority. When I later told Tony and other members of the LFH about Thomas's conduct, they were shocked and angry and told me they'd never had a similar experience. Apparently, Thomas has never again been invited to serve as a field master.

With the exception of Thomas (and unfortunately, his failure as a field master hadn't yet ended), the ride was phenomenal. Most of the jumps that day were banks rather than over stone walls. (The terrain of different clubs varies and with it the type of jumping.) I loved the challenge and adored the sensation of flying across ditches, landing solidly on the opposite bank, and galloping onward. It's heart-pounding excitement. During the breaks, I talked to a number of the riders. Some I knew, others became comrades by the shared experience. We had many long trots and canters during the day, and although I wasn't feeling much pain from my purple monster, I appreciated the occasional breaks when the hunt came to a halt as the foxes were outsmarting the hounds.

At the current break, as we rejoined the band of jumpin' divils by the farmer's gate, I was reminded of the Irish way of manners and circumspection.

Much of foxhunting is politics, not just the debate at the national level whether to continue or terminate the sport, but at the local level in developing good relationships with as many farmers and other landowners as possible, so the club in the area can have access to as much land as feasible.

The MFH dismounted, took off his helmet, placed it under his arm, and approached the farmer. As I well recalled when I'd first seen Captain Vinnie Bligh having his chat with his crabby German neighbor in Sligo, the last thing you want to do when you're petitioning a landowner to ride across his property is to appear haughty, literally up on your high horse and all done up in your riding fineries. Instead, as Vinnie Bligh did, as the MFH did, you have to come down to ground level, avoiding any appearance of superiority, and talk about everything except what you really want.

"Afternoon, Sean. That 'twas a fierce storm two nights ago, wouldn't you say?"

"Aye. Rain's comin' in from the west, I'd say."

"I'd say."

"Don't think it's blown itself out yet, do you?"

"No, I reckon it's still got a' ways to go."

"So, did ye hear that the O'Donovan lad is off to Clongowes?"

"No, I hadn't heard. Is this his transition year, so?"

"Not sure."

While this talk was ongoing, our job was not to interfere, but to cool out our horses by walking them in large circles. Obviously we were on a pig farm because we were walking out our steeds near a large round in-ground tank containing a huge amount of liquefied pig manure. Even with the dilution, the consistency was like that of a loose mud and the odor was evident. Suddenly one of the hounds excitedly bounded over the top of the tank and landed in the middle of it. He dog-paddled to a side, but couldn't get out. The top was too high. He turned and swan across the tank, but had the same problem. Strong as he was, eventually exhaustion would get the better of him, and he'd sink and drown.

Two riders dismounted. One peeled off his riding jacket and put his stomach on the edge while the other held him by his boots, trying to extend him far enough over the edge so he could grab the hound without falling in himself. It was no use. They couldn't reach the hound and he was too panicked to stay still long enough for them to grab hold of him anyway.

The rider with his jacket off stepped over the top and into the tank. It sloped steeply toward the bottom which he realized by taking just one step and finding the solution well up his thigh. One more step and he'd have to start swimming, all to a hopeless end. We all urged the hound to swim toward our hero. Eventually, more by luck than intention, he did. The rider grabbed him from the back, wrapping his two arms around his chest. By then the hound was so tired, he let himself be lifted up. A few other riders had dismounted by then, were at the side, and pulled the hapless hound over the top and onto terra firma, then gave a hand to the rider to help him out.

Someone had been prescient enough to find a garden hose and had it at the ready to wash down the hound before he started shaking himself. He was so exhausted by then he just stood there and took his shower, then gave himself a half-hearted shake. Then the rider got his shower. We all admired him, but stayed upwind of him for the rest of the day.

The MFH, engaged in his chat, was unaware of the hound-rescue drama, but just as it was ending, thankfully the farmer finally got to the periphery of the subject at hand.

"So, it looks like you've got a large field there."

"Oh, forty I'd say."

"And the hounds look fit, don't they now?"

"Oh, that they are, Sean. Got a good workout all summer. Will is a wonder at workin' with 'em."

"I'd say so. Seen him myself working them hounds down the roads, him on his bicycle and all."

"Did you make it to the puppy show this year?"

"No, couldn't."

"Shame. Will put them through their paces and they were brilliant."

"Is that so?"

"'Tis."

"So I 'spose you want to be ridin' over my property today?"

"Why, Sean, if it wouldn't be too much trouble that would be just grand."

"Well, you know now, I'd say fourteen, maybe fifteen years ago, yer group rode over the property here and caused some damage to some of the fences that never got fixed proper like."

"Why, that's just not right. Is there anything I can have any of the lads fix tomorrow for you?"

"No, I 'spect everything is okay now, so."

"Well, you just let me know, Sean."

"So, I guess it'd be fine for the field to have a go at it today. I'm sure we'll have none of those same problems."

"Why, this is grand, Sean, but only if you're sure it wouldn't be too much trouble."

"No, I guess it'd be fine, so."

"Now, I'll have some of the lads come out tomorrow, and you let them know if anything at all needs fixing from the riding. And let's have a pint or two soon for me properly to thank you, but meantime, please give my regards to Kathleen."

"Oh, I will, so, and God bless."

The MFH turned to remount, rolled his eyes as if to say, *This isn't easy, but thank you, Lord* as the farmer opened his gate. We entered, slowly and respectfully at a walk, each rider saluting the farmer by placing his bat to his helmet as we passed into his pastures, he nodding to each in return. Only after we were out of his view, with the rest of the field did I stand in my stirrups, lean forward a bit, pick up a canter, then a gallop, morphing into a part of a thundering herd, the bite of the cold wind tearing my eyes, and the rain spotting my glasses and soaking my pants.

Once during the hunt, a group of riders erroneously entered a pasture on which the farmer didn't want hunters riding, and I heard two blasts. Karen, back in the village, had also heard them and asked her guide John, "What's that?"

"Some farmer using his shotgun. 'Spose he doesn't want riders on his land."

"So he's using a *shotgun*?"

"Oh, I'm sure he's shooting over their heads."

Karen thought, *Where's a church when I really need one?*

At one point, three of us were taking up the rear: Sue Foley, her brother Ivan, and me. I took a jump down a small bank into a stream, up the bank on the opposite side, ready to follow the rest of the field into a forest, but if I'd done so I'd have been gone from view in a flash, leaving Sue and Ivan alone. I knew they weren't far behind me, so I waited. They got to the bank and also crossed relatively easily. But by this time, the sound of the hunt group, disappearing in the trees, grew dimmer. They weren't intentionally leaving us behind, but the foliage was so thick that I'm sure they didn't even realize a few riders were still to come. Or perhaps it was another screw up by the field master. Whatever. We were on our own. All we could hear was the occasional faint bark from one of the hounds. But on the wind, it was difficult to say exactly from which direction. We entered the forest.

As we did, three things quickly became apparent. First, the trees were so close together that frequently you had to pull a leg out of a stirrup to avoid knocking against one. Second, the forest was filled with many waterways, intentionally introduced when it was planted years earlier. That was fine for the trees, but it made for hard riding; the fords were just high enough and wide enough that the horses preferred to pop over them rather than to go into them and up the other side. This wasn't easy with the trees so close. Also, by this time, my purple monster was acting up, and I was squirming a bit in my saddle. Third, we had no idea whether we were going in circles, or heading toward or away from the rest of the hunters. We stopped and tried in vain to pick up sounds. We yelled, "Hello! Any riders out there?" Silence. Sue started getting claustrophobic. I assured her that we'd be out of the forest and into an open field in a few minutes, having no idea if that was true.

Ten minutes later, after pulling my right leg out of a stirrup to avoid smashing it into a tree, I brushed against it. In doing so, my right leather, stirrup and all, came off. It fell on the forest floor, and disappeared from view. Taking jumps with only one stirrup is tough under any circumstance, but particularly difficult in a thick forest, and even tougher when you're dealing with a Purple People Eater. For balance, it's better to ride with no stirrups, so I pulled up my left stirrup, placed it across my saddle, and silently thanked my instructor in California who had me practice jumping without stirrups. I'd never done it well, but at least I'd done it. I resented the hell out of her at the time, but now I was grateful.

Grateful or not, for a grown male rider, inexpert in the art of jumping without stirrups, this method hurts a lot where the sun don't shine, but it was jump and grind or smash into trees. I opted for jump and grind, thankful that I already had grown kids. At the same time, I tried not to think too much about the Purple People Eater, which, by this series of unfortunate circumstances, was *really* beginning to act up.

While we were still lost in the forest, we heard a series of notes, horn blasts to call the hounds together, and then barking. We waited. In another few minutes, out of nowhere, like an apparition, the whipper-in appeared in the forest. I thought, *We've been saved. Surely, this magnificent man, this hero in scarlet, who'd ridden his horse up that steep muddy bank with such grace and perfection is here to guide us to the rest of the group straightaway.*

Not so. He was intent on trying to find a few of the hounds who'd dashed into the woods following what we learned later was one of three foxes. At least he nodded to us, confirming we were there, and he'd tend to us eventually, but at that point he kept riding through the woods blowing on his horn and yelling, "Leave it!" and "Get back to 'em!" commands intended to get the hounds to return to the pack. At the time, all I knew was that this scarlet apparition disappeared and reappeared, blowing his horn and yelling funny words, coming from this side, and then that side five minutes later. We stayed put on our horses.

Finally, he came back and said simply, "Let me get you out of here." With a group sigh of relief, we followed, except that when we emerged from the forest, we were exactly at the small stream from which we'd first entered.

Then, as a reminder that the modern world intrudes into everything, he took out a cell phone and called Will. Will told him that the lost hounds had appeared and were with him. So the whipper-in said, "I guess we'd best be started."

"Where are we going?"

"Through the woods."

This is an Irish joke, I thought. *He's going to turn around and a few hundred yards up, he'll join us with the rest of the riders.*

He jumped into the stream and up the opposite bank. He turned to us and asked, "Are you ready?"

Christ. He's not kidding. We've got to do it all over again. We've got to return to the tightly packed trees, the impossible jumps across the mini-streams—me with my groin about to explode and no stirrups. I looked up and thought, *Lord. It's really time for you to stop these tests. I get it. Job had a hard time so, by comparison, we shouldn't be complaining, but enough already.*

But as had happened with my faux finish of the Ruan hunt, I had to ready myself to finish this one. We had to get to the damn opposite side of the woods, and we weren't about to allow our leader to disappear from view. Behind him was Ivan, and then Sue, and finally, your faithful narrator, still grumbling a bit about the Fates.

About five minutes into the trail, I heard Ivan shout, "I see it!" I suspected the strain had been too much for him, and while I'd only railed at God, he thought he'd seen God forming out of some tree branch. I shrugged, saying to myself, *Don't be so judgmental. If Moses saw God in a burning bush, why can't Ivan see God in a shadowy forest?*

But it wasn't God that Sue's brother had seen, it was my leathers— stirrup and all—on the forest floor. I was never good at math, but I've calculated the odds of finding them at something like 5,327,415 to 1.

The problem was I couldn't possibly dismount to get them. I'd never be able to remount my twenty-five foot tall steed without an extension ladder and a shot of morphine and neither appeared handy. Ivan was taller than I am and riding a smaller horse than mine, so he graciously offered to dismount and get my leathers. When he slid it back where it belonged on my saddle, and again I had two stirrups, I felt like a born-again rider.

Somewhat sheepishly, I looked up and thought, *Sorry for that crack a while ago about you needing to stop these tests—and I never agreed with Nietzsche. I know you do exist, that you are a benevolent God, and that your countenance is shining upon me.*

Getting back my stirrups was such a relief that I forgot I needed my morphine injection to tame the Purple People Eater, and from that point forward, the ride out of the forest seemed like a snap. About ten minutes later, we emerged on the other side where the whole group was waiting for us.

Michael walked his horse up to me. "Are you all right?"

"Fit as a fiddle. We were just enjoying the flora."

Michael told me that while we'd been lost, the riders, all Irish except for him, started joking about the last Yank who got lost in the forest.

"Never did find him, did we now?"

"Nope, but we had a nice Mass said for him anyway. Beautiful service it was, and with a lovely homily about horses, riders, and all."

But Michael said that Jamesy chimed in, "Well, this Yank we'll wait for and take back alive with us."

"So, Jamesy, you've become sweet on this Yank, have you?"

"Oh, he's an okay fella, but I'm not leaving here without him. He hasn't paid me yet for using me horse on this hunt."

From our woodsy experience, I was feeling a bit tired and ragged, but although I was hurting, I wasn't feeling disease tired. Besides, how many more times would I get to ride in a hunt in Ireland? So I remained a part of the field, determined to see it through.

Maybe fifteen minutes farther along, Thomas did it to us one last time. Ahead of us, he took a jump off a dirt path, up a bank, and down the other side. He didn't tell us that at the base of the other side the mud was three-to four-feet deep. I took the jump easily, but when Hillman landed in the muck up to his chest, he started thrashing about to get the hell out. Finally, from the exertion, he rolled onto his left side with me still on his back. As he was falling, I pulled my left foot out of my stirrup so my leg wouldn't get caught beneath him, pulled my right leg out of my stirrup, so that as he fell onto his side, I could roll as far from him as possible so he wouldn't crush me. I ended up on my back, and as I got up, I coated my riding pants and jacket with mud. Hillman got up and shook off his excess mud, splattering all nearby.

The next trick was remounting him. Doing so was like trying to step onto a second-story roof from the ground. I'd mounted him by using the side of a truck in Kildimo, but there weren't any handy in this isolated area.

One of the riders said, "Jest walk him in."

I thought, *Are you nuts?* But instead I said, "I'm riding this big boy home." I found a good-size mound of dirt, and walked Hillman next to it. Michael walked Dolores to the opposite side so Hillman wouldn't side step as I stepped up. I put my left foot in the stirrup, and as quickly as the Purple People Eater allowed, brought my right leg over him, and I was in the saddle again.

Just then, we heard the hounds yelping in a manner peculiar to identifying their quarry, and then another "Tallyho," but this time a legitimate one. Next we heard a "doubling the horn," a "gone away" sign, to alert the field when the fox leaves the covert. Though this was late in the hunt, the hounds bolted, and we were off like the wind. After a solid twenty minutes of hard riding and jumping more banks than I could count, the huntsman ended the hunt when the fox got to ground.

As I later learned, while Sue, Ivan, and I were in the woods, not one, not two, but three foxes, broke covert virtually simultaneously. Each ran off in a different direction, confounding the hounds and bringing the hunt to a temporary standstill. It seemed that the three foxes had formed a quick huddle. The quarterback fox said, "Okay, here's the plan for foiling our scent. You run through some manure. You run through that flock of sheep downwind a bit. I'll dash through that stream and into the forest up ahead." Whatever their precise methods, they won that day. Eventually, they were all run to ground. The hounds had been outfoxed. Thank God I could honestly tell Karen that, once again, I'd been on a hunt when no fox was killed, or in hunt speak, was bowled over. Tony confirms that it's his experience that it's rare that one is caught. They are foxes, after all.

As the hunt ended and the field of forty or so riders came down the wet Kildimo village road with that clippety-clop sound I love so much, I was tired and hurting, but once again, well satisfied. It had been a long chase and that was all that mattered to me—the longer the chase the better. This one had more stop-and-go than the Ruan drag hunt, as the hounds chased real foxes, but in all, we were in the saddle just under four hours. Once again I felt like an Olympian. I had endured, I had finished another hunt in Ireland, and I had more lifetime memories. Those memories caused by Thomas didn't seem so pleasant then, but with time and perspective, at least I could say to myself, *Well, he gave me some good stories.*

Before the hunt, Jamesy had told Michael and me to go to the Five Sisters Pub, dismount there, and wait, the same pub where Karen and I had once attended the seven o'clock feis that started at half nine. We did so. Nobody was in sight. Soon a truck pulled up, spotted us, and pulled over. "Jamesy 'sposed to send a truck for you?"

"That's right," I said.

"Well, no need to wait; we'll take you back to the meet."

With that, the driver hopped out of his truck and opened the back, which had a number of horses in it, all standing freely side-by-side. In the States, when horses are hauled, they're separated by stall slots, but this was Ireland. It seemed he didn't have room for my horse after squeezing Michael's in, but he walked Hillman up the ramp, turned him horizontal at the end of the truck, said, "There's a good boy," and gave him a friendly slap on the neck. Then he hopped off the rear of the truck, closed it up, and told us to get into the cab.

That horse didn't just stand there, I told myself.

I must have had this look of incredulity on my face, because the driver said, "Anything the matter?"

"No. Everything is just fine; in fact everything is grand," I said as I struggled to lift my legs up into the cab. You never know how tired you are until you stop, the adrenaline disappears, and you allow the exhaustion to wash over you. And it didn't help to be feeling the pain now throbbing from the injury from which I'd lost a quarter of my blood to internal bleeding less than a week earlier. What the hell. I was in Ireland. I just finished my second hunt. I'd done it—again.

Within ten minutes, we were back at the starting point where riders were dismounting and putting horses into trailers. Karen came up to me and gave me a long hug and a kiss. Then she started to brush off the mud, by then crusted on the back and side of my jacket and pants. I pulled away. "What are you doing?"

"I'm cleaning you up. You're a mess."

"You're brushing off my mud badge of honor. I wasn't thrown. This is because of a gobshite field master."

Karen rolled her eyes and shook her head. "Men."

From there, we went into a local pub where other riders had already gathered. Ivan was buying drinks and regaling all with how he'd saved his sister and me in the forest. He bought me a pint. I let him regale to his heart's content. The Purple People Eater had just finished a hunt in Ireland.

Harvey after the LFH Hunt, Disheveled, Tired, with a
Mud Splattered Face, but Hoisting his Pint from Ivan

Chapter 32

"You're a Fierce Local, Harv"

After the thrill of the hunt with the County Limerick Foxhounds, Karen and I looked forward to returning the following year and doing what we adore most about Ireland, just living in the village, no longer Yank tourists, but a couple of locals.

When we shop at the local centra, just like locals, we not only bring our own bags, but we do our own bagging. If you don't bring your own bags, at checkout, you have to pay for them, and if you don't do your own bagging, at most places you'll be there, with your bags still not packed, until closing.

Also like the locals, we go to church—yes, I accompany Karen. Adare has three churches. What is now Holy Trinity was founded in 1230 as a Trinitarian Abbey. The Trinitarians were suppressed during the Reformation; the church fell into ruins, and the first Earl of Dunraven restored its remains as the Holy Trinity Catholic Church in 1811. It was further restored in 1852. At the back of the abbey is a dovecot, or columbarium, in which doves and pigeons were housed and from which the Dovecot restaurant in the Heritage Center derives its name.

During our times in Adare, Karen and I often go to Holy Trinity. As Karen enters, she dips her fingers in holy water, crosses herself, and then goes to a side chapel where she continues her quest to burn down the country as she lights candles. Then, she crosses herself again, genuflects, and silently prays. I sit in a nearby pew, breathe deeply, and close my eyes. Sometimes I pray, knowing I'm in a house of God, and sometimes I just allow the peace and tranquility of the surroundings to settle over me.

As my disease progressed, without ever saying a word about it, we reached this compromise. As we enter the church, she dabs some holy water on my forehead but doesn't make the sign of the cross. The first time she did it, she said, "Can't hurt." Works for me. I hadn't allowed the sign of the cross placed on my forehead in Knock during the Mass for the sick, and I still won't allow it, but when Karen spritzes me with holy water, I smile and say, "Amen."

Outside the church is a graveyard. Just like in Carracastle, you know who the big shots are by where they're buried. One headstone right off the street in front of the church caught my eye. It reads, RIP, Marv Clifford. I got in the habit of saying "hi" to Marv each time we passed the church, until one day Karen asked me what I was doing. I explained. She looked at me and said "Marv? I don't think so." She walked up to the headstone and shook her head. "It's 'Mary,' my dear. It's just that the tail of the *y* got a bit worn down by the wind and the rain."

"Duh. You don't think I knew that? What do you take me for, an eejit?"

She gave me that same look, that same tilt of her head she always gives me at such times, as she did in Dublin when I made a telephone call to stop her silliness about trying to find a synagogue where I could say Kaddish for my father. Still, whenever we pass the grave, we both say, "Hi, Marv."

There was an evening in 2006 when Karen and I went to the Dunraven for a nightcap. As it turned out, the youngest Lohan sister had been married that day. Typical of Irish weddings, the women stayed at the reception and the men congregated in the bar, where we were. Andrew Lohan was there. As I went to pay for our drinks, I was told that "the gentleman" had bought them for us. I turned to Andrew, raised a glass to toast him, and then walked over and said, "Thank you, Andrew. That was kind of you."

"My pleasure."

"But I do have a bit of bad news."

He took a sip of his Guinness and looked at me a bit quizzically. "What's that?"

"Well, when I ordered our drinks, I added to our tab a bid to buy the Dunraven. So if that's accepted, along with the drinks, you'll also have to pay for the place."

He took another sip and said, "Why, that's grand. Sean and I have always wanted to own a hotel." Then, he leaned toward me and said in a conspiratorial tone, "And I think we can run it a might better than the Murphy's."

Craic. Gotta love it.

And, one of the times we went to the Treacy's for dinner while they were still living in the village, we had another local moment, one for which you had to know the origins of the village. Etched on the outside of their house is a large *H* for hydrant. Earlier that day, I prepared a sign and taped it next to the *H* before entering. The sign was: "arvey's House." At the bottom of the sign was: "By order of the Earl of Dunraven" with a bold signature. When we walked inside and received our usual hugs and kisses from the kids, Karen brought them outside to show them the sign, and they just about fell down laughing, yelling, "Dad! Dad! You've got to come see this."

We went back outside as Tony came for a peek. He looked at the sign, shook his head, and as I was reentering the house, he closed the front door, leaving me standing on the street. Within thirty seconds, I heard Victoria say, "Where's Harv?"

"He couldn't make it tonight."

"Tony, *what* have you done?"

"Mom, Dad locked him out on the sidewalk!"

"Tony!"

"He deserved it."

The door opened. Victoria walked outside, saw the sign, and burst out laughing. "You're very welcome, Harv," she said as she took my arm and led me inside, "And do come in. I've got dinner prepared in *your* house—by order of the Earl of Dunraven."

Something happens nearly every day that ties us closer and closer to the locals, and we love more and more living in Adare. Because the village is so small (perhaps twelve hundred), and because outsiders stick out like a sore thumb, you can't just blend. You're either accepted, or if not shunned, at least treated coolly.

We knew by first name virtually every merchant. We'd been introduced to and become friendly with a number of Tony and Victoria's family and friends. I'd ridden in a hunt with the local hunt club. It remains a joy to walk down the street, see Joe O'Dwyer, who used to water the hanging plants at the Adare Cottages, wave to him, and see him give a hearty wave back.

We knew Sue Foley from Clonshire. We'd established a fond relationship with Donal and Patsy Noonan. We had local library cards, knew every restaurant in town, and we knew the postmistress well enough that she allowed us to use the post office as a drop off by Fed Ex, because its driver couldn't find Purtill.

We knew Margaret and I'd shared the craic with her. We bought sheep from a local farmer, were offered the specials at Collins Pub, and like any local, we hid from ugly Americans who descended on the village for photo ops. We felt like we belonged there and believed that the feeling was mutual. But it was Martin Treacy who confirmed our status on the ride back from the Treacy's dentist in Limerick. Victoria was otherwise occupied, so Karen and I drove the kids to their appointments. When we returned to Adare, I took a turn.

Martin said, "Harv, you should turn around. We need to go in the opposite direction."

"I know," I said, "but it's easier if I just follow this little side street. It's shaped like a horseshoe and it brings us right back to the same street. It's better than backing into this traffic to turn around."

As I turned into the side street, I saw Martin in the backseat, smiling and shaking his head. As we came out on the opposite side, back to the same street, but now safely able to go in the opposite direction, I said, "Is anything wrong, Martin?"

"Wrong? Nothing's wrong. It's just that you even know the shortcuts. You know more about this village than some of the villagers. You belong here. You're a fierce local, Harv."

It was a grand confirmation of our own sense of acceptance into the life of the village and somehow it codified the status I felt. It was now official. A Jewish kid from Chicago had become a fierce local in an Irish village. Still, I wasn't yet a full-blooded Irishman, but that was to come.

Chapter 33

⌒

"We're Going to a Restaurant in Rathkeale?"

I find it ironic that the Irish, who've been subject to overt and repressive discrimination by the British for hundreds of years, have a way to go before learning tolerance for minorities. One of the groups for whom most Irish have no tolerance is the Travelers. In years past, they were known as tinkers who served a useful function in a number of communities by doing minor repairs. They went from village to village in their horse-drawn carts, setting up shop and tinkering at odd jobs, typically fixing tin utensils, until it was time to move on to the next village.

Today they're still mobile, but now when they move around in familial groups, it's by a convoy of cars, some pulling caravans (RVs), others pulling horse boxes (trailers), and the remainder just part of the group. Often they camp on the side of a highway and usually put their horses in some nearby pasture. Sometimes, not far from one of these camps, they set up tables on each side of the highway where young children sell strawberries or some other crop.

The stereotype and negative hype about Travelers is that they're squatters, burgle houses and small businesses, dump garbage in inappropriate places, and are a general drain on any locality where they perch. There's probably some, though not much, truth to the stereotyping. Still, the negative feelings persist and arguments that these folks aren't so bad fall on deaf local ears.

One summer, we heard about a restaurant named An Seabhac in Rathkeale, about ten kilometers from Adare. We were told it wasn't well known and the establishment didn't advertise. I called. The woman who answered said, "Hello."

I asked, "Is this Ann Sea Buhack?"

She laughed and said, "Yes, this is An Seabhac" (pronounced Ahn Shwock).

After my butchered beginning, I learned they did take reservations. I made one, still having no idea whether we were going to a restaurant with a flashback to the eighties style Irish cooking.

When we arrived, we thought we had the wrong place. From the outside, you couldn't see any lights on. The front door deposited you in an entryway that had two doors. I opened the one to the left and stepped in to find half a dozen dining tables, none set, and an empty bar.

"Hello. Is anybody here?" No answer. A bit louder, "Hello! Is anyone here?" After roughly a thirty-second wait, a woman appeared from behind the bar. Yes, she did have our reservation, and she asked that our group enter the other door from the entryway. With some trepidation, we did.

As we entered the other room, a fire glowing in the fireplace spread a warm and wonderful earthy smell of peat. Our table was set simply, but nicely. There were two other tables in the room, one with a group of four people engaged in animated conversation. When it came time to order drinks, we asked a question about an Australian wine unfamiliar to us. Between the waiter and the host, we learned that it was red. We weren't ugly Americans so we went with it. The wine was delicious. After a variety of appetizing starters, salads, and entrees, we all were well satisfied that we'd found a gem.

That same trip, we returned to An Seabhac a few more times and began to know the owners, all women. We also learned that if you wanted to eat duck, you had to order it when you called for reservations. I tried it, and from that time forward, I ordered it along with our reservation.

In 2004, we were guests one night for dinner at Kathy and Martin O'Farelly's house. To reciprocate, we told them we'd like to take them out. Of course, as a fierce local, you're obliged to know places that tourists don't. When we collected them on the appointed night, we told them we were taking them to An Seabhac.

Martin said he'd never heard of the restaurant and asked where it was located. When we told him, he just about had a stroke.

"Rathkeale! Did you say Rathkeale? Me mum was raised there and moved out as soon as she could. It's almost entirely taken over by Travelers. You'll see a caravan and a horse box in every front yard, and often the houses are vacant for months on end while a group of them are off and about doing whatever it is they do."

Of the two ways into the town off the highway, we always took the one at the far end of town, which is closer to the restaurant. Martin insisted we take the first exit and drive through the village so he could show us all the front yards littered with caravans and horse boxes. Although he's about nine foot three, I swear that while he was sitting in the back of the car, at various times he tried to slide down in his seat to become invisible. Much to his surprise, we made it through the rough-and-tumble of the town and arrived at the restaurant all in one piece and with none of our pockets picked. In a stance something akin to that of a ninja, Martin made sure we all made it into the restaurant safely before he carefully entered backward, making sure no rear guard attack caught us by surprise.

Even after we were greeted and seated by someone we'd come to know, Martin was still wary. His suspicions started to slip away as the food was served. As always, the meal was good and plentiful. By the time the evening was over, Kathy and Martin were singing the praises of the restaurant and laughing that it took a couple of Yanks to turn them on to a great eatery, virtually in their own backyard.

The following year, Martin called to say he and Kathy wanted to take us to dinner. "We'd love that, Martin. Thanks so much."

"Grand, and if you don't mind too much, we thought we'd take you to An Seabhac, where we've gone back a number of times now."

"Martin, that would be lovely and perhaps I'll call and order duck for myself."

"Why, although we already have reservations, Harvey, if you'll be callin', perhaps you wouldn't mind orderin' a duck for me as well?"

"Not a' tall, Martin."

And so I saw one more piece of evidence that often, even long-held prejudices melt away in the face of actually meeting "the other." Those whom we know to be bad only by myth and gossip, often turn out to be as decent as our next-door neighbors. And so it was in this case. Or maybe it's just that the duck is so good.

Chapter 34

"Say Nothing to Simon"

One of the shops in Adare has no name and no regular business hours. Whenever the owner, Simon, decides to open the store, it's open—perhaps two days in a row, perhaps three, and then closed for another week, or more. It's crammed with antiques covering two floors. You have to watch where you're going or you'll end up walking into a protruding chair leg, an edge of a mirror, a frame of a painting tilted into a walking space, or a side of an armoire door left ajar.

What originally enticed us was that when the store was open, Simon displayed some grandfather and grandmother clocks on the sidewalk. Karen loves clocks. She purchased some on her travels to Asia and bought some in the States at a few auctions, so his display hooked us. Once inside the shop, three things were apparent. First, the last time anyone had cleaned any part of the store was when the first Lord Dunraven was still alive. Second, Simon wasn't bashful about pricing. Third, although a lot of mediocre stuff was stashed all over the place, if you spent enough time hunting, you could find some lovely pieces, pricing aside.

We mentioned all this to Tony, who gave us the scoop. Simon was a Traveler and a shrewd businessman. He probably had more money than Donal or God. How did he get it? Villagers adhered to a version of President Clinton's "don't ask, don't tell" policy. Where did he get the items to put in his shop? Same answer. What Tony did say was, "Look, Simon most definitely marches to the beat of his own drummer—no store name, no regular business hours, sometimes he's not even there when it's open and his son is running the show—and his shop is right next door to the village garda station."

I asked, "How can he make money running such an irregular operation?"

"Because he has some great stuff in his shop. Though he sells plenty to tourists, locals, us included, have bought many items from Simon over the years. Don't feel sorry for Simon. He's doing just fine."

Karen said, "We agree. He has nice items. You have to spend some time scouting them out, but they're in there."

"Well," said Tony, "if you find anything in his store that you like, show no apparent interest in it. Don't even ask a question about it. Say nothing to Simon. Then, let me know what it is, where it's located, for how much he has it priced, and how much you're willing to pay. As I said, we've bought a number of items from Simon over the years, and I'll negotiate with him for you."

I said, "Okay, but why the mysterious method?"

"I was in Simon's shop about six months ago. A man walked in. I didn't know him, but he was Irish. After looking around for a while, he picked up a painting that had a price tag on it of five hundred. He handed it to Simon and said, 'I'll give you four-fifty.' Simon said, 'It's five hundred.' The man reached into his pocket, took out four-fifty, held it out to Simon, '*Here*,' he said.' This man was acting imperious. I could see Simon stiffen. He looked at the man coldly, took the painting out of his hands, and said, 'It's five hundred.' The man walked out. Ten minutes later, he returned, 'Okay, five hundred,' he said. Simon looked him squarely in the eye and replied, 'It's not for sale.' The man pulled his head back, a bit stunned. Hell, I've known Simon a long time and I was stunned. Anyway, the man said, 'But I was here just minutes ago and …'

"'It … not … for … sale,' Simon repeated slowly. With that, he took the price tag off the painting, turned, walked to the back of the store with the painting, and placed it in a new location. The discussion was over. The man left in a huff.

"Not ten minutes later, an American woman came into the store and announced that she was staying at the Adare Manor. Simon knew that most Americans who stayed there had a goodly wad of money, and he was only too happy to separate them from some of it through purchases at his store. She said the concierge at the manor told her she should let Simon know where she was staying and he'd give her a break. *Break,* I said to myself. *The only thing he'll break is her bank.* Almost as though staged by some writer with a perverse sense of humor, she spotted the same painting. 'How lovely,' she said. 'I like that very much. How much is it?' Simon put his hand to his chin, furrowed his brow as though calculating how much of a break to give her, and then said, 'Twenty-five hundred, but if you want it, I'll wrap it nicely for you and have it delivered to the hotel at no extra charge so you don't have to carry it there yourself.' 'Why that's very kind of you,' said the woman as she handed over her credit card.

"I left the store, barely able to contain myself," said Tony. "Now, I've been involved in many a business deal in my life, but never have I seen someone so coolly turn down a deal because of the manner in which he was spoken to and then, within minutes, as sweetly as you like, turn the matter into a five-times profit. It was truly stunning.

"So, I repeat, if you're interested in anything in the store, let me handle it. Say nothing to Simon."

Within days, Karen and I were back in Simon's store. We spotted four small paintings we liked and managed to convey our mutual interest without Simon seeing us. We noted the posted prices and the locations. Then we made sure to spend another fifteen minutes in the store, never returning to look at the paintings before we wandered out. We gave Tony the whole rundown: what we liked, where the paintings were located, the asking prices, and what we were willing to pay.

Two days later, Tony called to say he'd bought the paintings. He said, "I've got good news and bad news."

"What's the good news?" I asked.

"The good news is I bought the lot of them, not only for less than the posted prices, but less than your buying prices."

"That's grand, Tony. What's the bad news?"

"The bad news is my commission is three hundred percent."

"Sounds reasonable to me. So tell me, how did you do it?"

"Well, certainly I relied on the fact that I've known Simon for many years, and we've bought a number of items from him, so he knows that I know the game, and I never talk down to him. Second, though, I played this the Irish way. I looked all around the store and eventually found your four paintings. I disregarded them and looked at other items, asking him for prices. When he said what they'd cost, I just politely said, 'I don't think so.' Then I returned to the paintings. He followed me. I looked at them, making sure he saw me look at the posted prices and heard me say, 'They're nice, but a bit high, wouldn't you say?' I had the advantage of knowing the total price of the four paintings before entering the shop. I also knew how much you were willing to pay for the lot, so I put less cash in my wallet than you'd said you were willing to pay for all of them. I pretended to count my money, and then said, 'Simon, what I've got on me I'm willing to pay for these four paintings and what I've got on me is …' I then counted my money again, and announced what it came to, all in a friendly not a haughty manner. Without missing a beat, Simon said 'okay,' which probably means I left money on the table, but we'd closed the deal. I gave him the cash, and I walked out with the paintings and now I'm holding them for you."

The next time we were at their house, Tony brought down the paintings. I said, "I've got good news and bad news."

"What's the good news?"

"The good news is the paintings are nice."

"What's the bad news?"

"The bad news is those aren't the ones we wanted."

Tony looked at me, shaking his head, a smile on his face.

"But I'll tell you what I'll do," I said as I pulled out my wallet, having placed in it exactly half as much as Tony had paid. "I'm willing to pay for these four paintings what I've got on me, which comes to …" as I counted my money. "Well, it comes to half what you paid."

Tony said, "Oh, I've still got so much to teach. If you're to learn the Irish art of negotiation, study at the hand of a master. Don't face the person when you're going into your wallet. Turn your back to him, as I did to Simon, and as you're counting your money, give a little turn of the head as though you want to make sure he's not approaching you."

"I guess I've still got a thing or two to learn from the Irish."

"That you have."

Those four paintings now happily reside in our house in San Francisco. Occasionally, I turn my back to them, take out my wallet, and tell the paintings I'm willing to buy them for what I've got in my wallet. Then I look over my shoulder to make sure they're not creeping up on me as I wait for the nice men in white jackets to come and take me away.

That same year, there were some new paintings at Purtill. Earlier in the season, a professional artist had stayed there and had painted some oils of the cottage. We told Tony and Victoria how lovely the paintings were and they gave us one, which also now proudly resides in our house in San Francisco. To reciprocate, before we left that year, in crayon and in the style of a six-year-old, I drew Purtill. It had such artistic touches as a black stripe outside the cottage with the words, "Pump that doesn't pump" and an arrow pointing to it. We left it for Tony and Victoria on the day we returned home.

The following year, we found my drawing framed and hanging on the cottage wall, next to one of the professional's renderings.

Tony told us that visitors who'd been there said, "How adorable. How old is the youngster who drew this?"

Tony said he told them, "Trust me, you wouldn't believe it. It's a long story."

Chapter 35

⌒

The Pleasures of Travel

Traveling to Ireland from San Francisco isn't a walk in the park, and air travel anywhere in this post-9/11 world, has made it even tougher. There's no direct flight from San Francisco to Shannon. Our usual route was to fly to Heathrow, and then to Shannon. It might not sound so bad, but it can be a killer. The flight to Heathrow is about ten hours. We leave at noon and land at 6:00 a.m. local time, but for us it's still 10:00 at night. We then have a layover of about five hours when your bodies don't really know what they want to do, but they know they don't want to be upright.

At Heathrow, you have a 126-mile walk to get to the bus that takes you to the terminal from which Aer Lingus departs. Then you have a 327-mile trek to the Aer Lingus gates, mostly in a torture chamber built to test who'll faint first from the length of the walk and the poorly ventilated hall. Long ago, I decided this was designed as part of England's continuing punishment of the Irish and anyone bound for Ireland, just because the Irish made them look bad over that potato-famine thing. If you survive the sweatbox and actually arrive alive at the Aer Lingus gates, you still have another four-hour wait. About then, you realize you've been up roughly a full day and you're still wearing the same clothes.

In 2005, in an attempt to avoid the layovers, marathon walks, and the Heathrow torture chamber, we tried a new route. We left San Francisco on United Airlines for JFK in New York where we'd catch a connecting flight on Aer Lingus to Shannon. Ah, but the Fates decided to play their games with us.

The United flight was delayed in San Francisco for ninety minutes due to weather in New York. When we arrived at JFK, it took the ground crew twenty minutes to open the door, so we'd lost almost two hours of our connection time. Once we got out, we took an airport train to the correct terminal, and then ran to the Aer Lingus flight, not taking time to stop for boarding passes, figuring we'd be late if we did and we'd get them at the gate. We arrived forty minutes prior to departure.

The security guard wouldn't let us into the area without boarding passes. We explained the reason. He asked an Aer Lingus worker what to do. She said, "They can't come in; the flight is closed."

The security guard fidgeted for a few minutes, and then mumbled, "This is crazy. Let me call the supervisor."

She arrived. We told her our story. The plane was still tethered to the building. She said, "Our paperwork closes forty-five minutes prior to flight."

We said, "The plane is still here."

She said, "Our paperwork closes forty-five minutes prior to a flight. It's our policy."

I said, "I've never said this to any stranger before, but I have a rare blood cancer. My disease exhausts me. For health reasons, we can't afford to miss that plane and be stuck here overnight."

She looked at me. I thought I saw her weaken. *I have her,* I thought. *At last, my shameless use of my disease has served us well in the broader world. Ha!*

Then she said, "Our paper work closes forty-five minutes prior to flight. There's nothing I can do. You can't get on." And she walked away. Apparently, my trial lawyer skills still needed honing.

Karen and I walked away in a daze. Since our luggage was on its way to Shannon, we needed some place to buy toothpaste, underwear, and T-shirts. It's not easy finding that stuff at 11:00 p.m., even at JFK.

Then we walked to a hotel-booking stand where we were told the only hotels available were in Manhattan. We knew that couldn't be true. We called maybe eight hotels in the airport area. None had any availability. We finally returned to the UAL terminal, looking for any help we could get. After waiting forty-five minutes in a queue of other passengers who had their own tales of woe, we got to the counter. Expecting more double-talk and no help, we actually ran into a helpful agent who gave us a voucher for a hotel and a meal. After another airport train ride, a hotel bus ride, and three pilots with priority check-in rights at the hotel, we got our room. My belief in God was reaffirmed because a restaurant in the hotel was still open, a good thing, because by then I was ready to eat Karen's arm.

At eight the next morning, Karen was on the phone to Aer Lingus. They had no flight available that day. I started doubting again that there was a God. (I'm fickle that way. My belief or lack of belief in an Almighty tends to depend on what's happening at the moment.) The next flight available was the following night. Karen booked it.

We returned to the airport for another voucher for the additional night and met another helpful UAL worker, this one a supervisor, David Melendez. David booked us on a United flight later that night to Heathrow—Business Class—and arranged with Aer Lingus for a connecting flight to Shannon. He also gave us a pass for the UAL Red Carpet area, rebooked our return flight, and arranged a backup flight out of JFK, because the connecting time was tight. I was back to believing there was a God.

The first leg of the flight went well, but damned if we weren't back at Heathrow. So we had to face the 126-mile hike to the bus to change terminals and the 327-mile trek through the walk of torture we'd tried to avoid. But what the hell. We were there and it was early enough to catch an 11:00 a.m. flight to Shannon, though to be safe we'd booked the 3:00 p.m. flight. This was good. We'd take the earlier flight and get in hours earlier than we'd planned.

Then, for the first time, we heard about our luggage. The Aer Lingus ticketing agent told us, "We can't locate it and without your luggage we can't put you on the earlier flight even though there are seats."

I said, "But we checked it in at San Francisco. Here are the vouchers. We haven't seen the suitcases since then. We're willing to get on the earlier flight, even knowing our luggage won't be on it."

"Sorry, but for security reasons we can't let you go on the earlier flight unless we locate your luggage and can load it on the earlier flight with you. Without the luggage, you'll have to wait until the scheduled flight at three p.m."

Stupidly I asked, "What if our luggage still isn't found by the three p.m. flight?"

"No problem; you can still take that flight."

By then, I'd regained part of my senses and refrained from asking why that wouldn't be a security risk. Even with serious brain fry, I knew that I'd already asked too much. I didn't understand the security-risk thing, but feared that if I raised the question, they'd say I was right and we'd have to remain at the airport until our luggage was found, whether that took three hours or three weeks.

Here's how you can tell when you're really tired: if you lie down in an airport waiting lounge atop a series of three or four wavy plastic chairs and go to sleep. My head in Karen's lap, her stroking my head, although I had ongoing visions of the torture tunnel from which we'd recently emerged; I drifted into the land of nod, wishing instead that we were in the land of the Old Sod.

Inexplicably, as the 11:00 a.m. plane was boarding, the you-can't-get-on-this-flight-because-of-security-risks agent approached us and asked if we wanted to get on the flight. As I awoke from my nightmare about the torture tunnel, I said, "You found our luggage?"

"No, but if you want to get on this flight, you can."

I'd realized by this time that in travel, you take good news as you would if you were in the woods, starving, and then find tiny morsels of edible food on the forest floor. You never ask why. You just say, "Yes! Yes! Yes, and I'll rename my children after you."

So, we received our boarding passes from the Shannon agent, right as the flight was boarding, remembering the JFK Aer Lingus supervisor telling us of the policy of closing the flight list forty-five minutes prior to departure. I guess the policy amounts to, "We close our list forty-five minutes prior to a flight if we were able to sell your seat. If not, our policy is we can issue you a boarding pass as passengers are boarding. Security?

Don't be silly, boyo. So we don't know where your luggage is. You didn't misdirect it, did you? Be a good lad and get on the flight."

I was a good lad and we got on the flight, knowing what it meant to live in a world seemingly created by Kafka.

We arrived in Shannon. When we told the Aer Lingus baggage agent that we wanted to report our lost luggage, he said, "Wait till all the luggage comes off the flight. Maybe 'tis on there."

We knew 'twasn't, but we waited. Meanwhile, I started charging our European cell phone on the tab of the Shannon Airport electricity bill. The baggage agent finally took the information and gave us a telephone number to call to check on delivery when the luggage would likely arrive the following morning.

We picked up our car rental and took off. The Fates weren't through with us just yet, though.

Just as we were entering the outskirts of Adare, only a couple miles from Purtill, I was downshifting for a roundabout when suddenly the car felt permanently in neutral.

"Damn! Don't tell me. I don't want to know that the clutch just blew." It had. I managed to inch the car forward to a spot just past the roundabout, but in a position to force every car entering the village to have to wait for oncoming traffic to clear before going around us. Normally, that wouldn't have been a big deal. Since the population of Adare is about twelve hundred, though there's only a single lane into and out of the village, even with tourists, the delay normally wouldn't have been that bad for traffic that early in the day.

However, in furtherance of our unusual Irish luck during this ongoing saga, which seemed to have started ten years earlier and in a galaxy far far away, the Adare Manor was sponsoring a Pro-Am golf tournament with Tiger Woods and other golf luminaries.

Consequently, for the next two days and starting the minute we were semi blocking the road into the village, the first of fifty-thousand people started passing by, every one of them giving us a dirty stare as they snaked around our car. I wondered in exactly what Circle of Dante's Hell we were then situated. I knew it was one of the deeper ones.

After the car's forward motion ended, I sat for a full ten seconds with my hands on the steering wheel, and staring somewhere into the deep recesses of the universe. I knew this wasn't really happening and I'd wake up in a minute. I didn't.

"Okay, let's be grown-ups. Kar, I'll call the car rental place and ask for help. They gave me a road emergency number to call." I placed the call.

A person asked, "How can I help you?"

"The clutch on our rental just blew and we need roadside service."

"Where are you?"

"Just on the outskirts …" and the phone went dead, the battery not having received a sufficient charge at Shannon.

My brain was now fully fried. In total frustration, Karen got out of the car. "Don't leave me now, Kar! Besides, you can't walk back to San Francisco."

As she was milling in front of the auto, a young man with a bicycle that had a flat tire came walking our way. "This is Ireland, Kar. He'll have a cell phone. Everyone in Ireland has at least three. Tackle him. Do anything, but get his phone."

He had one and Karen got it. We called Tony and Victoria. They answered. They said they were heading our way and would be there shortly. (In Ireland, that could mean five minutes or five hours.) Thankfully, it was closer to the five-minute mark. They pulled in front of us. We had a few quick hugs and kisses. Victoria called the emergency roadside service and arranged for a spot to meet the tow truck, because we couldn't wait where we were.

At last, we could begin to unwind. We were with our friends.

We were safe. Until, after the briefest small talk, Tony, then about fifty, told us that he had just gotten out of the hospital yesterday, after having a heart attack six days earlier, and he'd been in ICU the entire time. (In the Irish manner, he dubbed it the Event.) Victoria and Tony had intentionally not told us, figuring that if we'd known we would have canceled our trip, which is exactly what we would have done, to let Tony get the fullest rest possible. In fact, they'd just been at the Mid-Western Regional Hospital in Limerick for a follow-up checkup and were on their way home when we'd called. What else could possibly befall us? A meteor shower? I heard President Bush, somewhere in the recesses of my fried brain, swaggering, "Bring it on!"

Victoria drove to the designated meeting place to meet the emergency road-recovery guy, Pat Byrnes. His brogue was so heavy, not even Victoria could understand all that he was saying, but eventually we figured out that he needed my car keys and the copy of the rental contract, both of which I dutifully handed him. He said he'd pick up our broken-down car, and deliver us a new one. Victoria gave him directions to get to Purtill. "Down this road you go, and you know where the McIlhaney's used to live?"

"I do."

"Well, don't do anything there. Straight on with you a bit past the dying tree and on the right there, oh three hundred maybe five hundred meters past that, straight up the unmarked drive you go."

"Aye."

"You know, right next to the mustard-colored house that used to be pink."

"I remember the pink one."

"Well, it's been mustard-colored now for years."

"Has it now?"

"It has. Anyway, couldn't miss it if you were blind."

"That's just lovely," said Pat. "I'll have them a new car within the hour, so."

Meanwhile, he already had another car piggybacked on his tow truck. I didn't ask how he was going to tow our car. All I wanted was my mommy.

Standing on the road as Pat Byrnes pulled away, it struck me that even with my thirty-five years of practicing law and the sophisticated legal matters that I'd handled, I'd just given a total stranger our rental contract and car key. Consoling myself, I thought, *"Tis Ireland, no concern. Right?* Sloshing around in my brain I heard, *Eejit!*

We've been to Ireland enough to know that in Oirish time, one hour can mean two or three. But after five had passed, to the extent my brain was functioning at all, I was beginning to get concerned. Just then, Pat pulled up the long driveway to Purtill with a new car rental. He offloaded it, handed me the keys, and said, "So, you wouldn't be so used to driving a standard shift, would ye?"

Even with his thick brogue and my exhaustion, I understood him perfectly. I tried not to be an ugly American, but he'd challenged my manliness. I explained that I'd not only owned standard shift cars, but also had at least twelve prior rentals in Ireland—all standard shifts and all without a problem.

He responded as most Irishmen would to avoid an argument or stop listening to what they think is blarney, "Lovely weather, isn't it?" He handed me the keys and the same contract I'd given him and left. Only later did it dawn on me I had no contract referring to the car he'd delivered to us. (But this is Ireland and upon its return that actually proved no problem though, the agent, after punching up information on the computer, said, "So, you had some trouble with the clutch?")

We sat down to allow some of the tiredness to settle in. We took a few deep breaths. But just then, we heard a car coming up the driveway. A garda got out of his car and walked toward our front door. I went outside to meet him.

"The gate at the bottom of the drive is open, don't you know?"

"No, I didn't," I said. I recalled our first trip to Ireland and my interchange with a garda at Dublin's airport, when I thought then and now, I'd never been in a jail, much less one in Ireland. So I engaged him in a bit of the Irish sport of "Do ye know …?"

"Well, now I'd be knowin' him, but not so well as to go to his house or anyt'ing like that, but I'd say more to know him by sight, I'd say, so."

"How about Margaret at the library?"

"Oh, yes, of course I know her."

"Why, my wife and I have local library cards."

"John O'Hara, the horse trainer, do ye know him?"

"We do, almost bought a horse from him. And how is his fine daughter, Mary?"

"Oh, she's a darlin' girl and doin' fine. Off to school, she is, and still ridin'."

Then I moved in for the killer information. "My wife has many a Duffy and Towey family member buried in a church graveyard at Carracastle. Her grandparents came from the area."

"Does she now? Did they now? Well, isn't that just grand."

I thought Karen's dead relatives probably wouldn't think so, but now I was hoping they were getting me a free pass from the local jail.

Karen couldn't stand it any longer. She stepped out of the cottage. "Good evening, officer. My name is Karen Duffy and my husband here is Harvey Gould. We'll be in Ireland for six weeks, renting this cottage from Tony and Victoria Treacy, as we have for a number of years in the past."

"Oh, now, so you know the Treacy's, do ye? Well, that's just grand," he said, hearing what he'd apparently wanted to hear all along. "You're very welcome."

For what, I wondered. We hadn't thanked him for anything. Then I remembered. In Ireland "You're very welcome" doesn't come after a "thanks." It's an honest-to-God greeting.

After the garda left, Karen said, "He didn't need all the schmoozing. He just wanted to be sure that we knew the Treacy's name. They're building a new house on the property while they still have their house in the village, so there's plenty of stuff here to steal. If we knew them, we weren't burglars."

"He didn't need all the schmoozing?"

"Nope."

"So, all my fancy footwork and 'Do you knows' didn't count for anything?"

"Nope."

"Confusing, these Irish," I said. "I still can't get it straight when they want information and when they just want good craic."

As Karen and I were trying to find the energy to go out to get something to eat, our angel in Ireland, Victoria, came by with a fully cooked dinner. We told Victoria we'd build a shrine to her, wolfed down her dinner, and then collapsed into bed. By then, it had been almost forty-eight hours since we'd left San Francisco. We slept a solid two hours. A few years later, we learned that Aer Lingus no longer has international flights into or out of Shannon. I can't wait for the upcoming adventure of getting there.

But the delight of travel on this occasion wasn't over yet. Our luggage didn't arrive for five days, so we had to go to Limerick to buy some clothes till our suitcases showed up. When they did and the driver arrived in Adare, he called for directions to Purtill, but even for the Irish, if they don't know the countryside of a particular area, giving directions is a bit like explaining how to get to Mars. When it became evident that the driver had no idea how to get to us, I said, "Do you know where the church is on Main Street in Adare?"

"I do."

"Just wait there for me."

I drove into town to rescue our bags.

Welcome back to Ireland.

Chapter 36

What Do Ewes Want?

The residence the Treacy's built on the Purtill grounds is a gorgeous family home in one of the most breathtaking settings I've ever seen. The view from one direction looks out at the horses in the pasture with fences that curve rather than square off giving an extra soothing feel to the view. In another direction, you see a large rolling pasture with grass that seems hand cut, and where their two dogs, Nelson and Fred, romp and pretend to be ferocious with each other. In a third direction is another pasture, which, when they built the house, was crying out for sheep. Finally, they created a man-made lake (although Karen insists that I call it a pond) with an island, all of which you can see from their house.

The island is about thirty-by-fifteen feet, and the lake is sixty-by-thirty. The lake is designed so that if the water level gets too high, the excess drains off through a pipe and is carried underground to a small stream (per Tony, a river) on their property. If the level gets too low, water automatically flows into it from a different set of underground pipes. A little pier protrudes into the lake where Gordy frequently sits and suns himself. A small rowboat, to get to the island, is docked at the pier.

Some years earlier, Karen and I had masks made with the image of my face which we sent to Victoria. On Tony's birthday, she and the children, each wearing one of the masks and singing "happy birthday," walked into the room where Tony was sitting. Tony swears the shock of that scene, some years later, caused his Event.

I needed to do better than the masks, so I threatened to erect a life-size statue of me on the island. The face would be an image of mine in a rictus, reminiscent of the Joker in Batman, and a hinged and motorized arm constantly waving at the house. Tony said it was a grand idea, because he needed target practice.

Tony and I laughed so much that eventually he named the lake and island Harvey Lake and Harvey Island. I'm still waiting for the spots to make it onto Irish maps. I've quoted Tony the fare for going to Harvey Island time and again, but to this day, the cheapskate hasn't paid me his first euro for any trip.

In 2005, the fourth time we'd stayed at Purtill (including our two trips the preceding year), Victoria and Tony said they'd no longer accept money for the rental of the cottage. Karen and I protested vigorously. "Rental of the cottage is a business." Our arguments fell on deaf ears.

"Our kids love you. Besides, did you charge us when we stayed at your house when we came to the States for Ashley's wedding?"

"That's not a fair comparison and you know it. We never intended that apartment as a profit center. We don't rent out guest space in our home."

No sale. They remained steadfast.

"You're no longer customers. We've told you time and again that you're the only folks who stay here who aren't tourists, but who literally live in the village, know the locals, are involved in events, and are friends with a number of the villagers. Nobody else does that, and more importantly, you're our friends. We don't charge friends."

Neither Karen nor I are accustomed to losing arguments, but this one was going nowhere.

Karen and I discussed various alternatives. If we sent them a check, they'd tear it up. If we bought gift certificates from some local department stores, they could turn them in for cash and send the money back to us. The one thing we knew for sure was that we would not stay at the cottage and fail to pay for it. The trick was how to do that.

A few nights later during dinner, Tony told us of his plan to buy ten or so sheep to graze in one of their pastures. He said they'd be little lawnmowers and would add a pastoral touch to their property.

Later that night, I said to Karen, "So Tony wants sheep? Let me ask you this. If we bought sheep, could they return them?"

"I don't think you can return sheep," Karen said.

So we started our hunt to purchase sheep. As it turned out, it wasn't difficult. When Margaret arrived on her Rolls Royce to clean Purtill one day, we asked if she knew of a local sheep farmer. She didn't, but she asked her son. He called us and gave us a telephone number for Michael Power who lived in Cappagh, a nearby village. I called Michael and said we wanted to buy ten sheep for friends who lived nearby.

"Rams or ewes?"

"Uh. Well. Hmm." I could tell by the silence on the other end of the phone that he thought he was dealing with a whack job. Who buys sheep as a gift, and worse, who doesn't know if he wants to buy rams or ewes? "Ewes, I guess. Are they the females?" He almost hung up.

"Okay, so. When would ye like to come over to pick them out?"

"Well, we can come pretty much anytime, but we'll talk to you when we get there about the selection and when they're to be delivered." I asked roughly how much it would cost per sheep.

"Oh, I'd say eighty to eighty-five euros each."

I figured that meant one hundred each, so we went to the bank, and I had one thousand euros in my pocket when we arrived to meet Michael at his farm.

Finding him was no easy trick. "Do ye know how to tarn at the crossroads to go into Adare from where yer stayin'?"

"Yes."

"Well, don't. Go 'tother way. Then at another crossroads where the road bends to the left near a big tree—"

"Yes, I know the crossroads."

"Don't go that way either. Jest keep goin' till you get farther ahead, and then ye'll tarn left."

"Is there a sign for Cappagh?"

"Not exactly, but you'll see another crossroads sign."

Okay, I thought, *here we go again with the damn crossroads signs.*

"Don't do anything there."

"Uh huh. So we keep going how far?"

"Not very. Then ye tarn right fer a bit, which will take you to a charch."

"A charch?"

"A charch, lad. Where they say Mass."

"Oh, a church, okay, and then?"

"Then, when you're at the charch, you've gone too far."

"Uh huh."

"So, tarn around and be takin' a left tarn at a dirt road."

"Uh huh."

"Then you just find me at the shed."

"The shed?"

"Yes, I'll be workin' at the shed."

"Okay, we'll be there this afternoon and Michael, please keep your cell phone with you and turned on today."

I don't know why I was a tad confused with the directions, but I concede that I made a few wrong turns along the way and was sure we'd end up in Iceland. I managed to get us to the church, and from that point forward, called Michael six times. A good way up the dirt road we spotted a shed a few hundred yards across a field. A house was nearby. We knocked on the door and peered through the windows. No lights were on, but before making the trek to the shed, I acted as lookout in case a garda happened by, while Karen rifled through the mailbox to make sure it was Michael's house. It was.

We then walked across the open field to meet him at the shed, but found a deserted skeleton of a building and no Michael.

I phoned Michael a seventh time and told him where we were.

"No, not *that* shed, lad. The *workin'* shed."

"How do we find the working shed?"

"Just keep comin' down the road and take a tarn to the right—no I guess to the left—and not too far up from there is another shed." Then I heard the dreaded words "Can't miss it."

"How far down the road after the turn?"

"Not very."

"Okay." We continued down the road, took the tarn to the left, damaging our kidneys with every major bump, when suddenly, we found him. My faith in the guiding hand of an all-powerful God was restored.

Michael had a fat ram in a mechanical contraption that held the animal upside down. He was trimming the ram's feet and giving him an injection of some kind. Finished, he pushed a button, which rotated the ram right side up and sent him gingerly walking away.

"This old ram had done his service over the years," he said, "and now he's past his prime. Aye, 'tis the truth. He's earned his retirement. So I'm just tryin' to make him comfortable."

We felt good about that. Here was a farmer who didn't just throw his over-the-hill animals away on a garbage heap. Good sign.

I held out my hand to shake. Slowly Michael rotated his hands so that I could see them as he said, "Not sure you want 'ta do that." His hands had more dirt, sheep dung, and other toxic substances than any hazardous materials dumpsite—the EPA would have ordered him off limits. Dispensing with a handshake seemed a good idea. Instead, I gave a mild wave. "Hello, Michael. Good to meet you."

"Hallo, Herbert."

"It's Harvey."

"Okay then, Herbert, Missus ..." I remained Herbert for the transaction and forever after with Michael.

If you've ever seen a *Seinfeld* episode, you know there can be great humor in talking essentially about nothing. That was our discussion with Michael. Though zilch said was particularly funny, the episode was hilaaaaaaaaaarious, because he just wanted to talk and talk, and we just wanted to finish transacting our business about the sheep and be on our way. It was cold, and I mean Irish cold. Karen and I had been foolish enough to think we'd meet Michael, talk over a cuppa, and leave, so we weren't dressed for the North Pole, and we were slipping into hypothermia. He was so starved for human companionship that he yakked for thirty minutes about everything *except* sheep.

Karen has told me many times that I should be elected president of the Slow Talkers Association of America, but compared to Michael I was a speed freak. Making matters even more difficult, he spent so much time with the sheep that he often turned his head to look at them and the Arctic breeze carried his words away.

Finally, we got around to the subject at hand. "So, Michael, we're here to buy some sheep for Tony and Victoria Treacy."

"Are ye now, Herbert?"

"Yes, we are."

"Well, is that so? I know Tony Treacy, now. Well, I'd not say I know him. It's just that I know him. Do you know what I mean Herbert?"

"We understand," I said as our core body temperatures entered the danger zone. It took awhile, but we agreed that we should buy ewes only, no ram.

"Ye can always rent a ram if they want more."

Hmm, I thought to myself. *Rent-a-Ram. Has an interesting ring to it. Maybe I can come up with an advertising campaign built around the slogan.* Then I snapped out of my drift, realizing that I was probably beginning to hallucinate from the cold.

We told Michael that Tony would be putting up sheep fencing within the next few months, so the ewes didn't have to be delivered until September or so. We gave him Tony's telephone number and asked him to call in about six weeks to let him know that ten ewes were coming and to arrange for delivery.

I asked how much it would cost for the ten ewes, including delivery.

After much hemming and hawing, he said, "Oh, so. I'd say 'bout a hundred euros each and if it comes out less, I'll give ye back what's left over."

Without hesitation, I handed him the one thousand euros, thinking that Karen and I probably shouldn't plan our retirement on any refund. I think even Michael was surprised at the speed with which I handed over the money and that I gave it all to him in cash without awaiting delivery or negotiating. But I was just trying to keep Karen and me from turning into human icicles. There I was again thinking of some bulletin from the US State Department: "American couple found frozen in dung pile on an Irish sheep farm."

Michael looked at the cash in his hand and asked if I needed a receipt.

"No need. I know you're a man of your word, Michael."

"And what do ye do Herbert?"

"I sue people when they break their promises."

He laughed.

Actually, I do sue people when they break their promises.

"Okay, so. I'll pick good ones for ye and take good care."

"One more thing, Michael."

"Yes, Herbert?"

"When you deliver the sheep, we want you to give the Treacy's what's in this envelope."

Inside the envelope was the following signed document:

KNOW ALL MEN BY THESE PRESENTS:

Delivered herewith to one Tony (aka Tiger) and Victoria Treacy and to their rightful heirs at law, Martin, Rebecca, and Gordon are the following ewes: Bacardi, Banrion [pronounced Bahnreen and meaning Queen], Buaiteoir [pronounced Boowahr and meaning Winner], Cara [meaning Friend], Daisy, Milis [pronounced Meelish and meaning Sweet], Mo chuisle [pronounced muh khwish-la or muh kooshla and meaning My Darling], Harvette, Snow White, and Tonette.

BY THEIR ACCEPTANCE OF DELIVERY OF SAID EWES Tony and Victoria, for themselves and for their rightful heirs, hereby create a bailment on behalf of Karen A. Duffy and Harvey Gould, the Island Owner, until such time and under such circumstances as said glorious personages shall reside permanently in Ireland.

Go ye now in peace and contentment and accept into your charge the aforesaid ewes so that they may do their work beside their eternal friends Roger, Honey, and Ollie.

DONE AT ADARE, COUNTY OF LIMERICK, REPUBLIC OF IRELAND

IN THE YEAR OF KAREN'S LORD 2005

WITNESSETH OUR HAND:

_____

Karen A. Duffy

_____

Harvey Lawrence Gould
(Island Owner)

Karen advised me before we arrived not to seal the envelope. "If you do, he'll be insulted and think you don't trust him."

"It's not sealed, Herbert."

"That's okay, Michael. Just be sure to give it to Tony and his wife when you deliver the sheep." Not that we didn't trust Michael on this score, but we gave Margaret a duplicate of what was in the envelope.

Six months later, Michael hadn't called Tony, let alone delivered the ewes. I called him from San Francisco, got his voice mail, and left a "What's up with the delivery?" message. That morning at 3:00 a.m., the phone rang and our hearts jumped. Karen scrambled for the phone. It was Michael. Although Karen's heart was still thumping, she sounded sleepy. "Did I get ye out of the cot, Missus?"

"Yes, Michael. It's three in the morning here."

"Oh, so. Is Herbert there?"

I got on the phone. "Yes, Michael."

"So, I was jest t'inkin' about ye and wantin' to know what ye want me to do?"

"Oh, did you get my voice mail?"

"No. I was jest t'inkin' about ye."

"Uh huh. Well, why don't you call Tony, tell him you have ten ewes to deliver, arrange for a delivery date, and when you deliver them, give him and his wife the envelope we left with you."

"Oh, so, is that how ye'd like me to handle this, Herbert?"

"Yes, that will work fine. So, you'll do this soon, Michael?"

"Indeed I will and sorry fer gettin' ye and the Missus out of the cot. God bless."

"Good-bye, Michael."

Another six months later, in July 2006 when Karen and I were back at Purtill, one full year after we'd made the deal, Michael delivered the ten ewes. Since we were there, Michael said, "Well, now, this worked out jest fine, didn't it, Herbert?"

"Yes, Michael, perfect. I'd say even grand."

Shockingly, Michael failed to bring the envelope, but after our arrival, we'd asked Margaret for her duplicate, so we had it with us to give to Tony and Victoria upon the delivery. Also, shockingly, there was no refund from what we'd paid Michael.

Sometime later, Victoria found an article in a local newspaper with a picture of Michael holding a lamb and standing next to his mother-in-law. The article reported that "some of us might have found the weather miserable. Michael says that it couldn't have been better for the lambing. It was bitterly cold, but it was mainly dry." I read the article and had flashbacks of hypothermia.

The ewes didn't fully cover rent on the cottage for 2006, so we bought each of the Treacy kids super-duper iPods and carrying cases, making sure they couldn't be returned by having them engraved with their initials. Payment via this surreptitious route had worked, but it hadn't been easy. From then on, however, we vowed to pay for our stay at the cottage without Michael's help.

Michael Power Delivers the Ewes

Chapter 37

~

Harvey Becomes a Full-Blooded Irishman

In 2006, the night before we left for Ireland, I got sick and was up most of the night. Karen and I both wrote it off to too much sushi at dinner. The next day we traveled to Eire, a comparatively uneventful trip.

Because of my disease, I'm always tired. I learned long ago to push through the exhaustion, giving in only when I can't fight it anymore. But the tiredness I was feeling in Ireland was of a different order. Not only was I constantly exhausted, but I also found it difficult to walk without having to stop every few feet, heart racing and out of breath. This was new. As I lay in bed I could literally hear my heart thumping in the quietness of the night. I remember thinking that if I explained the sensation well enough to Edgar Allan Poe he could write a story about it. Slow deep breathing didn't help. Taking an extra pill to relax myself didn't work. My chest hurt from the pounding. I tend to be fairly stoic, so these developments were disturbing.

We were expecting a number of guests that summer. Before any of them arrived, we had our first misadventure that pushed my exhaustion beyond its limits. The Treacy's left for a brief holiday in Portugal and asked if we could give their vegetable garden a good watering every few days and let their dogs out for a good run.

Nelson is a lovable Dalmatian who literally smiles when you ask him properly. Fred's a terrier. He doesn't know he's a quarter the size of Nelson and when the two of them are let out of their dog run, they romp on the grass and growl fiercely at each other, Fred barking the whole time and nipping at Nelson's hind legs. Nelson takes it all in stride, opening his mouth like he's about to eat Fred. Fred accommodates Nelson by sticking his head in his mouth. Nelson growls ferociously, licks Fred and the two of them roll around in mock battle, and then chase each other across the large rolling lawn in front of the Treacy's house, into the pastures, and around and sometimes into Harvey Lake.

We knew Fred was a roamer. Tony told us when he lets the dogs out, Fred often takes off into the pastures, but returns as soon as he yells for him. In the few instances when he doesn't, Tony returns Nelson to the enclosed dog run and Fred runs back to join his pal.

Though I was feeling weak when the Treacy's left on their trip, I walked down to their house with Karen. A few times, I sat in a chair as Karen watered the garden and let the dogs have their romp. One day, Fred and Nelson took off into one of the pastures. Nelson came back. Fred didn't. We sat there with Nelson for twenty minutes, occasionally yelling Fred's name. No response.

We put Nelson in the enclosed dog run to use Tony's trick of luring Fred back. Thirty minutes later, still no Fred. "Don't tell me that we've lost Fred," I said to Karen.

"Don't be silly. Just sit there for another ten minutes and he'll be back." Twenty minutes later, still no Fred.

"Holy shit. We've lost their dog."

This time Karen didn't say, "Don't be silly," so I knew we were in trouble. She went down the back driveway to Purtill and I started walking out the front. I got to the end of the driveway and started walking the loop. Huffing and puffing, I passed five houses; I walked about a mile. I knew I still had to walk back and had already pushed my limit. Still, before heading back, I rang the doorbell at the fifth house to ask if they'd seen Fred, but no one answered. Despondent, I gave up and started the slow and difficult walk back. I managed to make it, hoping against hope that Fred had returned and Karen had put him in with Nelson.

Karen was at the cottage waiting for me. No Fred. By then both of us were exhausted and panicked. I had to lie down. I couldn't really sleep, but I was just about immobilized. We rested for about an hour, and then took our car and drove up and down the road. No Fred.

We returned to the cottage. Our cell phone rang. It was Tony, calling from Portugal. Great. Did I confess our crime, or play it as if nothing had happened so as not to ruin their vacation? Tony asked if everything was okay.

"Welllllllll, everything is sort of okay, but—"

Tony interrupted, "If you're looking for Fred, our neighbor has him. Go out the front driveway and turn to the left: it's the fifth house."

"I was there! Rang the bell and no one answered!"

"Well, they're home now. Our neighbors know Fred. They called to ask if I wanted to drive over to pick him up. I said that since we're in Portugal, it would be a bit of a long drive, but I knew someone who might be willing to come get him."

Thirty seconds after hanging up, I was in the car and heading back to the house where Fred was waiting for me. The man who answered the door said Fred had ended up at their house before. He had the dog in an enclosed area. As I walked toward Fred, he was yapping and jumping, tail wagging in friendly recognition. When we let him out, for a second I thought he might bolt again, but even for Fred, he'd had enough for the day and he darted for my car. I opened the door. He hopped in like a youngster happy to be heading home after a long afternoon of hard play. I thanked the man profusely. "No problem a' tall," he said.

The short drive back to the cottage, Fred yapped, telling me of his exciting adventure. As soon as I got back, Karen and I put him in the dog run with Nelson, who opened his mouth and Fred obligingly stuck his head inside. They rolled around a bit, and then Fred drank what looked like a few gallons of water and lay down for a nap.

For the remainder of the time that the Treacy's were on holiday, we let Nelson out for romps, and took Fred for rides in the car.

Company came, but I felt progressively worse. I wasn't shaking whatever had a hold on me. When the Treacy's returned from Portugal, they invited us to dinner. Victoria took Karen aside and told her that even the children had commented on how horribly pale I looked and how unusually quiet I was. Karen agreed and asked for the name of a doctor. Victoria suggested a private practitioner in Croagh, five miles outside Adare. Tony gave me directions on how to get there, providing further evidence that no one, under any circumstances, should ever take directions from Tony.

We went on a Friday. I gave the doctor a brief history of my disease and told her what I'd been experiencing since the night before leaving for Ireland. She took my blood pressure, which was fine. That was puzzling, because I knew something was wrong. She said if I didn't get better over the weekend to return on Monday. I had a rotten weekend, so we were back on Monday.

She drew some blood. Although understandably she didn't know much about myelofibrosis, she knew that of the many effects of the disease, one is abnormally low hemoglobin. She had us drive my blood to a lab at the Mid-Western Regional Hospital in Limerick, the same place where Tony had spent time recuperating after his Event. Three hours later, the doctor called Karen and said, "Get your husband to the casualty now. His hemoglobin is at six-point-one. He needs a blood transfusion—fast."

The high normal range for hemoglobin is 17.5. Since the onset of my disease, mine had hovered between 11.5 and 12.5, and that was with the aid of injections I'd taken for years. At 6.1, you're in serious trouble. Much later, after figuring I'd been in that dangerously low territory apparently for many days, my doctor in the States said he was amazed I hadn't had a heart attack or stroke because my heart had to work that much harder to make up for the dramatically decreased oxygen supply to the muscles and organs. Ah ha! So that heart thumping wasn't just my runaway imagination about a possible new Edgar Allan Poe short story.

One of the things Dr. Damon had told us in our first meeting was that I'd never crash. We well remembered him saying that while my disease was chronic and terminal, "At least it tends to move slowly so you'll never fall off a cliff."

That's not the kind of news you forget and even a week before we left for Ireland that year, my blood counts were what, for me, were abnormally normal. Unfortunately, my doctor was wrong about me not crashing.

Not long after I was diagnosed, Karen found a cartoon. It depicts two people walking out of a cancer ward. One says to the other, "Do you want the bad news or the good bad news?" For anyone with a chronic or terminal disease, that pretty much sums it up, but it seemed that during our summer in Ireland in 2006, I had only bad news.

We drove immediately to casualty where we went through the same nightmare that people all over the world experience in emergency rooms. I told the young woman at admissions that my doctor had said I needed a transfusion immediately. I put her on the phone with the doctor. That was nice. Then we waited three hours before they finally located a gurney for me. Meanwhile, because of liability insurance concerns, no hospital personnel would move our car, which I'd parked outside the emergency room. We were told that within a short time it would be towed. Karen can't drive the cars we rent in Ireland.

"I'll move the damn car," I said as I struggled off the gurney. I drove the car into the hospital's car park and slowly, with great difficulty breathing the whole way, walked back to my gurney, my heart feeling like it was about to explode.

Hours later, we were told there was no room available in the hospital, so I couldn't be admitted. I could remain all night on the gurney, essentially in a hallway, or return the following day for a transfusion as a patient at the Cancer Day Ward. The air was stifling in the area, the gurney was barely large enough for someone half my size, and they told us that even if I did wait all night, I couldn't get a transfusion until the morning, because they were short staffed. A hematologist tried to talk us into staying the night, but we said, "No thanks." Before I left, though, they drew some more blood.

I drove us home, a roughly twenty-minute ride. Honestly, I still don't know how I managed that, or driving us back to the Cancer Day Ward the next morning.

When we got in, a young woman sat with us, clipboard in hand. I figured this was where the bureaucratic hassle would begin about insurance, but her questions were routine. She never did ask about insurance; it wasn't until we'd returned the third time that anyone even took a credit card number (which was not processed until my insurance company finally paid me the amount of the bill a year later).

One of the questions she did ask was, "What's your religious preference?" I hesitated before answering. I didn't mind the question. It's that it struck home that some of the patients at the ward would need last rites, or the Protestant equivalent, and they wanted to know, when the need arose, whether to summon a priest or a minister.

I flashed back to a scene more than fifty years earlier. My family was vacationing at a rented summer house outside Chicago. We were heading out to a movie and I skipped to the car, hopped in the backseat, and slammed the door leaving some fingers inside the doorjamb. I immediately passed out. My mother saw me, gasped, opened the door, grabbed me, and ran back to the house carrying my limp body—my head back and my arms dangling spread eagle.

A priest playing a round of golf nearby saw what was happening, ran up to my mother, and asked, "Madam, do you need last rites?"

"Hell no!" my mother screamed. "What I *need* is a doctor!"

I shook off the memory, but briefly wondered if the hospital could get the *shomer Shabbos* leprechaun from Dublin for me, if necessary.

Finally, I answered, "Jewish."

In one motion, the young woman's head snapped up from the clipboard, her mouth opened, her eyebrows raised, and she said, "This is exciting! You're my first!"

I almost said, "You don't look like a virgin." Instead, I replied, "Glad to be of service."

A hematologist was assigned as my primary care doctor. In turn, she'd conferred with Dr. Damon. When I spoke to him myself, he assured me that the doctor in Ireland, while not familiar with the specifics of my disease, fully understood my crisis and was well trained to know how much blood to give me and how often.

We met the doctor the first day I was at the ward. She told us from the blood that had been drawn the night before, my hemoglobin had dropped to 5.6. Since it had been 6.1 from blood drawn earlier that same day, this news was frightening and stunning. The doctor said something else, but my brain put her volume on low and all I heard in my head like a reverberating echo was, *You'll never fall off a cliff. You'll never fall off a cliff. You'll never fall off a cliff.*

Hell, I was in freefall, a virtual nosedive. I received two units of blood that day, my first blood transfusions ever. As it turned out, I needed twelve units, which I received on seven separate days during the course of three weeks, a fair slug since a body typically holds ten.

The time we spent there could have been horrible had it not been that the day ward was something of an oasis in a desert. It was comparatively new, well lit, and airy. Though there were examining rooms for privacy, all receiving treatment did so in the same large open area. At UCSF where, by that time I'd been a patient for six years, the treatment rooms were cramped and without daylight. Best of all, not only was the ward staffed with well-trained professionals, as also was true at UCSF, but also with many volunteers who took time to chat without being intrusive and who took a serious interest in trying to make you as comfortable as possible. By the second time we returned to the Cancer Day Ward, the staff already knew us by name. They were organized, polite to a fault, and efficient.

At UCSF if you wanted something to eat, you'd bring something with you or go hungry. At the day ward in Limerick, they served lunch and late-afternoon tea with biscuits (cookies) for patients and their companions.

Still, death sat at some of those treatment tables, and there were a number of patients in their twenties and younger. One day a beautiful young girl started sobbing as she sat alone at a table receiving chemo. It broke my heart to see her struggle with what was happening to her body. I hadn't had time to play out my life as fully as I wanted to, but I had children and grandchildren. I'd had a long career as an attorney. I was married to the love of my life and my best friend. I'd traveled and done some living. This young girl hadn't even had a chance yet to dance the dance of life. She was at a stage when a primary issue for her should have been whether to wait for some boy to ask her out on a date or whether she should make the first move. Instead, she was forced to contemplate her own death. The eternal unfairness of it was overwhelming. Tears began to stream down my face. I didn't want to add to her grief, so I turned away so she wouldn't see me.

This could have been a dark time for me, but because of the surroundings, the good care generally provided in a convivial atmosphere, and that a number of other patients were able to slough off the deadly seriousness of it all and instead engage in wonderful discussions, it was Ireland at its best.

During those visits, I had some of my best conversations and best laughs ever. Not that all my chats ended on a high, but they all ended in an Oirish way.

One day I was talking to a man whom I'd seen there several times previously. In the midst of one of his jokes, a nurse waited till he'd finished, and then told him he'd only be admitted to the hospital if some test results revealed his condition was critical. We continued to yammer. A while later, the same nurse, then looking somber, told him that he was being admitted. He and I knew that he'd just been handed his death warrant, but we continued telling jokes, laughing, and having a grand afternoon. When I was finished for the day and while we were both still seated, I reached over and shook his hand. Before I had a chance to say anything, he put his second hand over mine, patted it, and said, "Now be a brave lad and keep up the good fight."

"That I will, my good man; that I will. And God bless you."

I stood, but he wouldn't let go of my hand. Instead, he continued patting it, cocked his head to one side, looked straight into my face and with a twinkle in his eyes asked, "Now, would that be the Hebrew one?" Craic at death's door.

"That would be anyone you want."

Karen and I slowly walked out of the ward. For the man's sake I held myself together until we got outside. Then I broke down. Karen held me as I sobbed like a baby. I never saw him again.

When it was time for us to leave for the States, my hemoglobin was at around nine, still not good, but a hell of a lot better than five, at least high enough for me to make it home with the help of wheelchairs at the critical points.

Back in California, my doctor gave me another two units of blood. We compared bills for my one transfusion at UCSF with the many at the hospital in Limerick and the cost in the States was roughly three times as expensive.

It took seven months for my numbers to come back to their normal abnormal level and to this day, no one really knows what happened or why I crashed that summer in Ireland.

I also checked in with my internist. After reviewing all the blood work that had been done in Ireland, he determined that I now also had diabetes. By that time, Karen and I were so beat up that we almost yawned. The following year, I learned that I had gallstones and had to have my gall bladder removed. "What else?" I asked Karen. I shouldn't have asked.

Before my gall bladder surgery, I had a routine checkup by a cardiologist. He heard something he didn't like and had me take a stress test. I flunked. Within a week I was on an operating table, not to have my gall bladder removed, but for an angioplasty. The stress test revealed a 90 percent blockage in one of my major coronary arteries. Because I'd be under a general anesthetic for the gall bladder surgery, they required that the blockage be opened, which was done by using balloons that are inflated inside the artery.

A few weeks later, I had my gall bladder removed. Six months after that, I was on the table again for my second angioplasty, this time to have two stents implanted after a subsequent stress test revealed that the blockage had returned.

Even with the major medical challenges I'd had during the preceding twelve months, I had time to reflect on my overall positive experience in the Cancer Day Ward at Limerick. Before we left Ireland, Karen and I delivered a round of goodies for the staff and they'd posted our note of thanks from "the Yanks."

The more I thought about it, though, the more I concluded I was more than a Yank, even more than a fierce local. So on October 19, 2006, I wrote the following letter to Ireland's Prime Minister, Taoiseach Bertie Ahern:

HARVEY L. GOULD

SAN FRANCISCO, CALIFORNIA 94118

October 19, 2006

The Honorable Bertie Ahern
Taoiseach
Department of the Taoiseach
Government Buildings Upper
Merrion Street Dublin 2
Ireland

Taoiseach Ahern, a chara,

Ba maith liom me fein a chur in aithne duit. Although I was born in Chicago, and am descended from Jewish grandparents from Poland and Russia, I am writing to request that you certify me as a full blooded Irishman. Here's why.

In 1988, my wife brought me to Ireland for the first time. Although I had no emotional connection to the country (and making matters worse, had never had a Guinness), quickly I fell in love with the beauty of the countryside, the Irish people and the good craic.

Ever since then we've spent a holiday in Ireland every year. First, we did the typical tourist stuff, but now we just "live" in your country, always staying at the same cottage outside of Adare. We know the local postmistress, the librarian, the grocer and the owners of many local businesses. We know a local sheep farmer and bought ten ewes from him as a gift for friends who live in Adare. We know the Master of the Hounds for the Limerick Hunt Club. Sometimes, he stops by our cottage in the summer surrounded by his forty hounds which he is training for hunt season. I've gone on two hunts, both in Ireland, one in Clare and one in Limerick, and both the thrill of a lifetime.

Perhaps none of this qualifies me to be an honorary Irishman, but here's what does. I have a rare blood disorder and while we were in Adare this past July I ended up receiving 12 units of good Irish blood at the Cancer Day Ward at the Midwest Regional Hospital in Limerick. In fact, as I was getting my twelfth unit, for cross checking purposes, the nurses asked me my name. I said, "After this next transfusion my name will be either Taoiseach Ahern or Seamus Heaney so either I'll make a political speech in Irish or I'll recite a poem for ye -- or both."

I know you have a few other items on your agenda, but what could be more important than a Taoiseach deciding who is Irish? In my case this should be an easy decision. Since a person typically has ten units of blood or less, literally I am now a full blooded Irishman, so I'm just looking for you to officially recognize my already existing status. Besides, this will help you with the Jewish vote, which could mean up to another six or seven votes at the next election.

Tugaim buiochas leat roimh re as do chabhair.

Lea meas,

Harvey L. Gould (soon to be O'Gould)

p.s. After receiving word from you confirming the certification, I'll let you know when we'll next be in Ireland this coming summer. In that way you'll know when you can stop by our cottage; have a cup of tea (or something stronger if you prefer) and a scone or two and drop off the certificate, unless you want the ceremony nationally televised. Just let me know so I'll be sure to bring the appropriate attire on our holiday. Slainte chugat.

I figured that if any country had a government that would get a laugh out of such a request, it would be Ireland, the land of craic.

On November 7, 2006, I received the following letter from the Office of the Taoiseach:

Oifig an Taoisigh
Office of the Taoiseach

7 November 2006

Mr. Harvey L. Gould

San Francisco
California 94118

Dear Mr. Gould,

The Taoiseach, Mr. Bertie Ahern T.D., has asked me to acknowledge receipt of your letter of 19 October, 2006 which has been referred to the office of the Minister for Foreign Affairs, Mr. Dermot Ahern T.D., for attention and direct reply to you.

Yours sincerely,

Michael Sludds
Taoiseach's Private Office

Telephone: 01-6194020
E-mail: privateoffice@taoiseach.gov.ie

Oifig an Taoisigh, Tithe an Rialtais, Baile Átha Cliath 2.
Office of the Taoiseach, Government Buildings, Dublin 2.

293

Okay. This wasn't the rollicking response I was hoping for from the Taoiseach, but at least he'd handed it off, so I was still in the game for a worthy reply.

The good thing about letters to politicians in Ireland is that you don't have to wait long for an answer. One office seems literally to hand carry the letter to the next office, so the next day, November 8, 2006, I received the following letter from the Office of the Minister for Foreign Affairs:

OIFIG AN AIRE GNÓTHAÍ EACHTRACHA
(OFFICE OF THE MINISTER FOR FOREIGN AFFAIRS)

BAILE ÁTHA CLIATH 2
(DUBLIN 2)

Mr. Harvey L. Gould

San Francisco
California 94118
U.S.A.

8 November 2006

Dear Mr. Gould,

On behalf of the Minister for Foreign Affairs, Mr. Dermot Ahern T.D., I wish to thank you for your letter of 19 October 2006, which was forwarded here from the office of An Taoiseach.

As this is a matter for the office of the Minister for Justice, Equality and Law Reform, I have taken this opportunity to refer your correspondence to that office for attention and direct reply to you.

Yours sincerely,

Ciarán Madden
Private Secretary

Good Lord. I was getting the bureaucratic shuffle. Still, I had to have faith. I told myself, *"This is the land of craic. These aren't bureaucratic bumpkins like we've got. These people are the Irish. They have a sense of humor."*

On November 15, 2006, I received the following letter from the office of Justice, Equality, and Law Reform:

TÁNAISTE AND OFFICE OF THE MINISTER FOR JUSTICE, EQUALITY AND LAW REFORM
TÁNAISTE AGUS OIFIG AN AIRE DLÍ AGUS CIRT, COMHIONANNAIS AGUS ATHCHÓIRITHE DLÍ

15 November, 2006

Dear Mr Gould,

I write to acknowledge receipt of your letter dated 19 October, 2006 addressed to Mr. Dermot Ahem T.D., which I will bring to the Tánaiste's attention.

Yours sincerely,

Private Secretary

Mr Harvey L. Gould

San Francisco
California 94118
U.S.A.

CUIRFEAR FÁILTE ROIMH CHOMHFHREAGRAS I NGAEILGE
94 ST. STEPHEN'S GREEN, DUBLIN 2 / 94 FAICHE STIABHNA, BAILE ÁTHA CLIATH 2
TELEPHONE/TEILEAFÓN: (01) 602 8202 LO-CALL: 1890 221 227 FAX/FACSUIMHIR: (01) 661 5461 E-MAIL/RÍOMHPHOIST: INFO@JUSTI

Uh oh. Now, not only was I getting the bureaucratic shuffle, but they'd even stopped reading my letter. It had *not* been addressed to Dermot Ahern, but to Bertie Ahern. *Don't tell me this is going to end with gibberish. I don't want to hear it. It can't be.*

On January 5, 2007, at last I got my formal reply from the Private Secretary for the Tánaiste from the Office of the Minister for Justice, Equality, and Law Reform:

A Fíerce Local

TÁNAISTE AND OFFICE OF THE MINISTER FOR JUSTICE, EQUALITY AND LAW REFORM
TÁNAISTE AGUS OIFIG AN AIRE DLÍ AGUS CIRT, COMHIONANNAIS AGUS ATHCHÓIRITHE DLÍ

5   January 2007

Dear Mr. Gould,

I am directed by the Tánaiste and Minister for Justice, Equality and Law Reform Mr. Michael McDowell T.D. to refer to your correspondence addressed to An Taoiseach, Mr. Bertie Ahern, regarding your wish to become an Irish citizen by association.

The Irish Nationality and Citizenship legislation allows the Minister the power to waive some of the statutory conditions for naturalisation. However, it should be pointed out that while it is not strictly necessary, it is desirable that an applicant is living in the State at the time of the application. In the past, the Minister has held that applicants who are not residing in the State do not have sufficient Irish association to warrant waiving the conditions, in particular the residency requirement. Since it appears that you are not permanently resident in the State, naturalisation is not an option at this point in time.

Yours sincerely,

Private Secretary

Mr. Harvey L. Gould

San Francisco
California 94118
U.S.A.

CUIRFEAR FÁILTE ROIMH CHOMHFHREAGRAS I NGAEILGE

94 ST. STEPHEN'S GREEN, DUBLIN 2 / 94 FAICHE STIABHNA, BAILE ÁTHA CLIATH 2
TELEPHONE/TEILEAFÓN: (01) 602 8202 LO-CALL: 1890 221 227 FAX/FACSUIMHIR: (01) 661 5461 E-MAIL/RÍOMHPHOIST: INFO@JUSTICE.IE

I was crestfallen. "Waiver?" "Applicant?" "Statutory conditions for naturalization?" "Residency requirement?" Who did they think they were, some United States senators giving a stump speech about illegal immigration in the US and our need to kick out twelve million people and make them all start over again? I wanted to write back and say, "For Christ's sake, wake up and take a joke. All I was looking for was the following letter: 'Boyo, excellent try. How about a drink at any pub of your choice next time you're in the Old Sod and we can hoist a few pints too many together and have a good laugh over your letter, maybe even show it to a few of the patrons as we all get pissed. Deal?'"

Karen told me I should write back and say that on their road to becoming an economic powerhouse, they'd become bloody Brits and had lost their sense of humor in the process.

Still, not all was lost. In December 2006, Jim Duffy, one of Karen's cousins, was honored as Man of the Year for an Irish-American organization that works with physically handicapped Irish and American children. We went to the dinner in New York honoring him. What I didn't know is that privately, Karen had sent Jim's son Scott my letter to the Taoiseach and all the desiccated responses. As one of the coordinators for the event, Scott met Tim O'Connor, then Ireland's Consul General to New York. He showed the ambassador my letter to the Taoiseach and the responses I'd received to that date. In an effort to make up a bit for the sourpuss replies, the consul general wrote a letter to put a human face on the correspondence, and he presented it to me that evening as part of a surprise private ceremony, while I was surrounded by the entire forty or so Duffy clan members present. With Ambassador O'Connor standing next to me, Bill Broderick, head of the organization honoring Karen's cousin that evening, read to me the ambassador's letter, which follows:

ARD-CHONSALACHT NA hÉIREANN
TEILEAFÓN: 212.819.2555
FAX: 212.980.9475

CONSULATE GENERAL OF IRELAND
345 PARK AVENUE, 17TH FLOOR
NEW YORK, NY 10154-0037

1 December 2006

Mr Harvey L Gould
San Francisco
California

A Harvey, a chara,

I have learned from our good mutual friend, Bill Broderick, of your great interest in, and support, for Ireland. As the Representative of Ireland in New York, I am very pleased to welcome you to this City for the Annual Dinner of the Physically Challenged Irish and American Youth Team, a wonderful charity that does so much good for Irish and American young people. This year the Honoree of the Dinner is a valued and proud member of your extended clan, the great Jimmy Duffy – and given all that Jimmy has done for the Youth Team over the years, there could not be a worthier recipient. I know that Jimmy will be delighted that you are here.

I want to say to you, Harvey, how much we appreciate your interest in Ireland. You have made your home over the years in beautiful Adare (which, by the way is only about 20 miles from my own home Parish of Killeedy in West Limerick – olam katan, as your Jewish grandparents might have said!)

I was sorry to hear of your illness, but very pleased to hear that you were well looked after by the Regional Hospital in Limerick last year – and that you were the recipient of good Irish blood! I wish you well for a continued recovery and express my deepest thanks to you for being such a great supporter of my country. We hope that you and your wife will continue to visit us regularly and that you will continue to get a great céad míle fáilte – a hundred thousand welcomes.

Míle buíochas arís as ucht do chuid suime – is cara dílis thú. Go n-eirí an bother leat.

Is mise, le meas

Tim O'Connor
Ambassador, Consul General

301

The ambassador presented his letter to me, framed. Also standing with me as the ambassador made his presentation was Phil Coulter, one of Ireland's most respected contemporary songwriters, performers, and informal ambassadors, who was the lead performer that evening. I was surprised and immensely pleased that an Irish ambassador had bothered to prepare and present me with such a letter. Karen was so thankful she wanted to go light some candles.

Jim Duffy and Phil Coulter with Harvey Holding the
Framed Letter from Ambassador O'Connor

Some months later, I sent Phil Coulter a letter, telling him how much Karen and I were touched by his participation in the fundraising event. I also sent him a copy of my letter to the Taoiseach and a copy of my CD set. I explained that many of my songs contained a message similar to many of his—what a gift life is. I told him I hoped he got "even a tad of enjoyment" from the three discs, and if not, to just use them "in lieu of peat on some cold night."

He wrote back, thanking me for my CD and my correspondence, commenting that I'd argued my case with the Taoiseach effectively and saying, "Surely if he has any heart, or any sense of humour, he must say 'yes'!" Though Phil Coulter's prediction of the Taoiseach's reply proved wrong, the consul general's reference to *olam katan* in his letter still leaves me an opening. Olam katan is Hebrew, meaning, "It's a small world."

As striking as it was that Tim O'Connor used Hebrew in his letter to me, even more remarkable is that he's married to an Israeli, and though he returned to Dublin to serve as what we'd call the chief of staff for Ireland's president, apparently he and his wife plan on retiring to Israel. Hmm. Chief of staff for the Irish president married to an Israeli? Maybe my quest to be recognized as an honorary Irishman isn't over yet. Olam katan.

Chapter 38

⌒

Reverend Harv

Shortly after their engagement, Maggie and David asked me to write them a wedding song. David was then a high school teacher and Maggie was going to law school. Happily, I agreed. Although I've played guitar and written songs since I was a teenager, the first time I publicly sang one I'd written was for my parents' fiftieth wedding anniversary in 1980. From that time forward, at every major event—a niece or nephew's bat or bar mitzvah, my own children's b'not mitzvot, my wedding to Karen, and eventually my daughters' weddings—I've written and performed a song for each.

I don't read or write music. So unless I make a recording of a song I've written, usually on a handheld device, eventually I forget it, and more times than not, I did fail to make a recording. As my children grew older, occasionally they'd ask me to sing one, but often I'd forgotten the chords, the melody, or the words. As a birthday gift, they bought me time in a recording studio, so I could at least record those songs I'd written and still remembered.

By the time I finished, I had a three-CD set, filled not only with songs, but also with stories of the people for whom the songs had been written, and in some instances, audio edited in from videos of the various events. I was also able to work with other musicians and add music to the songs I'd originally sung solo. The effort turned out to take about a year, became something of an obsession, and although at times it was physically exhausting, in the end I was delighted to have created a form of a partial oral history of and for our families. I sent a copy of this set to Phil Coulter.

When David and Maggie asked if I'd write them a wedding song, Maggie immediately added that her dad played guitar and sang. Clearly, the die was cast. "That's great. I'll ask your dad if he'll join me in the writing and playing," I said, thinking, *Maggie will make one hell of a lawyer. She knows exactly how to back someone into a corner from which there's no escape, all the while making it appear as though she had no idea of the trap she'd just sprung. Good for her. But damn, what if her dad plays like a ten-year-old pounding on his first fifteen dollar plastic guitar and sings like an off-key rooster?*

Soon thereafter, Karen and I invited Maggie's father Russ to dinner at our house. I asked him to bring his guitar so we could jam a bit and see if we could begin to find a tune for the wedding song. I needed to find out if Russ had any conception about how to tune, let alone, play a guitar, and whether he sang any better than a crow with a sore throat.

After a pleasant dinner, Russ, Karen, and I retired to the living room. Russ is a quiet guy. We'd met at a few previous holiday events and he was always polite to a fault, but he wasn't outgoing. With me, all you have to ask is how things are going and I'll tell you my life history, starting with the time in Chicago when, as a five-year-old, I had my picture taken on a pony that some enterprising bloke managed to bring into the concrete backyards of apartments. And it wouldn't take much for me to drag you around to show you the photo.

With Russ, I was reminded of the story about President Calvin Coolidge, also known as Silent Cal. One evening a man approached him and said, "Mr. President, I've placed a wager with this gentleman that I can get you to say more than two words," to which the president replied, "You lose."

It worried me that Russ could be another Silent Cal, because I thought that to be a good musician you have to be someone willing to talk, to be forward, and then doing so by playing an instrument. So with some trepidation, I asked Russ to play anything on his guitar he liked, which would give me a feel for just how serious a problem this was going to be, as I kept saying to myself, *How in the hell am I going to cut this guy out of doing the wedding song without bruising Maggie?*

While pondering my question, he started to play. After his first five chords, he started finger picking up and down the neck of the guitar. I was transfixed. He wasn't playing the music. He wasn't talking the music. He was *feeling* the music. I couldn't even pretend to keep up with him. Once again, I'd proved to myself what I've always known. I'm a complete snob.

I have a baby grand piano I'd bought for my girls fifteen years earlier. I'd initially rented an upright as a test to gauge their interest. All three girls played it every time they were with me and enjoyed it immensely. So as a surprise gift one Hanukkah, I bought the baby grand and that was roughly the last time they ever played piano. Take it from me. Kids will get you with a sucker punch every time. But the purchase wasn't all for naught. It serves as a large stand for all the important family photos.

Russ eyed the baby grand and appeared to have something different in mind. "Do you mind if I fool around a little on the piano?"

Still in a mild state of shock and not even knowing he also played piano, I said something intelligent like, "Uh, um, I, uh."

While I'd just been blown away by his guitar playing, once he got going on the piano, he switched with ease from blues and contemporary show tunes to those neglected sixties rock and roll rubies. This guy wasn't just good. He was fantastic.

Then when he started singing, I wanted to dig a hole and climb in. I was sure he'd read my previous concerns and as he was sounding better than Elvis, or Lou Rawls, or Fats Domino, he was just laughing at me. And so our journey to sing and perform David and Maggie's wedding song as a duo had begun.

Just about this time, something else had started—a budding romance between Russ and Leanna, whom he'd met by chance at a wedding some months earlier.

For all his talents, however, Russ hadn't written songs, so the plan was, I'd write the song in Ireland, which we'd sharpen up after Karen and I returned.

Having spent most of my time in the Cancer Day Ward, I had little time to work on the song. Two nights before we were scheduled to return home, we had dinner at the Treacy's, where Tony told me that Gordon had written a piece for the piano. I asked Gordy if he'd play it for me and the two of us sneaked off.

The melody was beautiful. I borrowed one of Gordon's guitars, asked him the chord sequence, and started playing along. By then I'd gotten in the habit of carrying around a small digital recorder, so I recorded several versions of us playing his tune. Soon, Tony, Victoria, and Karen drifted into the room, and we wowed them with Gordy's song. Victoria said, "How do you know what to *do,* Harvey?"

Gordon answered, "He has a good teacher."

I added, "I'm learning at the hand of the master."

In fact, I told Maestro Gordon right then that with his permission, I planned to borrow his melody and use it as the base for the wedding song I still needed to write. Gordy agreed.

When Karen and I arrived home, I expanded the tune a bit and wrote the lyrics. Though Russ and I performed it at the wedding, we also recorded it with a number of musicians and included that version on a compilation CD that Maggie and David gave as gifts to all attending their wedding.

We spent two days in the studio playing separate guitar parts, singing separate parts, singing harmony, working with other musicians, and then adding production elements to the tune. This was my first experience working with a partner in a recording studio; I alone had made all the decisions on my CD set. When you're making production decisions on a piece of music in which two people are invested, you'll either end up really good friends or you'll murder each other. In our case, it was the former, and sealed by our duet at the wedding, Russ and I became, and remain, dear friends.

I sent a copy of the CD to Gordy with a recorded introduction: "For anyone listening to this recording, you should know that the music was written by Gordon Treacy. If you like the song, it's because of his music; if you don't, it's because I messed up his melody."

Meanwhile, in the run-up to the wedding, when Russ and I got together to rehearse, Russ's hot flame Leanna sat in the peanut gallery and burst into applause every time we did the song, while Karen sat coolly saying, "Not so good. Do it again." It was obvious which couple was into serious courting and which one was accustomed to ruthless objectivity.

Two months after David and Maggie's wedding, Russ asked Leanna to marry him. To no one's great surprise, she said yes. To my great surprise, however, they asked *me* to marry them—in Ireland!

Russ and Leanna wanted a private marriage, performed by someone with whom they shared a special relationship and who knew them well enough (and would be schmaltzy enough) to perform a memorable ceremony. The rub was I thought it a tad improbable that the state of California would recognize a wedding ceremony performed in Ireland by a nice Jewish guy, originally from Highland Park, who became a reverend in the Universal Life Church—online no less. So the plan was that I'd perform the ceremony in Ireland, but upon their return, they'd go to city hall and have a judge perform the official version.

Karen and I planned to be in Ireland in 2007 from late April until early June, staying, of course, at Purtill Cottage. We knew we wanted the wedding ceremony to take place on the grounds of the Mustard Seed with dinner afterward. Before we left for Ireland, we booked the date, Dan Mullane gave us his blessing to perform the ceremony anywhere on the grounds, and he agreed to cooperate in any way he could.

Before the happy couple arrived, Karen ordered a bouquet for Leanna to match the colors of her wedding dress and a boutonniere for Russ. We bought Waterford champagne flutes as their wedding gift and for their first toast to each other on their wedding night. Karen also arranged for Leanna and her to have their hair, nails, and makeup done on the wedding day, and she lined up a videographer and photographer. And we decided that you simply couldn't have a wedding in Ireland without a piper, so we hired one as a surprise.

I spent a fair amount of time writing the ceremony. Finally, Karen and I agreed that we needed to buy them mead for use in the ceremony.

Mead is a drink of white wine and honey. In ancient days in Ireland, it was reserved for kings, but over time, became traditionally used by a bride and groom on their wedding night. Also traditional was for the bride and groom to be given enough to last them for one full cycle of the moon, and hence the word, "honeymoon."

Four days before Russ and Leanna arrived, and for the two days afterward, it rained. We're accustomed to the Irish soft rain, a light mist, then sun, and then rain. We'd also been in some lashin' rains, but none that lasted and lasted and lasted. But on those six days, it poured, relentlessly, and while neither Karen nor I would say it out loud, both of us were thinking, *We want the ceremony outside where we've planned it, especially since the site had a symbolic significance that was written into the ceremony.* But the odds for an outside wedding weren't looking good.

Shortly after we got them to the cottage on the day of their arrival, they brought out what they wanted me to wear during the ceremony: a white robe, borrowed from an Episcopal minister, and a purple-fringed stole to be draped over my neck. A friend of theirs had done some embroidery on the stole. On one side of the front was a Star of David sprinkled with shamrocks. On the other side was a symbol of the Claddagh. On the back were the words, "The Rev. Harvey O'Gould, Doctor of" and underneath those words, a heart with the word "Love" inside it.

On the wedding day when we awoke, it wasn't raining. The skies looked patchy and threatening, but it wasn't pouring. As the day wore on, the weather held. I figured this had something to do with the Boss deciding it would be unfair to ruin this wedding for a couple who'd flown in from the States to be married outside by Reverend Harv. (Although my mother died in 1990, she'd have *another* stroke if she learned that her nice Jewish son was now a reverend.)

Hour after hour, the rain stayed away. By the time we got to the Mustard Seed, the fog lifted and you could see the spectacular view. Russ and Leanna went off with the photographer for about a twenty-minute photo shoot, while Karen and I reconnoitered with the piper, who was hiding out in the Mustard Seed's sitting room, kilts and all. (I know, I know. A bagpiper is Scottish and the Irish don't play bagpipes, they play Uilleann pipes, but we love the sound of bagpipes and had a piper at our wedding.)

By this time, of course, I was now in full dress: white robe, stole, and all. Youngsters in the room, sitting with their parents who were having a drink before dinner, wanted to know if I was going to marry someone. I was definitely getting into my role. "Yes, I am, child. God bless you."

The skies began to gray. Karen and I got anxious for the set of photos to end so we could have the piper escort us to the wedding site. "Don't you dare," I said, looking up and wagging a finger at the heavens, a bit carried away with my title and my power.

Russ and Leanna reappeared. When they first heard the piper, Leanna threw her head back and started to cry. The piper escorted us to the wedding site and the ceremony began. Russ and Leanna absolutely beamed. The photographer, videographer, and I all did our thing. So did the Boss. The weather held.

Processional Including Reverend Harv

As part of the ceremony, of course, I included a Celtic tale of sorrow, death, and eternal love. Hell, this was Ireland. And, in the telling, I let them know why we'd chosen their wedding site:

> In the ancient and mystical days of Ireland, Deirdre married Nesh, thereby violating a decree of King Conicher. Because she had violated his order, eventually the king had Nesh killed. Broken-hearted, Deirdre, too, died soon afterward and her people buried her in a grave next to the grave of Nesh. Two years later, beside the graves grew two beautiful new trees. Though the trunks emerged from the ground six feet apart, the trees grew together, twisting around each other and becoming so intertwined that the two became one. And so you are being married near these two intertwined trees behind me, because they symbolize the power of Deirdre and Nesh's eternal love for each other and because they represent our hope that your love for each other will be as intertwined as theirs.

The ceremony ended with a touch of an Irish prayer, a feel of some Irish imagery, and a recommendation from the sixties:

> May the roads rise to meet you; may the wind always be at your back. And just as the two of you brought the face of God to this ceremony through your love for each other, so may God forever hold the two of you in the hollow of his hand.
> Now that you have made your vows to each other and each of you has consented to be married to the other, I hereby pronounce you husband and wife—and since we are all children of the sixties, I say to the two of you that to end this ceremony—you may seal it with a kiss.

After they sealed it with a kiss, the piper piped us back up the hill, and as he did, for the first time in six days, the sun broke through and shone down on the newlyweds in all its glory.

"I guess I do have a few good connections," I said to Karen.

She smiled and said, "Don't get carried away."

"I don't know. Maybe I should set up a 'Reverend Harv' blog and go into a new business."

Russ and Leanna opened and used the flutes for their champagne toast in our own little reception area, and then lit a friendship candle (another of Karen's touches). I slipped out of my robes and donned the white dinner jacket I'd worn at Karen's and my wedding reception. Finally, we settled down to a perfect dinner.

During the meal, Dan came to the table to tell Russ and Leanna that he'd hosted many weddings at the Mustard Seed, some for sixty guests or more. He said that for most of them, he'd seen no wedding planners until the day of the wedding, but that he'd seen Karen and me, on separate days, meeting the photographer; meeting the videographer; meeting the piper; scouring the grounds for the site of the ceremony; picking out the table for dinner, and arranging for a special dessert. He said he was certain we'd spent more time in planning this wedding for all four people attending than was spent in planning all the weddings of all the ancient high kings of Ireland.

All in all, it had been a hell of a ride.

The next day, it rained.